Working Smart
in ADOBE® Photoshop® CS2

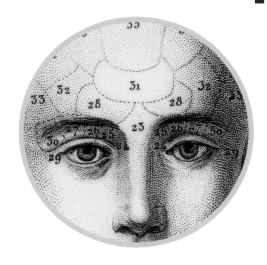

Working Smart in Adobe Photoshop CS2

Conrad Chavez

Copyright © 2007 Conrad Chavez

This Adobe Press book is published by Peachpit. For information on Adobe Press books, contact:

Peachpit
1249 Eighth Street
Berkeley, CA 94710
(510) 524-2178
Fax: (510) 524-2221

For the latest on Adobe Press books, go to www.adobepress.com

To report errors, please send a note to errata@peachpit.com

Peachpit Press is a division of Pearson Education

Project Editor: Corbin Collins
Project Editor: Becky Morgan
Production Editor: Kate Reber
Technical Editor: Adam Pratt
Compositor: Jerry Ballew
Indexer: FireCrystal Communications
Cover design: Charlene Charles-Will
Interior design: Kim Scott

ISBN 0-321-33539-2

9 8 7 6 5 4 3 2 1

Printed and bound in the United States of America

Contents

Introduction

We all know the cliché: "Work smarter, not harder." What exactly does it mean to work smart in Photoshop? To me, working smart is about getting the most done with the least amount of time and effort, and without being slowed by avoidable bottlenecks. Although this may not seem as exciting as ordering the newest, fastest computer, the advantages of working smart can be profound. For example, if you give the same job to two different users, and they have equally powerful computers, the difference in their productivity can come down to which person works smarter. Working smart can also potentially make you more productive than another person who has better equipment or more time.

Working smart has a lot to do with the idea that small changes can have large results. Small changes may initially seem inconsequential, but every little increase or decrease in efficiency makes a bigger difference as your workload scales up. If you perform a two-step task 100 times a day, and you find a way to perform that task in one step, then you double your efficiency—you cut your workload in half, or you can do twice as much in the same amount of time.

The number of images we process is certainly rising. A few years ago, the cost of film limited the number of images that were practical to shoot in a single session. Now, with a digital camera and a large memory card or tethered to a computer with an even larger hard disk, you can shoot far more images per session than you could have with film. A few years ago, most jobs were print jobs with fixed page counts; now there is no practical limit to the number of images you can upload to a Web site such as a stock photo agency or a retailer's online catalog. With the increased volume of images to process, and the fact that there are better things for you to be doing than clicking the same buttons all day long, working smart in Photoshop is more important than ever.

How This Book Is Organized

Working smart isn't just about shortcuts. It involves looking at your entire workflow holistically, paying attention to everything from the hardware you use to your day-to-day work habits. This book is divided into four major parts, and each part addresses a different aspect of working smart:

■ **Part I: Making Photoshop Your Own.** Photoshop makes higher demands of your computer hardware than most other programs do, and raw CPU power is not the only factor that affects Photoshop performance. It pays to make sure that all of your computer's subsystems—CPU, RAM, and hard disk—are configured for maximum Photoshop performance. The rest of this section helps you fit Photoshop to the requirements of your work by shaping your Photoshop workspace, developing efficient work habits, and creating presets for the tool configurations you use most often. If you lead a workgroup, you can create tutorials of your production standards and integrate the tutorials into the Help menu of Photoshop itself.

■ **Part II: Saving Time While You Work.** This part of the book focuses on specific tasks throughout an image-processing workflow, from opening files to printing. The book isn't big enough for me to cover every last detail of every workflow, but in this section I target some of the areas that can make a large difference in your productivity, such as selecting, using layers, and using transparency.

■ **Part III: Processing Images Automatically.** If you know what steps you require to process your images, and you know what settings you require for those steps, it seems natural that you should be able to make the computer remember all that for you. Photoshop gives you the power to do exactly that, by letting you condense and compress multiple-step sequences into a single step through actions (which are like macros), droplets, scripts, variables, and task-specific automation features such as the Image Processor.

■ **Part IV: Making Photoshop a Great Team Player.** Photoshop is often not the end of the line for an image. Images frequently move on to Web site programs, video-editing programs, or page-layout programs for print. This part provides workflow tips for using Photoshop documents with other programs, especially the Adobe Creative Suite.

Photoshop is both wide and deep. Many Photoshop books attempt to cover all areas of Photoshop in some detail. Other books focus on specific areas of Photoshop, such as compositing or color correction. This book doesn't fall squarely into either of those categories; instead, in this book I look at one aspect of the Photoshop workflow—efficiency—and how it works across the entire program. I hope you find this book to be successful in that way.

Tips for Reading This Book

There are certain features of both your operating system and Photoshop that I refer to many times in this book, because they're frequently used. To keep the text from becoming too redundant, I introduce those features in detail right here, instead of explaining what they are every time they appear in the book. As you read the book, if I make a reference that seems a bit vague, check here.

Context Menus

A *context menu* pops up under the mouse pointer and provides context-sensitive commands for whatever is under the pointer. On Windows, open a context menu by right-clicking in the document window. On Mac OS X, open a context menu by Ctrl-clicking the document, or right-clicking if you've connected a two-button mouse or Apple Mighty Mouse. If you use a Mac notebook, you may be able to simulate a right-click by clicking with two fingers on the trackpad; to see if your Mac notebook has this capability, go to System Preferences, open Keyboard and Mouse preferences, and in the Trackpad panel look for an option to simulate a right-click with a two-finger click.

Keyboard Shortcuts

Photoshop keyboard shortcuts are similar across Mac OS X and Windows XP, so it isn't too hard to use Photoshop shortcuts productively on both platforms. For most Photoshop shortcuts, the Command key on Mac OS X corresponds to the Ctrl key on Windows, and the Option key in Mac OS X corresponds to the Alt key on Windows. To save you the trouble of thinking through all of that, when I provide a keyboard shortcut I list it for both platforms, listing the Mac OS X shortcut first.

Throughout the book I point out keyboard shortcuts where I think they merit special attention, and in some cases I present tables of especially useful keyboard shortcuts. However, I don't list every shortcut for every feature I mention because that would become tedious reading. Listing shortcuts can also become irrelevant if you customize the keyboard shortcuts in Photoshop. If you want to know the current shortcut for a menu command, it's always listed on the menu right next to the command. When I mention keyboard shortcuts, I refer to the default Photoshop shortcuts. If you're really interested in keyboard shortcuts (and you should be), you can get the most out of them by taking a good long look at Chapter 3.

Palette Menus and Unlabeled Pop-Up Menus

When I talk about a *palette menu*, I'm talking about the menu that pops up when you click the round button with a triangle inside it that exists in the top right corner of many palettes (**Figure 0.1**). Keep an eye out for that little round button, because there are several places in Photoshop where an unlabeled pop-up menu exists and that button is the only way that you know about it.

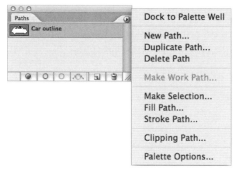

Figure 0.1: **When you see a round button with a triangle in it, there's a menu hiding under there.**

The Photoshop Application Folder

In this book I sometimes refer to some of the useful utilities and files that are installed by the Photoshop installer into the *Photoshop application folder*, the folder where Photoshop is installed by default. The location of this folder is slightly different on each platform. On Mac OS X, Photoshop installs into the folder:

    Computer/Applications/Adobe Photoshop CS2

In Windows, Photoshop installs into the folder:

    C:\Program Files\Adobe Photoshop CS2

It's best to leave Photoshop where the installer installs it. Moving the program may cause problems when updating it later.

The Utilities Folder (Mac OS X)

I sometimes refer to programs that live in the *Utilities folder* in Mac OS X. You'll find the Utilities folder inside the Applications folder. In Mac OS X 10.4 (Tiger), you can go directly to the Utilities folder from the Finder by choosing Go > Utilities.

The Preferences Command and Photoshop Preferences File

The Preferences dialog box comes up quite a bit throughout the book, but the location of the Preferences command in Photoshop is different in Mac OS X and Windows. In Mac OS X, choose Photoshop > Preferences. In Windows XP, choose Edit > Preferences.

The Preferences file stores both the settings of the Preferences dialog box and many other settings in Photoshop. It's located in the Adobe Photoshop CS 2 Settings folder. On Mac OS X, the path to the Preferences file is:

```
Computer/Users/<username>/Library/Preferences/Adobe Photoshop CS2
Settings/Adobe Photoshop CS2 Prefs.psp
```

In Windows, the Photoshop preferences file is located at:

```
C:\Documents and Settings\<username>\Application Data\Adobe\Photoshop\9.0\
Adobe Photoshop CS2 Settings\Adobe Photoshop CS2 Prefs.psp
```

Special Thanks

Although my name is on the front of this book, the book would not exist without the professional crew behind the scenes. My sincere thanks goes out to everyone who made this book happen. Pamela Pfiffner and Nancy Davis of Peachpit Press provided the support to get this project started. Adam Pratt of Adobe Systems used his seemingly encyclopedic knowledge of Adobe products to provide a thorough technical review, even during his well-earned holidays . . . now that's dedication! With clear, gentle guidance, Corbin Collins made sure that what I was writing actually made sense. The book's friendly, readable lay-out is thanks to the design and production team at Peachpit Press, led by Kate Reber, Becky Morgan, and Becky Winter; they put the book on paper and got it out the door.

I would also like to thank the Adobe Photoshop development team and community of users and authors for participating in a dialogue, in blogs, forums, podcasts, and conferences, that continually reveals the secrets of every corner of this amazing software. I would like to specifically thank Bruce Fraser and David Blatner for all of the Photoshop knowledge I've learned from them both directly and indirectly through their works.

My family and friends have been incredibly supportive during the time-consuming final phases of writing this book, and they deserve my most heartfelt thanks.

And finally, thank you for reading this book. If you'd like to contact me, you can e-mail me at workingsmart@conradchavez.com, or visit my Web site at www.conradchavez.com.

CHAPTER ONE

Optimizing Your Computer for Photoshop

GETTING GOING WITH PHOTOSHOP can be as simple as running the installer, just as you do with other programs. But Photoshop is not quite like other programs, and it's not even like basic image editors such as Microsoft Paint. Taking full advantage of the advanced features in Photoshop requires much more processor power, disk space, and RAM compared to most other programs you use.

The larger your images, the harder Photoshop and your system have to work, and if your system isn't up to the task, you'll find that "working harder" becomes "working slower." If you produce simple low-resolution images, such as those for the Web or for standard-definition video, you might be satisfied with using Photoshop on a laptop or low-end computer right out of the box. If you work in print media or high-definition television, or regularly work with images from digital SLR cameras (which can be 6 megapixels or more), you'll need to have a good system to start with, and you still might need to beef that up. And even if you think you only work with small images, the Photoshop optimization advice in this chapter still applies to you if your images usually start out as large original digital camera images or scans.

As you put together your Photoshop machine, it's very important to keep in mind that the raw performance of any one part is less important than how well all the parts are balanced. For example, don't obsess over getting the fastest, most expensive central processing unit (CPU) if you won't have enough money left over to buy enough RAM to prevent RAM from becoming a bottleneck.

The Processor

To do its job, Photoshop needs to process bit after bit of image data as fast as it possibly can, so having a powerful CPU obviously helps.

What exactly does "most powerful" mean? You can break down this concept into a few basic factors:

- **Gigahertz.** The most obvious measure of CPU speed is *gigahertz* (GHz), the number of cycles per second that a CPU can handle. Computer companies advertise gigahertz because it's one number that can be increased in ads over time to make it seem like it's time to buy a new computer all over again. It's easy to use gigahertz to compare CPUs of the same type, but gigahertz is less useful for comparing CPUs of different designs. Gigahertz is not the most reliable way to compare whole computers, especially of different brands, because there are other variables involved such as the speed of the disk, RAM, and video. You might think of gigahertz like revolutions per minute (RPM) in cars—more RPM can mean higher speed, but it depends on the car, the engine type, the gear you're in, and so on.

- **Number of CPUs.** Some high-end desktop computers contain two or even four CPUs (**Figure 1.1**). Two CPUs are better than one, but only if your programs are written to use multiple processors. Photoshop can use multiple processors, and so can Adobe Camera Raw. Some older Photoshop plug-ins may not be multiprocessor-aware.

Figure 1.1: **Processor configurations found in today's computers. From left to right: Single processor, dual processors, single dual-core processor, and two dual-core processors.**

■ **Number of cores.** Up until recently, the only way to have multiple processors in a typical computer was to add another CPU. Now, an increasing number of consumer-level CPUs have two processors in one CPU, and this is a very good thing. To distinguish between the number of CPUs and the number of actual processors, the processor inside a CPU is called its *core. Dual-core* CPUs have two processors in one CPU. Dual-core CPUs save space and are just as fast as having two single-core CPUs. If you use Photoshop on a laptop, rejoice: Thanks to the multi-core design, you can finally buy a reasonably priced laptop with more than one processor inside, enhancing performance significantly over traditional single-processor laptops.

If you can afford it, you can go all-out and buy yourself a desktop computer with two dual-core CPUs, giving you *four* processor cores to throw at your work. Of course, you'll enjoy their full benefit only during peak loads. But if you do spend a lot of time converting Raw files or running filters on large images, having all that CPU power can be worth it.

When Photoshop doesn't need all of the processors you have, Mac OS X and Windows XP are both able to apply unused processors to other programs you're running. If you have only one processor, it has to handle everything running on your computer, from processing a folder full of deadline-driven images to flashing that cute alert icon in your chat program. With multiple processors, the system can dedicate a processor to one task and move other tasks to another available processor, allowing the first task to finish faster by letting it work without distractions.

WILL A FASTER CPU HELP?

Before you go shopping for a new CPU (or two) to speed up Photoshop, check your machine to make sure it's already working the current CPU to the limit.

On Mac OS X, open Activity Monitor and click the CPU tab at the bottom of the Activity Monitor window (**Figure 1.2**). If the CPU Usage graph indicates very high usage (or low Idle percentage) as you work in Photoshop, that's one indication that the CPU may be at its limit. In the main Activity Monitor list, sort the list of processes by CPU usage by clicking the CPU tab to see which applications use the most CPU power.

On Windows XP, right-click the taskbar and choose Task Manager. Click the Performance tab (**Figure 1.3**) to see CPU performance statistics.

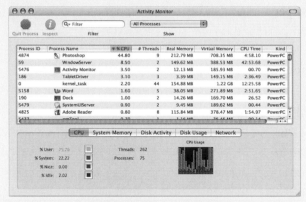

Figure 1.2: **The Process list and CPU Usage tab in Mac OS X Activity Monitor monitor system performance on Mac OS X.**

Figure 1.3: **The Performance tab in Windows Task Manager monitors performance on Windows XP.**

RAM

The term *memory* is often used too loosely, because there's more than one kind of memory in a computer, and it's important not to get them mixed up. The two kinds of memory we're most concerned with are *random-access memory* (RAM) and *hard disk space*.

RAM is the memory where your computer does most of its thinking. RAM comes as a set of chips on a small circuit board. In contrast, hard disk space is the memory where your computer stores documents, and I talk about that in the "Hard Disks" section later in this chapter. RAM is fast, so your computer and Photoshop do as much processing as possible using RAM, and therefore it's a good idea to install as much RAM as possible. The problem is that RAM is much more expensive per gigabyte than hard disk space, so not everyone can afford to install the maximum amount of RAM their computer can take. In some cases, the cost of the memory chips required to fill a computer to capacity with RAM is more than the cost of the computer itself!

How Photoshop Uses Memory

When you start Photoshop, it sets aside part of your computer's available RAM to use as its work area. If you start to do things that require more RAM than is available, Photoshop begins using hard disk space to extend its work area. Because large images require more RAM than small images, Photoshop will use your hard disk sooner with large images (such as high-resolution print images) than with small images (such as low-resolution images for the Web).

Using hard disk space as working memory is called *virtual memory*, to distinguish that use from hard disk space used simply for file storage. Virtual memory is nothing new; both Mac OS X and Windows XP use virtual memory so that running out of RAM doesn't mean you're out of memory. The only time you really run out of memory is if your hard disk is so full that there isn't enough room for virtual memory to stretch out. Photoshop creates its own virtual memory, separate from that of the operating system, because it works with files that are much larger than you typically work with on your computer.

Virtual memory can't always save you from not having enough RAM. Some filters and plug-ins can operate only in RAM, and if you run them on a large enough image, it's certainly possible for an out-of-memory alert message to appear. Adobe Camera Raw and Extract are two examples of plug-ins that must operate completely within RAM. If you use plug-ins and filters often, you'll probably need more RAM than someone who doesn't use those features.

If you're knowledgeable about RAM and curious about how Photoshop really works with RAM, you might find this interesting: Recent versions of Photoshop are designed to use virtual memory space as main memory, and to use RAM as a fast cache of what's in virtual memory. While that sounds backwards, it makes sense if you think about it. When Photoshop routinely handles more data than can fit in RAM, which is most of the time, Photoshop organizes the working data using virtual memory on disk, where there's more room, instead of in RAM. What does Photoshop put in RAM, then? It gives priority to the image data and Photoshop tools you're currently using. An advantage of this approach is that your RAM is completely dedicated to the part of an image you're actually editing. If you edit part of an image and don't come back to it, it can easily be moved to virtual memory to make your fast RAM available for whatever you've moved on to.

Do You Need More RAM?

To understand whether you've got enough RAM installed for Photoshop, use a few tools that are available both inside and outside Photoshop.

The Info palette in Photoshop can display key information about Photoshop's memory usage, but the information isn't displayed by default. Here's how to set up the Info palette for memory analysis:

1. Choose Palette Options from the Info palette menu.

2. Enable Scratch Sizes and Efficiency and click OK (**Figure 1.4**).

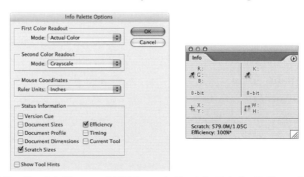

Figure 1.4: **Enabling Scratch Sizes and Efficiency in the Info Palette Options dialog box** (left) displays them in the Info Palette (right).

3. Open an image that's typical of the images you edit and perform several of the editing or correction steps you normally perform. It's important that the image be representative of the pixel dimensions and bit depth of the images you edit, too.

Take a look at the Info palette and interpret what it says in the following places:

■ On the Scratch line, the number on the left tells you how much RAM your open document currently uses. You'll see this number go up and down as you edit the image. The number on the right tells you how much RAM is available for Photoshop to use, which is set by the Memory Usage value in Preferences (I get to that in the next section, "Allocating RAM to Photoshop"). The number on the right can vary depending on other programs that may be running.

■ On the Efficiency line, see if Photoshop is operating at 100%. When Efficiency is below 100%, there isn't enough RAM for Photoshop to complete its work entirely in RAM, so Photoshop is starting to swap data between RAM and the scratch disk (Photoshop's own virtual memory), a process that slows Photoshop. If you typically see Efficiency at or near 100%, there's no immediate need for more RAM, but according to Adobe, if you consistently see an Efficiency value of 60% or less, you definitely need to add RAM.

Where All That RAM Goes

A typical reaction to watching Photoshop memory readouts is "Geez, why does Photoshop use up so much RAM?"

Here are some of the most important factors affecting how much RAM Photoshop uses (**Figure 1.5**):

■ **Number of pixels.** If your first digital camera created 4-megapixel files, and your new camera creates 8-megapixel files, the images from the new camera require twice the RAM compared to images from the older camera. Here's another example: A typical print-quality image can be 3000 x 2000 pixels, but the same image sized appropriately for the Web may be 300 x 200 pixels, which means the print image contains one hundred times the number of pixels as the Web image. That results in a *huge* difference between the RAM requirements of each image.

■ **Bit depth.** 16-bit images consume twice as much RAM than 8-bit images.

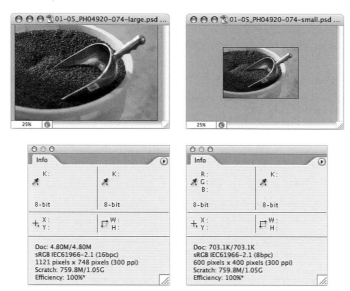

Figure 1.5: Examining an image (top left) compared to a smaller version of the same image (top right) using the first three status lines in the Info palette (bottom left and bottom right).

■ **Number of layers, masks, and channels.** Adding a layer, mask, or channel literally adds another image to the image. An RGB color image can be triple the size of a grayscale version of the same image, because the RGB version contains three color channels while the grayscale version has only one channel (black). If an image starts out as a 8-bit RGB file without layers, and you add a layer to it, the file now contains two 8-bit RGB images.

■ **Number of open documents.** You can tell from the other items on this list that just one layered print-resolution image can easily consume the moderate amount of RAM that most computers come with out of the box (1GB or less). If you open multiple documents, and they're all rather involved, they can start to crowd each other out of your computer's available RAM.

What does all this mean? For maximum efficiency, figure out the highest level of quality required for your workflow and stay within that range. If you can't afford the RAM and other hardware to accommodate the memory needs of your workflow, try to avoid creating files that are larger or more complex than necessary. This doesn't necessarily have to lower quality; for instance, if your workflow doesn't benefit from 16-bit images, stick with 8-bit images, and Photoshop will be much more responsive.

NOTE   Adding a mask or channel increases file size less than adding an layer does, because a mask or channel consists of just one grayscale channel. Adding a layer requires adding all of the color channels used by the image. Adding a layer to an RGB image creates a 3-channel layer, while adding a layer to a CMYK image increases file size more because it creates a 4-channel layer.

If you use system utilities such as Activity Monitor (Mac OS X) or Task Manager (Windows) to monitor RAM usage, you may have noticed that Photoshop grabs a lot of memory when it starts up. This has led some to believe, mistakenly, that Photoshop takes more RAM than it needs. Actually, the amount of RAM Photoshop "reserves" at startup isn't exclusive to Photoshop. If Photoshop needs that RAM first, it will take it and hold on to it until you exit the program, but if Photoshop isn't currently using it, the RAM is available to other programs.

 NOTE   For complete, up-to-date information about the Photoshop RAM explanations in this chapter, see the Adobe tech note at:
www.adobe.com/support/techdocs/320005.html

Allocating RAM to Photoshop

There's one more factor that affects how much RAM Photoshop uses: the Memory Usage percentage in the Preferences dialog box. Everybody seems to have a slightly different idea of what this preference is and how it affects Photoshop performance and efficiency, and I'm going to try and set the record straight.

I've already covered how Photoshop starts to use hard disk space as working memory when you do things that require more RAM than is available. A side effect of this is that before Photoshop starts to use your hard disk, it will use all of your available RAM first. Sometimes you don't want that to happen; you may want to keep enough RAM free to smoothly run another program alongside Photoshop such as Adobe Bridge, Adobe InDesign, or Adobe Illustrator. That means you want to limit Photoshop's natural tendency to use all available RAM. And that is what the Memory Usage preference does (**Figure 1.6**). The Memory Usage preference doesn't allocate more RAM to Photoshop; instead, it limits the amount of RAM that Photoshop can have.

You'll notice that the default percentage of the Memory Usage preference is 70%. Now, don't be tempted to top it off at 100%. Remember, Photoshop isn't the only program you're running on your computer. The operating system needs

Figure 1.6: Use Memory & Image Cache preferences to fine-tune the balance between Photoshop performance and RAM usage.

RAM to run, and so do all the more modest programs you probably use constantly without a second thought, like e-mail and chat programs, and your Web browser. If you set the Memory Usage preference too high, other programs may not run well. If you can't afford to install enough RAM to run everything efficiently, you have a choice. If you want other programs to run well on the same machine as Photoshop, lower the Memory Usage percentage in Photoshop. If you want Photoshop to run faster, run as few other programs as possible.

How do you know whether the Memory Usage preference should be increased or decreased? Answering that question puts us into geek territory, so if you're fine with watching statistics and graphs, read on. If not, leave the Memory Usage preference alone and move on.

To check the RAM performance of Photoshop on Mac OS X:

1. Open Activity Monitor, which is in your Utilities folder.

2. Click the System Memory tab at the bottom of the screen.

3. Notice the readout for Free memory, indicated in green (**Figure 1.7**).

Figure 1.7

4. Watch the Free memory readout as you edit your images in Photoshop. If Free memory regularly falls below 20MB, consider lowering the Memory Usage percentage in Photoshop preferences as described later in this section. You can also install more RAM or run fewer programs alongside Photoshop.

To check the RAM performance of Photoshop on Windows XP:

1. Right-click on the Taskbar and choose Task Manager.

2. Click the Performance tab.

3. In the Physical Memory section, notice the readout for Available memory (**Figure 1.8**).

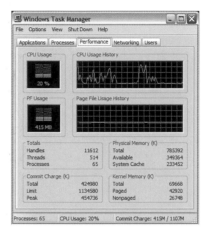

Figure 1.8

4. Watch the Available Memory readout as you edit your images in Photoshop. If Free memory regularly falls below 20,000K, consider lowering the Memory Usage percentage in Photoshop preferences as described later in this section. You can also install more RAM or run fewer programs alongside Photoshop.

 TIP   In Windows, advanced users can monitor RAM usage more precisely using the Performance utility, which is located inside Start menu > Control Panel > Administrative Tools. After it opens, click the Add button (plus sign) on the toolbar, select Memory from the Processor Object pop-up menu, select Available Mbytes from the list box, click Add, and click Close. The graph may be easier to read if you adjust the graph scale; right-click the vertical axis, choose Properties, and click Graph. Set the Maximum to a useful number such as the total number of megabytes of RAM installed in your computer.

To change the Memory Usage preference in Photoshop:

1. Open the Preferences dialog box.

2. Choose Memory and Image Cache from the pop-up menu at the top of the dialog box.

3. Adjust the Maximum Used by Photoshop percentage value. It's best to make an adjustment 5% up or down from the current value, but avoid going above 75% unless you have more than 2GB of RAM installed. For more about that, see the topic "Using More than 2GB of RAM."

4. Click OK and restart Photoshop.

5. Monitor Photoshop performance as described earlier, and make another adjustment if needed.

To summarize, Photoshop starts with the amount of unused RAM in your computer and uses the Memory Usage preference to set the amount of RAM that it ultimately uses (**Figure 1.9**). Anything that doesn't fit in RAM goes to the scratch disk.

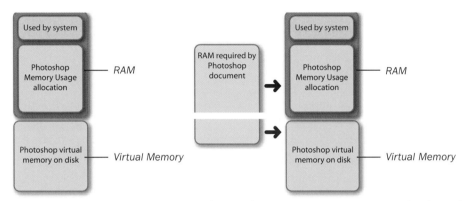

Figure 1.9: **Photoshop can use the RAM left over after the operating system gets what it needs (left). If a Photoshop document requires more RAM than is available, parts of the document are shuffled in and out of virtual memory as needed (right).**

 TIPS   In this post on his blog, Adobe engineer Scott Byer describes in more detail how to monitor your Photoshop memory usage:

`http://blogs.adobe.com/scottbyer/2006/03/reap_what_you_m.html`

The Dashboard widgets in Mac OS X are convenient and fun, but don't go overboard with them. Dashboard widgets don't consume CPU power when they're hidden, but each one constantly occupies RAM, as you can observe in Activity Monitor. Dashboard runs as part of the Dock, so to quit all running widgets and release their RAM, select the Dock process in Activity Monitor and then click the Quit Process button in the Activity Monitor toolbar. Note that widgets don't load until you open Dashboard for the first time after logging in.

NOTES You may have noticed that the Memory Usage preference displays an amount of Available RAM that doesn't match the total amount of RAM in your computer. That's because there's always a base amount of RAM that Photoshop and other programs can't ever use because the operating system needs that RAM just to keep your computer running.

Some Mac users initially interpret the Memory Usage allocation to be similar to the memory allocation feature in the Get Info dialog box in the OS 9 Finder. That's not the case at all. In OS 9, the system allowed manual control of RAM allocation. In OS X, there is no system-level user control over RAM allocation. The Memory Usage preference in Photoshop is provided by Adobe, not OS X or Windows, and can only limit Photoshop RAM usage—you can never use it to give Photoshop more RAM than it could have obtained on its own.

Advanced RAM Tweaks

If you've already read this far into this topic, you're probably not against a little work under the hood to tune Photoshop efficiency. In that case, I have a few more tips for adjusting the balance between performance and RAM usage. The way you want to think about these tips is in terms of how much RAM you've got installed. If you have more than 2GB of RAM installed, you've got enough room to tune for maximum performance. If you have less than 2GB installed, you need to make compromises to avoid slowing down Photoshop. OK, here we go.

Bigger Tiles Plug-in

When you open an image, Photoshop breaks it up into tiles so that the tiles loaded into RAM are only those involving the part of the image you're working on. By default, Photoshop tiles are on the small side so that they're easier to load into available RAM. If you have more than 1GB of RAM, you can enable the Bigger Tiles plug-in. Bigger tiles mean fewer tiles, and moving fewer, bigger tiles is more efficient than moving more, smaller tiles, if you have enough RAM.

To load the Bigger Tiles plug-in:

1. Go to the following folder, which is inside your Adobe Photoshop program folder:

```
Adobe Photoshop CS2/Plug-Ins/Adobe Photoshop Only/Extensions/Bigger Tiles
```

2. You'll find the Bigger Tiles plug-in with a tilde before the name (˜Bigger Tiles.plugin). Delete the tilde.

3. Restart Photoshop.

 TIP   You can disable any plug-in by adding a tilde (~) before the name.

Cache Levels

Photoshop can use a portion of RAM to remember how an image looks at different zoom levels, so that you experience less of a delay each time you zoom in or out on a large layered file. Of course, there isn't enough RAM to cache every possible zoom level, so Photoshop is set to cache six zoom levels by default. If you work with large layered files and aren't short on RAM, you can set Photoshop to use up to eight cache levels. If you want to make more RAM available for other Photoshop operations or you work with small, flattened images, you can lower this value down to one cache level.

To change the number of cache levels:

1. In Photoshop, open the Preferences dialog box.

2. Choose Memory and Image Cache from the pop-up menu at the top of the dialog box.

3. Adjust the value, click OK, and restart Photoshop.

RELEASING RAM IN A HURRY

Although Photoshop can normally avoid out-of-memory situations by using virtual memory, some filters and features need to do their work only in actual RAM. If the size of an image and the feature you're applying create more data than your computer's RAM can handle, it's possible to get an out-of-memory message. You can often save, exit and restart Photoshop, and try again.

In the worst case, you may see an alert that there isn't enough memory to save. This is bad because it means you can't exit Photoshop without losing unsaved changes. Luckily, Photoshop provides a way out that usually works: the commands on the Edit > Purge submenu (Undo, Clipboard, Histories, All). If you don't need your History palette history states, you might as well go straight to the Edit > Purge > All command and then try to save. Otherwise, you keep the most options open by choosing Edit > Purge > Clipboard and then try to save again; if that doesn't work, try the other commands. Note that even if you choose Edit > Purge > All, the History palette isn't fully purged until you manually delete the first history snapshot in the History palette.

Using More than 2GB of RAM

If you're fortunate enough to have more than 2GB of RAM installed in your computer, Photoshop works a bit differently than it does when you have less than 2GB of RAM—especially if you have a 64-bit CPU and operating system. The more RAM you have installed above 2GB, the closer you can set the percentage in the Memory Usage percentage to 100%—on a 32-bit CPU and operating system, Photoshop can't access more than 2GB directly, so once Photoshop gets its 2GB, the rest of the RAM will be used for the operating system and other programs you run.

If you have a 64-bit system and more than 4GB of RAM, things get quite interesting. On a 64-bit system, Photoshop can directly use 3GB of RAM, and Photoshop plug-ins can use the RAM between 3GB and 4GB. Above 4GB, you can get an unexpected speed boost: When Photoshop would normally move scratch data to its scratch disk, Mac OS X and Windows XP allow that data to move to the RAM above 4GB instead. We all know that RAM is much faster than hard disk space, so this use of RAM can really enhance performance. (Mac users should note the potential issue in the next section, however.)

What's the lesson in all this? If you work with very large files and are thinking about installing 2GB of RAM, think about installing 4GB instead so that Photoshop can reach its maximum RAM potential and still have RAM left over for the system and other programs. And if you edit large files on a 64-bit CPU and operating system, consider going all the way to 6GB or more so that you can take advantage of the faster scratch data storage in RAM, if your files are so large that this features applies.

Using More Than 4GB of RAM in Mac OS X

There is a bug in Mac OS X 10.3 and later that may cause a long wait cursor (that spinning rainbow wheel) when more than 4GB of RAM is installed. If you experience this, you may want to download and install the Disable VM Buffering plug-in from Adobe. The plug-in turns off the ability to move Photoshop scratch data into RAM above 4GB. If you have more than 4GB of RAM and you don't see the long wait cursor, you may not want to install the plug-in, so that you can continue to benefit from storing scratch data in RAM.

You can download the plug-in here:

```
www.adobe.com/support/downloads/detail.jsp?ftpID=3337
```

Using More Than 4GB of RAM in Windows XP

In Windows XP, a program can use up to 2GB of RAM. However, if you have more than 4GB of RAM installed in a computer running Windows XP Service Pack 2 or later, you can add a line to the boot.ini file that will allow Photoshop to use up to 3GB of RAM. This is called the /3GB Switch. It isn't guaranteed to work on all configurations, which is why it's turned off by default in Windows XP, but if it works on yours, any program you have that is written to use more than 2GB of RAM take advantage of it.

You should try this only if you're familiar with how to edit the boot.ini file, because it controls how your computer starts up. Careful!

For Microsoft's information about this switch, read this Microsoft tech note:

    http://support.microsoft.com/kb/833721/en-us#E05B0ABAAA

 TIP   Avoid putting large amounts of data on the clipboard. The clipboard is where data goes when you use the Edit > Cut or Edit > Copy commands, and the clipboard consumes available RAM. Fortunately, Photoshop provides better ways to move or duplicate than the Cut and Copy commands. For example, if you want to copy a selection, you can Option/Alt-drag it using the move tool. If you want to copy a layer to another document, it's easier and more precise to use the Layer > Duplicate command rather than copying and pasting. You have more control and use less RAM.

Hard Disks

It might not be obvious at first glance, but in many ways the hard disk you have is just as critical to Photoshop efficiency as the CPU and RAM you have. As I described in the RAM section earlier in this chapter, when you have Photoshop do something that requires more RAM than it's got, Photoshop starts to use hard disk space as an extension of RAM. Shuffling data between RAM and the hard disk imposes a performance penalty, because hard disks are slower than RAM, which means that RAM will be left waiting for data from the hard disk. With that in mind, you'll want to consider the performance of your hard disk whenever you buy a computer to use primarily for Photoshop. The faster the hard disk, the more responsive Photoshop can be.

Hard Disks as Scratch Disks

If you really want Photoshop to run efficiently, it's a very good idea to connect an additional hard disk and use it as a Photoshop scratch disk, and to avoid using your startup disk as the scratch disk. If you don't know why, an analogy can help.

Have you ever gone to a restaurant at peak dinner hour and discovered that there's only one server working all the tables, maybe because the other server called in sick? You know that the one working server has got to be overworked, and may not be able to give each customer the service they deserve. The server's attention is simply divided too many ways. When both servers are there, each of them can give their section of the restaurant the proper level of attention and service.

You can think of your hard disk in a similar way. On a typical computer, you have one hard disk, yet there are always multiple streams of data moving between the hard disk and RAM, such as the following:

- Operating system code

- The operating system's virtual memory scratch files

- The code of the program you're running

- Photoshop's virtual memory scratch files

- The document you're editing

A hard disk has a set of heads reading off the disk platters. The more each data stream demands use of the disk, the more each data stream has to wait for the disk heads to get the requested data that some other data stream wants, and everything slows down.

Of the data streams in the list above, the two busiest are usually the ones handling the scratch files for the operating system and for Photoshop. If you apply the restaurant lesson to the two scratch disk data streams, what you need to do is direct each stream to a different hard disk. That way, the operating system and Photoshop can each have the full attention of its own scratch disk (**Figure 1.10**).

To assign the scratch disk for Photoshop:

1. In Photoshop, open the Preferences dialog box.

2. Choose Plug-ins and Scratch Disks from the pop-up menu at the top of the dialog box.

Figure 1.10: **Using a single hard disk makes your operating system and Photoshop compete for the same single hard disk (left). It's best to assign a Photoshop scratch disk to a separate (green) internal disk (center) or external disk (right).**

3. In the Scratch Disks section (**Figure 1.11**), choose the name of your scratch disk from the first pop-up menu. If you're using additional drives as scratch disks, you can choose them in the other pop-up menus in that section.

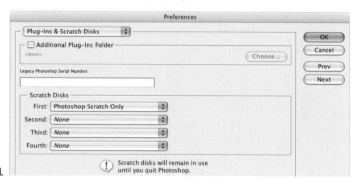

Figure 1.11

 NOTE   Only assign scratch disks that are completely dedicated to being scratch disks. Don't choose the disk that contains the swap file for your operating system. If you don't know which disk contains your operating system swap file, it's the startup disk, because that's where it goes by default. Also, don't use other partitions on your startup disk as scratch disks, because scratch disks are only faster if they are truly separate disks.

To be clear, all Mac OS X and Windows XP programs use the operating system's virtual memory. However, you don't often hear about enhancing performance by putting the virtual memory file on a different disk, because most programs don't move as much data as Photoshop does. You wouldn't notice the difference as easily. If you happen to hang around professionals who work with large databases or audio/video professionals, you actually might hear them talk about moving the virtual memory scratch file (often called the *swap file* outside of Photoshop).

TIPS   To make your Photoshop scratch disk as efficient as possible, assign a large, fast hard disk that isn't used for anything else. If you must use a disk that contains other files, it will work best as a scratch disk if you partition it, keeping one partition empty for use as a Photoshop scratch disk and storing the files in the other partition.

Another great way to set up scratch disks is as a RAID (Redundant Array of Inexpensive Disks). A RAID appears on your computer as a single disk. Because a RAID is actually made up of multiple disks, reads and writes are distributed among all the disks. That arrangement keeps up with RAM much faster than a single disk can.

MANAGING SCRATCH DISK SPACE

Photoshop can consume up to several gigabytes of disk space for maintaining its scratch files, depending on the size of the images you edit and how many images are currently open. That may seem excessive until you think through why so much space becomes necessary. You could say that Photoshop scratch disk space is the space where Photoshop keeps your options open. For example, Photoshop stores the History palette's history states on your scratch disk. If Photoshop didn't provide the great convenience of history states, those states wouldn't need a place to be stored. Each history state can represent an entire document, so if you edit a document that's 100MB on disk and you maintain 20 history states, you could easily build up a 2000MB (2GB) scratch file, and that's just for your history states.

To find out how much scratch disk space Photoshop is using, check the Scratch readout in the Info palette. The number on the left side represents both the current amount of both the RAM in use and the data being stored in the scratch file. However, what's probably more important is the amount of free space on your scratch disk. On Mac OS X, you can see the amount of free space by opening a folder window for a disk; on Windows, open My Computer and select a disk to display Free Space in the left column of the window. Note that Photoshop scratch files are temporary and are automatically deleted when you exit Photoshop.

On both Mac OS X and Windows XP, having less than 5GB of available disk space can lead to system instability. If your available disk space creeps dangerously toward zero as you work in Photoshop, it's a sign that your scratch disk is too small. That's yet another good reason to use a separate disk as a Photoshop scratch disk: You remove the risk that a Photoshop scratch file will consume all the remaining unused space on your startup disk.

TIP   If you like to load a lot of custom brushes into the Brushes palette in Photoshop, you might want to know that brushes are saved with the document, stored with its history states, and take up RAM. It's a good idea to delete any brushes you're sure you don't need.

Hard Disk Speed

There's more than one way to measure hard disk speed. The unit of measure you see most often in ads is revolutions per minute (RPM). For desktop computers, 7200 RPM is common, while laptops have been moving from 4200 RPM to 5400 RPM. However, measuring hard disk speed using only RPM is like measuring a processor using only MHz—it doesn't give you the whole speed picture. For example, a 7200 RPM 3.5-inch desktop hard disk is typically faster than a 7200 RPM 2.5-inch laptop hard disk. If you really want to compare the speeds of different hard disks, look at RPM, the sustained read/write speeds, and the cache size. *Sustained read and write speeds* are usually measured in megabytes per second (MB/sec) and are representative of what Photoshop does all the time. When Photoshop moves data between RAM and the hard disk, or when you save a file, that's a sustained read or write. A larger *cache size* saves time by keeping recently read data in a RAM cache that's part of the disk drive, so that your computer doesn't have to go all the way to the disk every time it needs data (as you know by now, disks are slower than RAM). Cache isn't the most important number to look at, but it makes a good tie-breaker when comparing two hard disks where the other factors are equal.

Determining Space for Storing and Backing Up Files

By now you realize that Photoshop is most efficient with at least two hard disks: one for the system and documents, and another for Photoshop scratch disk use. You might get your two hard disks and figure you're done. But you probably aren't done. If your projects are important enough that you're doing them using pricey software like Photoshop, you need to make sure your project files aren't lost during a major disaster. Let's say you've determined that a 250GB hard disk is big enough to store all of your current images and the images you'll create for the next year. Does that mean you should buy one 250GB hard disk?

No. It means you need to buy at least two 250GB hard disks. One disk for storing your images, and at least one more for *backing up* your images. And because hard disks can fail at any time, many professionals back up to more than one hard disk, or burn DVDs of each project. Never have just one copy of anything important.

It's a great idea to have an *offsite backup*—a complete copy of your important files that you store away from your main location. An offsite backup protects you from losing data to theft or to a disaster that destroys your home or office. If you live in an area that's vulnerable to disasters that can destroy an entire region, such as a flood, hurricane, or earthquake, consider maintaining an offsite backup outside your region. Whereas some keep their offsite backups in a bank vault, some find it sufficient to send their offsite backups to offices their company maintains in other regions, or to faraway relatives or friends. Some people agree to exchange and care for each others' offsite backups. At the very least, don't keep your only backup next to your computer, or connected to your computer—it's too easily lost to the same fire, theft, or electrical problem that would cause you to lose your primary data.

Debates rage about which backup medium is the best. Many of these debates center around the archival properties of a medium—the number of years a medium can reliably preserve data. I don't think media longevity is necessarily the most important factor, because media tends to become obsolete before it deteriorates. In other words, the reason people copy to newer media is not because the old media falls apart, but because it's no longer practical to maintain the old drives that read the old media (Syquest 44MB SCSI drive, anyone?). So what can you do after you realize you're going to have to move data every few years no matter what medium you choose? Simple: Assume that periodic data migration is a given, and make your long-term backup plans account for that. Based on that line of reasoning, my main backups would be multiple hard disks that are the same size as my main disk. Going with hard disks means that updating the backups or migrating to new hard disks is easy and fast.

Hard disk data can easily become corrupted, which can ruin a file. When I back up, the ruined file may replace the good copies of the files on my backup hard disks, wiping out all good copies of the file. To help safeguard data against this possibility, I also burn DVDs of the most important finished projects because DVDs can't be edited (although they can still deteriorate).

Whatever way you decide to back up, make sure your method is reliable, quick, and easy for you. If you choose a difficult or tedious backup plan, you won't back up as often as you should. The longer you go between backups, the more your valuable data is at risk. You should be able to back up as soon as you amass data that you can't lose; if that happens daily, then you should have a simple and reliable way to do a daily backup.

As you plan for your storage needs, be sure to think through all of the backup space you'll need. For example, because I wanted at least two full backups of my main 250GB image storage hard disk, I needed to buy three 250GB hard disks.

LAPTOP LIMITATIONS

As laptop computers have gotten more powerful, many people now use one as a primary computer, simply plugging in a mouse and big monitor when they get into the office. Dual-core CPUs give laptop computers a noticeable speed boost compared to the old single-core CPUs, and laptop hard disk sizes are now well above 100GB, allowing easy temporary storage of SLR-sized digital camera photos. For photographers and other creative professionals who spend much of the day on a location shoot or at a client site, a laptop is indispensable.

But there is one area in which laptops have not progressed, and that's the area of RAM capacity. While desktop computers that can hold 16GB of RAM are not new, laptops that can hold more than 2GB of RAM are still relatively rare. If you work with large images with many layers, the low RAM ceiling can be the most significant limitation of using a laptop, and a good argument for getting a desktop instead.

Laptops also lag behind in hard disk capacity and speed. While 250GB hard disks are commonplace in desktop computers, a 160GB hard disk in a laptop is an expensive luxury (or at least it is as I write this). In addition, it isn't practical to put a second hard disk in a laptop.

Finally, the screens on laptops are not to the same standard as good desktop monitors. As with other laptop components, laptop screens are somewhat compromised by the need for lightweight portability, mobile durability, and low power consumption. Fortunately, you can plug most high-end laptops into a good quality external monitor.

If you work with small images, you may have no problem using a laptop as your main Photoshop machine. But if you work with print-quality, high-resolution images in a workflow where color consistency is critical, you'll probably need a capable, expandable desktop computer and use your laptop for mobile work only.

Monitors and Video Cards

Photoshop requires a monitor set for at least 1024 × 768 pixels at a bit depth of at least 16 bits per pixel (thousands of colors). Fortunately, most new desktop and laptop computers being sold today are capable of well beyond the minimum requirements for Photoshop. Photoshop displays best if you set your monitor to 32 bits per pixel at the highest monitor resolution that's comfortable for you. You don't want to run at the minimum specifications anyway—1024 × 768 doesn't leave much room for palettes, and 16 bits per pixel doesn't represent color quite as precisely as the 24 bits per pixel (millions of colors) that color professionals use as a standard.

Another great efficiency booster is to attach a second monitor to your computer, so that you can spread out your work area and prevent palettes from covering the image window. If you want to run multiple monitors, make sure your computer or your video card has an additional monitor port available, and is capable of driving at least one of those monitors at the resolution and bit depth Photoshop needs. I talk about multiple monitors in more detail in the section "Optimizing for Multiple Monitors" in Chapter 2.

In most computers, monitors are driven by the video card that came with the computer, and that's usually fine. You can buy a different or newer video card if you want to:

- Upgrade to use a monitor with a higher resolution than your current card supports.

- Connect more monitors by installing a video card with one or more additional monitor ports.

- Add a monitor that uses a connector you don't have on your computer (VGA, DVI, S-video, and so on).

Video cards work in computers that have an expansion card slot. At this time, most video cards for desktop computers are PCI compatible; those for laptops fit in a laptop's PC card slot. If your computer doesn't have a card slot, there are some video solutions that connect to the USB or FireWire port, but they are not usually suitable for Photoshop use.

It isn't hard to shop for a video card to use with Photoshop. Thanks to gamers, who have continually demanded better 3D video performance, most video cards are capable of displaying millions of colors on large monitors and work great for Photoshop. When you shop for a video card, don't be concerned about 3D performance at all (unless you're a gamer). Pay more attention to the number and type of video output connectors, and make sure the card can drive your best monitor at the highest resolution it supports.

 TIPS   If you prepare graphics for video broadcast or DVD, you can buy a video card that has a television connector so that you can more effectively preview how your images will look on television. Many laptops have a TV output built in.

Some low-end computers use integrated video, which means that the computer drives a monitor by taking memory from main computer RAM instead of using RAM on a separate card that's solely dedicated to video. Integrated video lowers the amount of available RAM for Photoshop and may not perform as well as a separate video card.

Other Ways to Optimize Your Computer

There are a few other areas where your hardware habits can affect the efficiency of your Photoshop workflow.

Digital Camera Transfers

If you feed Photoshop with a steady stream of images from digital cameras, I hope you aren't still transferring your photos to your computer using the camera cable. It's much better to remove the card from the camera and insert it into a USB 2.0 or FireWire card reader connected to your computer. Using a card reader has the following advantages:

■   USB 2.0 and FireWire card readers are much faster than a camera cable. Cameras using USB 1.1 have very slow transfer rates over the cable.

■   You save your camera's battery power. When you use the cable, your camera must be switched on and involved in the transfer. When you use a card reader, your camera can be off.

■ You free up your camera. While transferring photos using a card reader, you can put another card in the camera and keep shooting. When you use a cable, you can't use the camera to take photos during a transfer.

Card readers are inexpensive, so if you don't already have one, you should definitely give them a look.

That Pointing Device in Your Hand

Yes, your humble mouse might actually be a hardware bottleneck. When using a mature product like Photoshop, you can potentially hold yourself back if you don't take full advantage of mice and other pointing devices. If you are a Mac user with a one-button mouse, you owe it to yourself to try a two-button scroll-wheel mouse. Photoshop takes advantage of both the right mouse button and the scroll wheel in powerful ways. Context menus, which you see when you right-click (Ctrl-click on Mac OS X), are all over Photoshop and can save you many trips to the main menu. You can use the scroll wheel to scroll and zoom in Photoshop.

To get the absolute most out of Photoshop, switch to a graphics tablet such as those made by Wacom Technology. A good graphics tablet comes with a pressure-sensitive stylus. Photoshop understands stylus signals such as pressure and tilt, so you can paint or retouch with almost as much control and subtlety as if you were using an actual pencil or brush. For example, you can use Photoshop brushes that make a stroke darker or wider as you press harder, and lighter or narrower as you ease up on the stylus pressure. I talk a little more about brushes in Chapter 4.

Get Rid of Excess Traffic

You know by now that Photoshop image editing works best when it has the full attention of your CPU, RAM, and hard disk. Every extra program you run can draw system resources away from Photoshop and slow it down.

If you have a spare computer lying around, consider running non-Photoshop programs on that computer. A computer that doesn't have the horsepower for Photoshop is often more than capable of running e-mail clients, Web browsers, and music and chat programs. Try to reserve your Photoshop computer for production tasks, freeing up more system resources for Photoshop.

Activation: Using Photoshop on Multiple Computers

If you spend as much time on your laptop computer as you do on your desktop computer, you probably want to run Photoshop on both machines. The Adobe Photoshop single-user license agreement says that it's legal to use your licensed copy of on two computers as long as you don't run both copies at the same time and you're the only one using the copies. In the past, compliance with this license depended on the honor system, but Adobe Photoshop CS2 is the first version to use *activation* on both Mac OS X and Windows. Activation is an online process that enforces the license agreement by making sure you're using only the number of Photoshop copies you're licensed to have. The Adobe Activation dialog box (**Figure 1.12**) appears automatically when you first start Photoshop, and it uses an Internet connection.

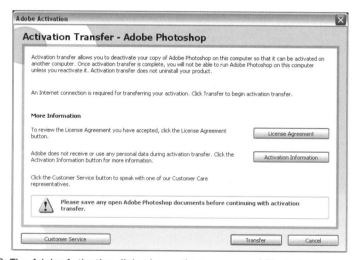

Figure 1.12: **The Adobe Activation dialog box activates a copy of Photoshop.**

How does activation affect your production efficiency? You need to think about activation when you radically alter the machine on which you're running Photoshop. For example, your laptop might develop a problem and you decide to move everything to a different laptop. In that case, remember to deactivate Photoshop on the dying laptop (Help > Transfer Activation) before you run it on the replacement laptop. You'll then need to activate Photoshop on the replacement laptop.

There are myths floating around about activation, so here are some facts about how activation works:

■ Activation doesn't need an Internet connection. If you are stuck somewhere without an Internet connection and you need to activate your software, Adobe provides a telephone number so you can activate over the phone. What if you're on assignment way out in the middle of nowhere, with no Internet *or* phone service? You're still not stuck. Starting from when you install, you have a 30-day grace period during which you can use the software before you must activate.

■ Photoshop doesn't "phone home" every time you use it. After you activate Photoshop, the program doesn't contact the activation server unless you decide to transfer activation. After you activate Photoshop, the only reason Photoshop needs the Internet is for online services like ordering prints or stock photos from Adobe Bridge. If you're just editing images, Photoshop doesn't need the Internet at all.

■ Activation does not limit you to two installations. You may be surprised, but nothing stops you from installing Photoshop on as many computers as you like. What activation does is prevent you from actually using Photoshop on more than two of those computers, because the activation server won't let you activate more computers than your license authorizes. The advantage of under-standing this is that you don't have to uninstall Photoshop just to change which two machines use Photoshop. So, for example, if you need to have one of your two Photoshop computers serviced and you want to temporarily use Photoshop on a third computer, in Photoshop on the computer being serviced simply choose Help > Transfer Activation (to deactivate it), and activate Photo-shop on the third machine. When the second machine comes back, deactivate Photoshop on the third machine and re-activate it on the second.

The mechanics of activation are kind of a pain to keep in mind, but Adobe seems to have anticipated most of the situations that would cause difficulty.

 TIP   The most important thing to remember about activation is to deactivate the software whenever you want to activate it on another computer or radically change the hardware on the same computer. As more companies use activation, remem-bering to deactivate has to become part of all of our system migration checklists.

From Beginner to Expert

To realize the full potential of Photoshop, your entire system must be free of performance bottlenecks. Due to the nature of heavy-duty image processing, Photoshop makes heavy demands on the CPU, RAM, and hard disk in your computer, and Photoshop performance can be held back by any of those three components. Of course, it can cost quite a bit of money to configure a great Photoshop system, so if your current system doesn't quite have the best of all worlds yet, here's how you might approach building a computer for Photoshop:

■ Start with an expandable system. A desktop computer should have extra empty bays so you can add internal hard disks. A laptop should have FireWire or USB 2.0 ports so you can attach fast external hard disks. Your computer should also have the capacity for at least 2GB of RAM, preferably much more.

■ Start with a multi-core processor, simply because you'll get twice as much processing power in about the same amount of space.

■ Start with at least 1GB of RAM. If you'll be processing large numbers of Raw format files from digital cameras or CMYK images for print, start as far above 1GB as you can.

■ If you must run Photoshop with one hard disk (such as on a laptop), start with a hard disk that has enough free space not only for file storage but also for operating system and Photoshop scratch disks. Although the size of such a disk can vary depending on your typical workload and files, this usually translates into "the biggest hard disk you can afford." On a desktop, try starting at 250GB, and on a laptop, try starting at 100GB. As your budget allows, add more fast hard disks to your desktop computer or replace your laptop hard disk with a bigger and faster one.

■ As your budget allows, add RAM, then add hard disk space.

■ As you gain experience and build a better system, start implementing the advanced Photoshop configuration tweaks I covered in this chapter, like the memory settings in the Preferences dialog box.

CHAPTER TWO

Optimizing Your Workspace

HAVING THE RIGHT TOOLS CLOSE AT HAND makes any project go more smoothly. When you're getting ready to cook, wouldn't it be great if you could push one button to bring out all of the bowls, utensils, pots, and pans needed to prepare a specific dish? That may still be a dream in the kitchen, but in Photoshop, it's a reality you can enjoy today. Photoshop workspaces can arrange windows, palettes, tools, and menus for you.

Optimizing workspaces isn't just about bringing out the tools you need; you can also use a workspace to hide everything you don't want in your way. With only the essential tools on screen, you can devote more of the available space on your monitor to displaying both the image and your favorite tools.

If you're just getting to know Photoshop, optimizing your workspace will be an iterative process, because you may not know enough about the tools to know which ones you really want up front. As you gain experience with Photoshop, expect to refine and update your workspaces over time. By the time you become an experienced Photoshop user, your workspace will look much different than it did when you were a beginning or intermediate user.

An important key to success is for you to learn how you work. Everyone does things a little differently, so you may need to adapt another person's great shortcut for your own working style. Keep an eye on what tasks you do most often and the paths you take through Photoshop to get those tasks done. If you catch yourself thinking "Man, this is the tenth time I've clicked that button today," you may have found an opportunity to learn or create a shortcut, or to refine a palette arrangement to make that particular task go a little faster.

Arranging Palettes

Arranging palettes is a concept so basic that it seems like I shouldn't have to discuss it. But like many Photoshop topics, you'll find a great deal of power hidden under the surface that can make a difference in your productivity. Photoshop has so many palettes that you can spend a lot of your valuable time showing, hiding, and pushing the palettes around the screen. Instead, let Photoshop remember your palette arrangements as *workspaces* so that you can apply any combination of palettes instantly.

To arrange palettes:

1. Open an image that's typical of the images you edit (**Figure 2.1**).

2. Open all of the palettes you want to display and close any palettes you don't want to display. You may need to ungroup or undock unwanted palettes to be able to close them individually (see nearby sidebar for more on docking).

3. Arrange palettes by dragging palette tabs or title bars. Be mindful of leaving enough space for the images you edit. Keeping palettes along the edges of the monitor helps to keep them out of the way of the image. On a widescreen monitor, it helps to keep palettes in vertical stacks along the left and right edges.

Figure 2.1

4. If there isn't enough space for all the palettes you want to display, dock and group them as needed (see nearby sidebar for more on docking). Start by docking, because docking maximizes palette visibility. If you still have too many palettes, start taking advantage of palette groups and the palette well. Send less-frequently used palettes to the back of palette groups.

 TIP As you drag the edge of the palette close to the edge of another palette or the screen, the edges snap to each other for your convenience. To force a palette to snap to the edge of the screen, Shift+drag a palette tab or title bar.

THE OPTIONS BAR: A SPECIAL KIND OF PALETTE

The options bar is the strip that runs across the top of the screen. Some people mistakenly call it a toolbar, but that isn't what it is. The options bar provides options for the tool that's selected in the toolbox. As you select different tools, the options bar changes accordingly. This is in contrast to palettes, which report on the state of the selection, cursor location, or the document.

DOCKING, GROUPING, AND THE PALETTE WELL

Docking and grouping are two ways to move multiple palettes together. When you want all palettes in a set to be visible simultaneously, *dock* them (**Figure 2.2**) by dragging a palette tab onto the bottom of another palette until a bold line appears, then let go of the mouse button. When you want to display multiple palettes on top of each other, *group* them (**Figure 2.3**) by dragging one palette tab onto another.

The palette *well* (**Figure 2.4**) is a place to keep palettes nearby without having them intrude on the workspace at all. To add a palette to a palette well, just drag a palette tab to the palette well, which you'll find at the right end of the options bar. To view a palette in the palette well, click its tab. The palette well is a good place to keep palettes that you only need to see or use briefly, because any palettes you open from there snap closed as soon as you click outside the palette. Any palettes you want to keep visible should be docked or grouped instead. A small monitor may not leave much room for the palette well.

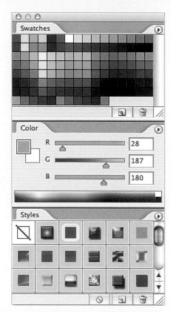

Figure 2.2: **Docked palettes are arranged as a vertical stack.**

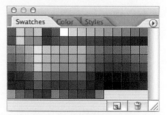

Figure 2.3: **Grouped palettes are arranged as a stack of palettes occupying the same space.**

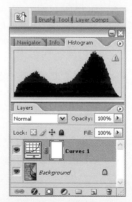

Figure 2.4: **At the top is the palette well, below that is a group of three palettes, and at the bottom the Layers palette is docked to the palette group above it.**

Saving Your Palette Arrangements

That's a nice palette arrangement you've got there . . . shame if something happened to it. Unfortunately, Photoshop has a way of resetting palette positions to the default arrangement at the slightest provocation. Your palette arrangement is stored in the Adobe Photoshop Preferences file, and if that preference file is reset or deleted, you lose your palette arrangement. You can also lose your palette arrangement by changing your monitor settings or connecting or disconnecting a monitor. To be able to recreate your palette arrangement no matter what happens, save it as a workspace.

And don't limit yourself to just one workspace. If you constantly switch between monitor layouts (for example, between using a laptop in the field and in the studio with another monitor connected), save a workspace for each monitor setup. The saved workspaces make it possible to switch palette arrangements instantly and protect you from the nasty surprise of having your palette arrangement reset by Photoshop.

To save a palette arrangement:

1. Choose Window > Workspace > Save Workspace (**Figure 2.5**).

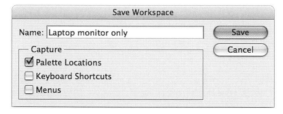

Figure 2.5

2. In the Save Workspace dialog box, name the workspace, make sure Palette Locations is enabled, and click OK. (I cover the other two options in that dialog box later in this chapter.)

To apply a saved palette arrangement, choose the name of the workspace from the Window > Workspace submenu.

 TIP To restore the Photoshop factory default palette locations, choose Window > Workspace > Reset Palette Locations.

Optimizing for Small Monitors

Although it's best to use Photoshop on a superfast desktop computer with a huge widescreen display or two, sometimes it's necessary to work with one small monitor when you're out in the field with a laptop, or when spending a week working in a client's under-equipped cubicle.

Fortunately, Photoshop provides enough flexibility for you to remain productive when your monitor is smaller than you would like. Consider these strategies:

- **The Tab key.** To hide or show all palettes at once, press Tab. This works great as long as a blinking text cursor isn't active in the document or in a palette. To hide all palettes except the Toolbar and options bar, press Shift+Tab—in many cases, this shortcut is more useful than hiding everything.

- **Careful palette docking and grouping.** Create a workspace that takes up as little space as possible by keeping all but the most critical palettes hidden. You'll probably want to group palettes more than you dock them, because grouping lets multiple palettes occupy the same space.

- **Alternate workspaces (Figure 2.6).** Save task-specific workspaces that you can quickly call up from the Window > Workspace menu to minimize the number of palettes that need to be open at any time. For example, when working with selections, you might create a workspace that focuses on the Layers, Channels, and Paths palettes.

- **The F key.** To switch among the three screen modes available on the Window > Screen Mode submenu (Standard Screen Mode, Full Screen with Menu Bar, and Full Screen), press the F key (the letter F, not an F-key or function key) until you get the mode you want (**Figure 2.7**). When you use the F key and the Tab key together, it takes just a couple of key presses to switch between full palette access to an image that fills all available screen space and with no distractions. Press Shift+F to show or hide the menu bar.

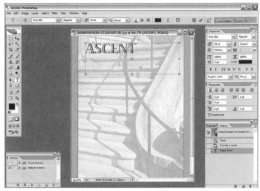

Figure 2.6: **The workspace on the left gives priority to palettes useful for correcting tone and color. The workspace on the right favors controls for typography.**

Figure 2.7: **Top left to right: Standard mode with palettes, Standard mode after hiding palettes by pressing Tab. Pressing F once enters Full Screen mode with menu bar and a gray background; pressing F again switches to Full Screen mode with no menu bar and a black background.**

■ **Navigation shortcuts.** Even if you hide the palettes and menu bar, you can get around with keyboard shortcuts listed in **Table 2.1**, "Shortcuts for Getting Around."

Table 2.1 Shortcuts for Getting Around

To...	...press
Zoom in	Shift+Command/Ctrl+= (plus sign)
Zoom in with zoom tool	Command+Spacebar+click/ Ctrl+Spacebar+click
Zoom out	Command/Ctrl+- (minus sign)
Zoom out with zoom tool	Option+Command+Spacebar+click/ Alt+Ctrl+Spacebar+click
Zoom in and out with a scroll wheel mouse	Option/Alt-scroll
Fit on Screen	Command/Ctrl+0
View actual pixels	Option+Command+0/Alt+Ctrl+0
Pan document freely (push it around)	Spacebar-drag
Scroll up one screenful	Page Up
Scroll down one screenfull	Page Down
Scroll left one screenful	Command/Ctrl+Page Up
Scroll right one screenful	Command/Ctrl+Page Down
Scroll by 10 pixels	Add Shift to a scroll shortcut
Scroll vertically with a scroll wheel mouse	Scroll
Scroll horizontally with a scroll wheel mouse	Command/Ctrl+Scroll
Scroll or zoom faster with a scroll wheel mouse	Add Shift to a scroll wheel shortcut

 TIPS I like to keep related palettes in different palette groups so that they can be viewed together. For instance, if I want to see both the Paths and Layers palettes, I don't put them in the same palette group because they obscure each other.

To collapse or expand a palette or palette group, double-click its title bar. This is a quick way to temporarily move a palette out of the way without hiding the whole thing.

FULL SCREEN MODE: CONCENTRATING ON ONE DOCUMENT

You can take all of the suggestions for small monitors and put them together into a sequence that you can use to move smoothly between complete tool access and undistracted editing of a single image.

Let's say you're starting out with the default view of a document window, the toolbox, and the palettes, and you're about to perform a retouching session with the spot healing brush tool. Here's how you might go about it:

1. Select the spot healing brush tool in the toolbox. (Pressing the J key should do it. If not, press Shift+J until the spot healing brush tool cycles to the front in the toolbox.)

2. Because you're ready to work with one tool for a while, press Tab to hide the palettes and F twice to enter Full Screen mode without the menu bar. Now you can use the entire screen to retouch without distractions. To get around the document while tools are hidden, refer to Table 3.1 in Chapter 3.

3. To show or hide the menu bar without changing the screen mode, press Shift+F.

4. When you're ready to move on to another tool or task, press Tab to get the palettes back, and F to restore the screen mode you want.

Using these shortcuts, you can get into a rhythm for focused work: Press tool shortcut, Tab, F, F to concentrate, then reverse the sequence to prepare for different work by seeing all the tools again.

Optimizing for Multiple Monitors

If you haven't used Photoshop with two or more monitors connected to your computer, you're missing out. A second monitor can boost productivity greatly because you can spend a lot less time showing or hiding palettes, and you free up display space to see more of your images.

Adding a second monitor doesn't have to cost very much money. If you have a good, calibrated monitor that you use for Photoshop work, your second monitor doesn't have to be top-of-the-line. It can be some faded old junker you pull out of the closet. Why? Because you can use the second monitor to display only items that aren't color-critical, such as palettes, dialog boxes, or windows of thumbnails in Adobe Bridge. You can also use your second monitor to keep an eye on e-mail , chats, the Web, or Photoshop online training materials while your Photoshop image remains on your other monitor.

Some desktop computers come with more than one built-in video port. If yours does, simply plug another monitor into the unused port. If your computer has slots for expansion cards, you can add video ports by installing one or more video cards.

1. With the second monitor connected in extended desktop mode (see the nearby sidebar "Setting Up Multiple Monitors in the Operating System"), start Photoshop and arrange palettes on either or both monitors.

2. Save a workspace as described in the the previous section "Saving Your Palette Arrangements." If you don't, you could lose your entire palette arrangement if the monitor setup changes or if you disconnect a monitor.

3. If you're using a laptop connected to an external monitor, create and save separate workspaces for when the external monitor is and is not connected. You can apply either workspace as needed by choosing the workspace name from the Window > Workspace submenu. Photoshop resets the palette arrangement whenever you connect or disconnect monitors, so using workspaces is the only way to preserve them.

SETTING UP MULTIPLE MONITORS IN THE OPERATING SYSTEM

After you connect a monitor to a video-out port, you may still need to tell the operating system (Mac OS X or Windows XP) how to relate that monitor to any others you've connected. The steps are not too different on either operating system.

On Mac OS X:

1. Choose System Preferences from the Apple menu and click Displays.

2. Click Arrangement (**Figure 2.8**). If Mirror Displays is on, turn it off. When Mirror Displays is off, the monitors are in extended desktop mode, combining the areas of both monitors.

3. Drag the icons of the two monitors until they match how you've got the monitors arranged on your real-world desktop. Now you can move the pointer and drag windows and objects between the two monitors as if they were one big monitor.

On Windows XP:

1. Right-click the desktop and choose Properties.

2. Click Settings (**Figure 2.9**). Select the new monitor and enable the option Extend My Windows Desktop Onto This Monitor to turn on extended desktop mode, combining the areas of both monitors.

3. Drag the icons of the two monitors until they match how you've got the monitors arranged on your real-world desktop. Now you can move the pointer and drag windows and objects between the two monitors as if they were one big monitor.

On either operating system, it can help to have two monitors with the same vertical pixel dimensions, such as two 1600 × 1200-pixel monitors (both 1200 pixels tall). When you use two monitors together and one has more vertical pixels than the other, the cursor can get caught in the portion of the taller monitor that extends past the height of the shorter monitor, forcing you to maneuver the mouse more carefully between monitors.

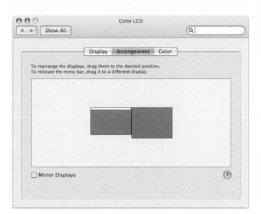

Figure 2.8: **On Mac OS X, the Displays system preference includes the Arrangement tab for telling the computer how your monitors are arranged.**

Figure 2.9: **On Windows XP, Display Properties lets you indicate your monitor arrangement in the Settings tab.**

 TIPS   When shopping for video cards for Photoshop, don't pay attention to 3D performance—that's for gamers. Graphic design in programs like Photoshop doesn't involve 3D video features at all. It's more important to make sure a card supports 32-bit color at the resolution of your monitor.

When you extend your desktop with a second monitor, you can drag any open dialog box to the second monitor. From that point on, Photoshop remembers to open that dialog box on the second monitor.

If you use Photoshop on a laptop, you may have support for a second monitor built in. Many of today's laptops include a DVI or VGA port that can drive a second monitor right away. If you don't have a built-in video port on your laptop but do have a PC Card slot, you can get a video card for that slot. If your laptop has both a DVI or VGA port and a PC card slot, you could conceivably drive two external monitors!

EXTENDED DESKTOP MODE VERSUS MIRROR MODE

When you connect a second monitor to a computer, you usually have the choice of *extending* your desktop or *mirroring* your desktop. For Photoshop, you want to extend your desktop, using the second monitor to add to your workspace. Mirroring means to show the same image on both monitors, and that isn't what you want.

Mirroring is intended for giving presentations or demonstrating software. During a presentation, you may be displaying material on a big screen that's behind you as you face the audience. Mirroring lets you use your laptop to see what the audience sees. It might be useful if you're called upon to teach a Photoshop class, but not while you're editing images.

If you're shopping for a laptop to use with Photoshop, keep in mind that although many laptops let you plug in an external monitor, some of them only support mirroring. If you want to use an external monitor to expand your laptop workspace, make sure your laptop supports extended desktop mode. For example, Apple MacBook, MacBook Pro, and PowerBook laptops support extended desktop mode, but Apple iBooks do not.

Editing Keyboard Shortcuts

As you learn keyboard shortcuts in Photoshop, you may discover that some shortcuts are inconsistent with shortcuts you use in other programs. For example, I'm used to the Mac OS X standard of pressing Command+, (comma) to open the Preferences dialog box. Adobe applications generally use Command+K, and it always throws me off. To solve this inconsistency, I used the Keyboard Shortcuts and Menus dialog box to change the Preferences dialog box shortcut to Command+, .

Note that shortcut inconsistencies aren't intended to be inconvenient. Shortcuts can naturally become inconsistent as different companies develop their own standards over time. For example, if you've used Photoshop since version 3, you're probably used to pressing Command+H/Ctrl+H to Hide Selection. But if you're a Mac OS X user, you're probably used to pressing Command+H to hide the current program. It isn't clear which shortcut is "correct," and in fact, it depends on your own experiences and preferences. If you've spent years in Photoshop, you probably believe Command+H in Photoshop should perform a Hide Selection; if you spend more time in Mac OS X programs other than Photoshop you may think Photoshop's use of Command+H is wrong. Fortunately, the ability to customize keyboard shortcuts in Photoshop means that you can make sure that Photoshop is always right from your own point of view.

To edit keyboard shortcuts in Photoshop:

1. Choose Edit > Keyboard Shortcuts (**Figure 2.10**).

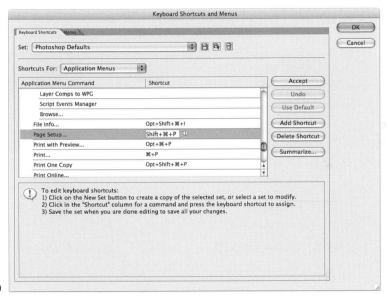

Figure 2.10

2. Choose a category from the Shortcuts For pop-up menu.

3. In the commands list, locate the command you want to customize by scrolling and clicking the disclosure triangles as needed.

4. Select the command and type the shortcut you want to use. Photoshop warns you if the shortcut is already in use or not available for use, so that you can try again.

5. Click Accept.

 TIPS   You can do much more with keyboard shortcuts than simply edit them. Developing work habits that take advantage of powerful modifier keys can enhance your productivity further. See the section "Get the Most from Keyboard Shortcuts" in Chapter 3.

If you can't locate a feature in the Keyboard Shortcuts and Menus dialog box, check Photoshop menus more carefully. For example, if you're used to creating a new Curves adjustment layer by clicking the corresponding button on the Layers palette, you'll probably try looking under the Palette Menus section to add a keyboard shortcut for that feature. However, you won't find a command for creating a new Curves adjustment layer there, because the Layers palette provides that feature through a button, not a palette. Fortunately, Photoshop replicates the functions of the Layers palette's Create Adjustment Layer button in the Layer > New Adjustment Layer submenu, and that's where you'd look in the Keyboard Shortcuts and Menus dialog box—under the Layers menu, within the Application Menus section.

Editing Menus

As Photoshop has developed over the years, its menus have gotten a bit overgrown. The Layer menu alone is now 29 items deep, and that's not counting the commands hidden on its submenus! This incredible range of choices has the unfortunate side effect of overwhelming a casual or beginning user. Part of the reason that so many commands exist is that Photoshop is very good at more than one specialized task; you can use it for print graphics, Web graphics, or pure photography. However, that means that for any given user's needs, entire sections of Photoshop's menus may not apply at all, and may simply be in the way.

As usual, Photoshop provides a way out. You can optimize menus by using the Keyboard Shortcuts and Menus dialog box. By optimize, I mean that you can emphasize the menu commands that mean the most to your workflow. You can emphasize your favorite commands either by applying a highlight color to them or by removing the commands you don't need.

To edit Photoshop menus:

1. Choose Edit > Menus (**Figure 2.11**).

2. In the Menus tab of the Keyboard Shortcuts and Menus dialog box, choose a menu set from the Menu For pop-up menu.

3. Scroll to locate the menu command you want to edit.

4. For the command you're editing, click the Visibility column to hide or show the command, or click the Color column to apply a color to the command.

5. Click the Save icon (the first one to the right of the Set pop-up menu) to save your changes to the current set.

6. Click the Save New Set icon (second from the left) to create a new set based on the current settings. After you create a new set, you can choose it from the Window > Workspace submenu.

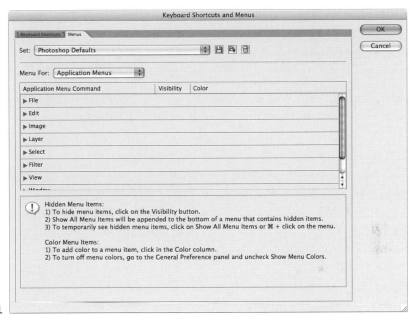

Figure 2.11

Your menu customizations are as flexible and editable as keyboard shortcuts and palette arrangements, because Photoshop can save a menu configuration as part of a workspace. The built-in workspaces found under the Workspace menu in Photoshop CS2 are examples of workspaces that change only the menus, not the keyboard shortcuts or palettes. To see what I mean, choose Window > Workspace and then choose any of the commands in the menu section, starting with the Automation command in the Workspace submenu. Choose one or two and take a look through the menus to see how they're highlighted. When you want to restore the Photoshop factory default menus, choose Window > Workspace > Reset Menus.

 TIP   To restore the Photoshop factory default palette locations, choose Window > Workspace > Reset Palette Locations.

Saving Your Workspaces

Earlier I looked at using the Window > Workspace > Save Workspace command to save a palette arrangement, and you may have noticed that there are two more boxes in Save Workspace dialog box: Keyboard Shortcuts and Menus. Although a Photoshop workspace can save the state of the palettes, keyboard shortcuts, and menus, you may not want to save all three every time. For example, you may have different task-oriented palette arrangements but one set of favorite keyboard shortcuts. If you want to remove any possibility of accidentally altering keyboard shortcuts when you change palette arrangements, don't enable the Keyboard Shortcuts checkbox when you save a workspace.

Moving Workspaces to Other Machines

Your workspaces only work on your machine. If you do a lot of work on other computers at a client's site or in a computer lab, though, you may want to save your workspaces to a disc or flash drive so you can load them onto the machine you're using. Workspaces are stored in the WorkSpaces folder, which is in the following folder paths

Mac OS X:

```
Computer/Users/<username>/Library/Preferences/Adobe Photoshop CS2
➥Settings/WorkSpaces/
```

Windows:

```
C:\Documents and Settings\<username>\Application Data\Adobe\Photoshop\9.0\
➥Adobe Photoshop CS2 Settings\WorkSpaces\
```

You can distribute workspaces to other computers in a workgroup or classroom by copying files from the WorkSpaces folder to the same folder on the other computers.

Resetting the Default Workspace

It's sometimes useful to set the Photoshop workspace back to the factory defaults; for example, when your machine will be used by someone who isn't familiar with your workspace configuration. You can start over by choosing Window > Workspace > Default Workspace.

Keep in mind that the Default Workspace command resets the current palette arrangement, keyboard shortcuts, and menus, so if you want to keep your customizations to any of those areas, save them before you reset to the default workspace. For example, save your current shortcuts as a keyboard shortcut set in the Keyboard Shortcuts and Menus dialog box.

Arranging Document Windows

By now you may realize that even the simple act of getting around in a Photoshop document offers many opportunities for saving time and effort. This idea also extends to getting around when you're working with multiple document windows in Photoshop. You can expend time and effort clicking and dragging windows to get them where you want, or you can try some of the ideas in this section.

The two most common challenges when working with document windows are getting to the window you want and keeping different windows out of each others' way. To address the first need, Photoshop provides window arrangement controls in the Window > Arrange submenu. The Cascade, Tile Horizontally, and Tile Vertically commands work just as they do in Windows; if you're not familiar with them, you can open three or four images and try out each command to see what they do. When windows overlap so much that you can't easily tell which one to click to bring forward, choose the name of the window from the bottom of the Window menu.

Arranging Windows Instantly

The Window menu includes several commands that can instantly arrange your open windows (**Figure 2.12**):

- To offset all open windows so you can see the title bar of each image, choose Window > Arrange > Cascade (**Figure 2.13**).

Figure 2.12

Figure 2.13

■ To arrange all windows oriented horizontally across the screen, choose Window > Arrange > Tile Horizontally (**Figure 2.14**).

■ To arrange all windows oriented vertically across the screen, choose Window > Arrange > Tile Vertically (**Figure 2.15**).

■ To cycle through open windows, press Control+Tab (Yes, this shortcut is actually the same on both Mac and Windows.) To cycle backwards, press Shift+Control+Tab.

Figure 2.14

Figure 2.15

 NOTE   On Mac OS X, the Photoshop shortcut for cycling windows does not match the system shortcut for this function, which is Command+` . In Photoshop, Command+` is the shortcut for viewing all color channels.

Examining Documents Side by Side

In Photoshop, you can compare multiple documents side by side, which is great for deciding between two very similar images from the same shoot. For example, you might want to decide which of two images is in sharper focus. You may think that this would be covered by cascading or tiling document windows, but Photoshop provides additional commands that make document examination much faster and easier:

■ To set all open windows to the same zoom level as the frontmost window, choose Window > Arrange > Match Zoom (**Figure 2.16**).

■ To set all open windows to the same location as the frontmost window, choose Window > Arrange > Match Location.

■ To perform both the Match Zoom and Match Location commands, choose Window > Workspace > Match Zoom and Location.

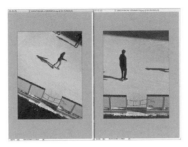

Figure 2.16: **Choosing the Match Zoom command sets all document windows to the same zoom level.**

- To scroll all windows together, select the hand tool, and in the options bar enable Scroll All Windows.

Let's take a look at an example of how this would work:

1. Open two similar documents that you want to inspect.

2. Choose Window > Arrange > Tile Vertically.

3. Select the hand tool in the toolbox.

4. In the options bar, click Actual Pixels and enable Scroll All Windows.

5. Choose Window > Arrange > Match Zoom.

6. Drag the hand tool within one of the document windows. Both windows move together, so you can compare them (**Figure 2.17**).

Figure 2.17

 TIP   You can scroll or zoom all windows using the Shift key instead of options bar settings. When you use the hand tool, adding Shift scrolls all windows; and when you use the zoom tool, adding Shift zooms all windows. For example, if you habitually press the spacebar to pan (scroll) a document in its window, pressing Shift+spacebar scrolls all document windows.

Comparing Views of the Same Document

Examining different documents is to be expected, but not everyone knows that you can also use Photoshop to compare views of a single document. Why would you want to see the same document twice? Actually, what happens is better than that. Photoshop includes the powerful ability to open multiple windows for the same document and set different view settings for each window. You can, for example, have one window showing an entire document, and another window of the same document zoomed in for detailed retouching work. You can therefore work in a detail view while seeing how your changes affect the big picture (literally).

To set up another view of the same document, choose Window > Arrange > New Window for <filename>. Now you can use the same commands that you would to manage multiple document windows.

Let's try the example of views at different zoom levels:

1. Open one document; don't open any other documents.

2. Choose Window > Arrange > New Window.

3. Choose Window > Arrange > Tile Vertically.

4. Choose View > Actual Pixels.

5. Select the hand tool in the toolbox.

6. In the options bar, click Actual Pixels and enable Scroll All Windows.

7. Drag the hand tool within the zoomed-in document window. Both windows move together, so you can compare the detail view with the overall view (**Figure 2.18**).

Figure 2.18

CHAPTER THREE

Optimizing Yourself

A POWERFUL AND EFFICIENT WORKFLOW DEPENDS on three factors: the hardware, the software, and you. In Chapter 1 I looked at optimizing the hardware, and in Chapter 2 I looked at optimizing the software (the Photoshop workspace). Now it's your turn.

Learning good habits is a great way to enhance your Photoshop productivity, because it's free, and you already have everything you need—yourself. To sweeten the bargain, many of the ideas in this chapter also work across the Adobe Creative Suite and in other parts of the operating system.

Getting Around Efficiently

Unless you work with small images, you'll spend a lot of time scrolling and zooming in and out. You could simply use the standard scroll bars that you see in every document window, and you can use the View > Zoom In and View > Zoom Out commands. There's also a magnifying glass in the toolbox; with that tool selected you can click a document to zoom in, or Option/Alt+click to zoom out. But Photoshop often provides much more efficient ways to achieve common tasks, and changing your view of a window is no exception.

Nobody's going to make you memorize every shortcut in this topic; you should simply be aware of all of the choices before you so that you can identify your favorite shortcuts and work them into your normal work habits.

TABLE: 3.1 Zooming Shortcuts

To do this...	...use these shortcuts:
Zoom in on a specific point in a document	Command+spacebar+click / Ctrl+spacebar+click*
Zoom in on a specific area in a document	Command+spacebar+drag / Ctrl+spacebar+drag*
Zoom out from a specific point in a document	Command+Option+spacebar+click / Ctrl+Alt+spacebar+click*
Zoom in using the keyboard only	Command+= / Ctrl+=
Zoom out using the keyboard only	Command+- / Ctrl+-
Zoom to Actual Pixels (1:1) magnification	Double-click the zoom tool, or press Command+Option+0 (zero) / Ctrl+Alt+0 (zero)
Zoom to a specific percentage	Enter the percentage value into the Navigator palette
Zoom using a scroll wheel	Option+spin / Alt+spin the scroll wheel*
Fit entire document on screen	Command+0 (zero) / Ctrl+0 (zero)

*If the zoom tool is selected, you don't need to press the Command / Ctrl key.

TABLE: 3.2 Scrolling Shortcuts

To do this...	...use these shortcuts
Scroll vertically using a scroll wheel	Spin the scroll wheel*
Scroll horizontally using a scroll wheel	Command+spin /Ctrl+spin the scroll wheel*
Scroll faster with a scroll wheel	Add Shift to the scroll wheel shortcuts
Scroll vertically one screenful using the keyboard	Press Page Up or Page Down**
Scroll horizontally one screenful using the keyboard	Press Command/Ctrl+Page Up or Command/Ctrl+Page Down**
Scroll by 10 pixels	Add Shift to the Page Up/Page Down shortcuts
Scroll to the top-left corner	Press Home
Scroll to the bottom-right corner	Press End
Scroll by pushing the image around (panning)	Press the spacebar as long as you're not editing text or entering values in a palette (shortcut for the hand tool) and drag

*To increase the scroll or zoom amount, add the Shift key to the shortcut.
**To decrease the scroll amount, add the Shift key to the shortcut.

Shortcuts for Zooming and Scrolling

Photoshop keyboard shortcuts for zooming are built around the plus (+) and minus (-) keys, while the shortcuts for scrolling are built around the Page Up and Page Down keys.

Photoshop also makes extensive use of the scroll wheel on a mouse that has one. In **Table 3.1** and **Table 3.2**, you see that you can change what the scroll wheel does by pressing a modifier key.

What's so cool about scrolling with the keyboard? Many Photoshop artists like to work in Full-Screen mode, in which the scroll bars simply aren't there, so pressing the Page Up or Page Down key can be quicker and more precise than scrolling with the hand tool. Also, there are times, such as when you're retouching, when you want to examine every inch of an image without missing a spot. Although you can use the scroll bars to scroll the document one screen at a time, it's too easy to overshoot or lose your place. When you scroll with the keyboard, you can move across a document one precise screenful at a time. If you ever lose your place, you can hit the Home or End key to return to a known location.

 NOTES Scrolling shortcuts don't work if the entire document is visible in Standard Screen mode.

When you're typing text, you type a plus sign by pressing Shift to get to the plus sign. With Photoshop, zoom tool shortcuts refer to the plus key only to make the shortcut easy to remember—don't press Shift when using the shortcut for View > Zoom In. To avoid confusion, in Table 3.1 I list the View > Zoom In shortcut literally, as Command and the equal sign (=).

 TIPS If you want your scroll wheel to zoom by default, open the Preferences dialog box and in the General preferences pane enable the Zoom with Scroll Wheel option. You can reverse the current behavior of the Zoom Resizes Windows preference by adding the Option/Alt key to the shortcuts.

Part of getting around efficiently is being in the right window. Photoshop includes commands and shortcuts for quickly arranging multiple windows so that the one you want is visible, or better yet, in front; see the section "Arranging Document Windows" in Chapter 2.

Navigator Palette

The Navigator palette (**Figure 3.1**) is feature packed, but many power users don't use it. This is probably because as you become more skilled at getting around with the keyboard, navigation techniques that involve the mouse often slow you down, and the Navigator palette is very mouse oriented. Now, if you like using the mouse, the Navigator palette can be a great help. It comes with a zoom slider, a field where you can enter a zoom percentage, and a red rectangle that you can drag to scroll the document. Its greatest advantage is that when you're zoomed in, the red rectangle shows you which small area of the whole document you're viewing. If you don't need that feature, you might prefer to use other methods to zoom and scroll and therefore hide the Navigator palette to free up some space on your monitor.

Figure 3.1: **The Navigator palette (left) provides several ways to quickly change the view to any part of a document (right).**

 TIP   If you zoom in and out using the View > Zoom In and View > Zoom Out commands or their keyboard shortcuts, your carefully arranged windows may change size, ruining your arrangement. To prevent this from happening, open the Preferences dialog box and in the General preference pane disable the Zoom Resizes Windows preference. You can reverse the current behavior of the Zoom Resizes Windows preference by adding the Option/Alt key to the shortcuts.

Get the Most from Keyboard Shortcuts

If you're used to getting around a computer by clicking controls with the mouse, consider adding keyboard shortcuts to the mix. Although getting used to keyboard shortcuts might seem like a bit of a time investment up front, learning them is one of the best ways to accelerate your work in the long run.

Keyboards shortcuts come into their own when you want to frequently use a feature that's buried deep within a couple of levels of menus. Instead of having to dig down into a hierarchical menu over and over, you only have to press a key combination. Of course, minimizing the amount of mouse movement you need to perform can preserve the health of your wrist, too.

If you don't like the shortcuts that Photoshop uses, you can edit most of them. See the section "Editing Keyboard Shortcuts" in Chapter 2.

Learning Keyboard Shortcuts Quickly

There's no need for you to learn shortcuts by memorizing long lists in advance. It's much more practical to learn them on an as-needed basis while you work, and that way you'll only learn the shortcuts that are the most useful for your own workflow. Most Photoshop shortcuts are easy to learn right away:

■ Keyboard shortcuts for menu commands are displayed on the menu itself, to the right of the command you're interested in (**Figure 3.2**).

■ Single-key shortcuts for tools are displayed in the tool tip that appears when you position the mouse over a tool in the toolbox (**Figure 3.3**). If you don't see tool tips, make sure Show Tool Tips is enabled in the General pane of the Preferences dialog box.

Figure 3.2: **If a menu command has a keyboard shortcut, you'll find it next to the command.**

Figure 3.3: **Single-key shortcuts appear in tool tips when you position the mouse over the tool.**

■ The Info palette suggests modifier keys for the current tool if you've turned on Show Tool Hints in the Palette Options dialog box (choose Palette Options from the Info palette menu) (**Figure 3.4**).

■ Other shortcuts are listed in the Edit > Keyboard Shortcuts command. To see all shortcuts in one place, click the Summarize button in the Keyboard Shortcuts tab of the Keyboard Shortcuts and Menus dialog box; this creates an HTML file you can view in your Web browser or print out.

■ In the Adobe Help Center, lists of keyboard shortcuts all have the word "keys" in the title. To find these lists, choose Help > Photoshop Help and enter "keys" in the Search For field (**Figure 3.5**).

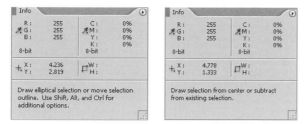

Figure 3.4: **The Info palette describes the current tool and describes the tool's modifier keys (left). With the Option/Alt key pressed (right), the Info palette tells you how that modifier key changes the tool.**

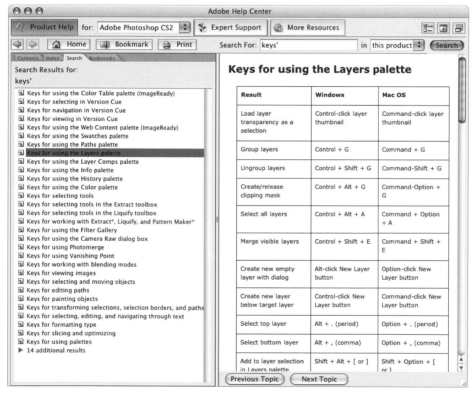

Figure 3.5: **The Adobe Help Center contains many tables of keyboard shortcuts.**

💡 **TIP**   When a tool is grouped with others in the toolbox, you can add the Shift key to cycle through all the tools in that group. For example, pressing L selects the lasso tool, and pressing Shift+L cycles through the polygonal lasso and magnetic lasso tools. If this isn't working when you try it, open the Preferences dialog box and make sure that Use Shift Key for Tool Switch is turned on.

NOTE   Adobe used to include a printed shortcut reference card with the software.
They no longer do this because the keyboard shortcuts are now customizable; any
shortcuts you customized would no longer match the card. Adobe's replacement
for the printed card is actually an improvement: If you click the Summarize button
in the Keyboard Shortcuts and Menus dialog box, the list Photoshop generates
always matches your customized keyboard shortcut configuration.

The Keys That Help You Everywhere

You usually hear about keyboard shortcuts as specific key combinations for
specific tasks. But certain keys affect Photoshop in a consistent way throughout many situations. For example, once you realize that the Shift key constrains
dragged objects along 45-degree angles, you can Shift+drag whether you're
dragging a layer, a text layer, a selection, or a path.

The Shift, Option/Alt, and Command/Ctrl keys are called *modifier* keys because
they only modify the functions of other keys—they have no effect when you
press any of them alone. In addition, you can combine modifier keys to achieve
even more precise control over what you do. If you know that Shift+dragging
constrains drags and Option/Alt duplicates a dragged object, you can drag a
perfectly aligned copy of a layer by Shift+Option+dragging/Shift+Alt+dragging
a layer. Feel free to combine the Shift, Option/Alt, and Command/Ctrl keys in
any way necessary to accomplish what you're after.

Let's look at some examples of how you can use the common modifier keys to
control what happens when you edit a Photoshop document with the mouse
(as opposed to entering numbers).

To constrain movement and scaling using the Shift key:

1. Select a layer in the Layers palette and select the move tool.

2. Hold Shift as you drag the layer. Notice that you can only drag along 45-degree
angles (**Figure 3.6**). You can try this with image layers, text layers, paths, and so
on—it works consistently.

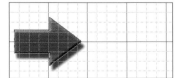 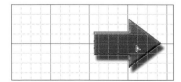

Figure 3.6

3. Choose Edit > Free Transform.

4. Hold Shift as you drag a corner handle. Photoshop maintains the proportions of the layer. To compare, also try dragging a corner handle without holding down the Shift key.

To copy using the Option/Alt key:

1. Select a layer in the Layers palette and select the move tool.

2. Hold Option/Alt as you drag the layer.

To resize from the center using the Option/Alt key:

1. Select a layer in the Layers palette.

2. Choose Edit > Free Transform.

3. Hold Option/Alt as you drag a corner handle. Photoshop resizes the layer from the center instead of the top left corner (**Figure 3.7**). To compare, also try dragging a corner handle without holding down the Option/Alt key.

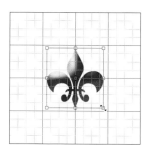
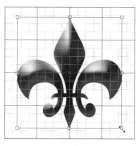

Figure 3.7

To enable distortion by using the Command/Ctrl key:

1. Select a layer in the Layers palette.

2. Choose Edit > Free Transform.

3. Hold Command/Ctrl as you drag a corner handle. Photoshop allows that corner to distort the object—except for type, where you're only allowed to stretch along one dimension (**Figure 3.8**). To compare, also try dragging a corner handle without holding down the Command/Ctrl key.

Figure 3.8

 NOTE   The range of distortion you can apply using the Command/Ctrl key is limited. For more control over distortion, choose Edit > Transform > Warp and change the settings on the options bar.

For a summary of common modifier keys see **Table 3.3**.

THE BEST OF BOTH HANDS

Photoshop is designed to let you use both of your hands to maximize productivity. You can keep one hand over the image to manipulate it using your mouse or stylus, and keep your other hand over they keyboard to change tools and options using keyboard shortcuts. I'm right-handed, so my left hand uses keyboard shortcuts to change the tools and options that my right hand then applies to the image, like an assistant handing tools to a surgeon.

For example, to use the two-handed method to make a selection and move it, with my left hand I press the L key to select the lasso tool, with my right hand I draw the selection, with my left hand I press the V key to select the move tool, and with my right hand I drag the selection. The great advantage of doing it this way is that instead of making lots of repetitive mouse trips between the image and the toolbox, I can keep my eyes and my mouse focused on the image as my left hand manages the tools.

Once you become comfortable with this technique, you can use it in other Adobe programs, most of which are also designed for efficient two-handed operation.

TABLE: 3.3 Useful Keys Across Photoshop

Mac	Windows	When you...	The key...
Shift	Shift	Move by dragging	Constrains to 45-degree angles
Shift	Shift	Resize by dragging	Constrains proportions
Shift	Shift	Change values with arrow keys or arrow buttons	Changes the value by 10x
Option	Alt	Move by dragging	Copies the layer or object
Option	Alt	Resize by dragging	Resizes from center of layer or object
Option	Alt	Open a dialog box	Uses the settings that were last entered
Option	Alt	Click a "New" button in a palette	Changes behavior of the button*
Command	Ctrl	Drag a corner handle	Allows distortion
Return	Enter	Edit a dialog box or number field	Applies all pending changes
Esc	Esc	Edit a dialog box or number field	Cancels all pending charges

* How a button changes depends on the palette. For example, clicking the New button in the Actions palette normally presents the New Action dialog box; Option/Alt+clicking skips the dialog box. In the Layers palette, clicking the New Layer button normally adds a layer immediately; Option/Alt+clicking presents the New Layer dialog box.

 TIP   When a menu is open from the menu bar or a pop-up menu, you can select an item by using the arrow keys, Page Up/Page Down, or type-ahead—typing the first few letters of the command you want to select. Type-ahead saves a lot of time when a menu is so long you can't see all of it on the screen at once. When you've highlighted the command you want, press Return or Enter to apply it.

Shortcuts for Entering Numbers and Text

Palettes and dialog boxes that are full of number and text fields often look like forms to fill out, and forms are not much fun. Many people select a number or text field with the mouse, type into it, select the next field with the mouse, and type again. But the alternating movements of clicking with the mouse, then typing with both hands, then switching between mouse and keyboard again isn't very efficient. I describe ways to enter numbers or text without using the mouse, but you'll also see how you can enter numbers without using the keyboard! Read on and you'll be able to blast through dialog boxes and palettes much more quickly. The shortcuts I mention in this section are summarized in **Table 3.4**.

Table 3.4 Numeric and Text Entry Shortcuts

To do this...	...press
Go to next field	Tab
Go to previous field	Shift+Tab
Increase or decrease a numeric value by one increment	Up Arrow or Down Arrow
Increase or decrease a numeric value with a scroll wheel	Spin a mouse's scroll wheel (if equipped)
Increase or decrease a numeric value by dragging	Horizontally drag a field label or Command+drag / Ctrl+drag a field number horizontally
Increase or decrease a numeric value by a large increment (usually 10x)	Press Shift key when pressing Up / Down Arrow keys, Command / Ctrl+dragging, or a scroll wheel
Apply changes (in a dialog box, same as clicking OK)	Return or Enter
Apply changes in a palette while keeping field selected	Shift+Return / Shift+Enter
Don't apply changes (in a dialog box, same as clicking Cancel)	Esc
Revert a dialog box to its default values without closing itl	Option / Alt+click the Cancel button

 NOTE   In this section, when I say "palette," I also mean the options bar at the top of the screen, because it's got number and text fields too.

Wandering Through the Fields

You don't need to precisely click to every text and number field in a dialog box or palette. Just press Tab to move forward through the fields until you select the field you want to edit. (If you're editing text or numbers in a palette, click in the first field you want to edit.) Press Shift+Tab to move backward. This is one of those shortcuts that usually works in programs other than Photoshop, too.

Adjusting Values with the Keyboard

You can, of course, simply type numbers or text into a field. But if you need to adjust a value just a little bit, over and over, it becomes tedious to type numbers constantly—you're not an accountant! Fortunately, Photoshop provides ways to make precise adjustments to values you've already entered.

The following techniques assume you've selected a value in a number or text field in a palette or dialog box. Here we go:

■ You don't have to drag to highlight a value in a number or text field. Click once on the field label to select the entire value and then you can start typing right away.

■ To increase or decrease a value, press the Up Arrow or Down Arrow keys.

■ To change values in bigger increments, add Shift to the shortcuts above; in most cases Shift multiplies the usual adjustment by 10. For example, pressing Up Arrow increases font size 1 point, and Shift+Up Arrow increases it 10 points.

■ In a palette, if you want to apply the value while leaving the field selected so that you can immediately type another value, press Shift+Return/Shift+Enter. What's the big deal with this one? If you simply press Return or Enter, the highlight goes away, and you have to select the value again before entering a new one.

■ To apply a change, press Return or Enter. In a dialog box, Return or Enter apply all changes made in the dialog box—it's a shortcut for the OK button.

■ To exit a field without applying what you entered, press Esc. In a dialog box, Esc discards all changes made in the dialog box—it's a shortcut for the Cancel button. By the way, pressing Esc in a palette may not revert the value if you were adjusting it with the arrow keys, because using the arrow keys immediately applies your adjustment.

TIPS   When you highlight a font name (for example, in the Character palette or options bar for the horizontal type tool), the Up Arrow and Down Arrow keys choose the previous or next font, respectively. That's a quick way to try different fonts by stepping through the list. You can also type the first few letters of a font; Photoshop automatically selects the first matching font name.

In most cases there isn't a difference between the Enter key above the Shift key (on Macintosh computers, this is the Return key) and the Enter key on the numeric keypad. But if you're editing text on a type layer, there is a difference. Pressing the Enter key above the Shift key (Return) types a paragraph break so you can enter multiple paragraphs. Pressing the Enter key on the numeric keypad applies the changes and exits text-editing mode. Another way to stop editing a type layer is to press Command+Return or Shift+Enter.

Scrubbing to Adjust Values

Now, there are plenty of people out there who just don't like using the keyboard. If you're one of them, there are fast ways to fine-tune values by spinning a rotary control or dragging. This is what the audio and video realm calls *scrubbing*, so I'll use that term here for convenience.

If you have a scroll wheel mouse, click in a number or text field and spin your scroll wheel up or down to change the value.

You can also scrub numbers by dragging a field label horizontally, or by Command/ Ctrl+dragging a number horizontally (**Figure 3.9**). Either method turns the field into an on-demand slider control. This is great if you don't have a scroll wheel or other rotary input device. It also lets you use the entire width of your monitor as a slider, which means you can adjust a value more precisely than you can by using the visible slider.

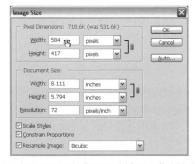

Figure 3.9: **Find the right value interactively, by scrubbing a field label (Command/ Ctrl+dragging a value).**

NOTE The shortcuts in Table 3.4 also work in Adobe Camera Raw 3.4, except for the ability to adjust values using a scroll wheel.

 TIP If you know the Windows XP shortcuts for navigating a dialog box or palette, you can use those in Photoshop, too. For example, if a pop-up menu is selected, press the spacebar to open it. Mac OS X has similar shortcuts but Photoshop dialog boxes aren't compatible with them.

Putting It All Together

If you haven't really worked with shortcuts before, you might think this section is just a long list of details to try and remember . . . what a chore! But that would be the wrong way to look at it. The real value of shortcuts comes after you've gotten familiar with which ones are important to the tasks you do the most. Here's an example that can help you pick and choose shortcuts to create just the right way to make precise adjustments in a particular situation.

Suppose you're trying to make fine adjustments in the Levels dialog box. The obvious way to do it is to drag the sliders. What can be tedious about that is every time you want to change a value, you have to move your mouse to the slider's new location to drag it. When repeated many times over the course of a day, your fingers can tire of the repetitive repositioning (**Figure 3.10**).

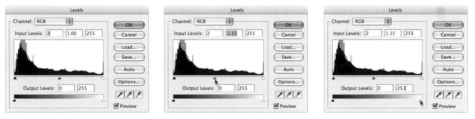

Figure 3.10: **Using the Levels dialog box usually involves moving the mouse back and forth among many different sliders and fields.**

Instead, take advantage of the scrubbing shortcut. With a field selected, drag horizontally starting from the field label, in this case Input Levels, and let go. When you want to refine that value, just start dragging from the field label again (**Figure 3.11**).

When it's time to adjust the next field, once again there is no need to reposition the mouse very far—just leave it where it is over the field label. Take advantage of the Tab key this time and press it to go to the next field, and with the mouse still over the field label, start dragging (**Figure 3.12**). You can keep progressing through the dialog box this way, using Tab and Shift+Tab to change fields as needed.

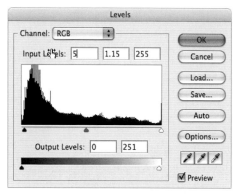

Figure 3.11: **Because you can scrub from any part of the field label, a field label is often a much bigger and easier target to drag instead of aiming for a tiny slider.**

Figure 3.12: **To scrub another field controlled by the same label, you can leave the mouse where it is and simply press Tab to change fields.**

In this way, you combine the Tab key and scrubbing to change values more efficiently than you would if you used the visible sliders. If you want, you can use the Up and Down arrow keys instead of scrubbing, depending on your working style.

 TIPS   It's often hard to see the difference between small changes, like increasing a tone or color value by one percent. I like to use Shift+Up Arrow or Shift+Down Arrow to change a value by larger increments so that changes are easier to observe. For example, instead of going from 10% to 11%, I'll go from 10% to 20%. If 10% is too little and 20% is too much, sometimes I'll just enter 15% and move on, instead of trying to observe 1% adjustments all day long. While 5% adjustments may be too coarse for color-critical work, they're often OK when applying filters.

If you use a rotary dial controller like the Logitech NuLOOQ or Griffin PowerMate, its driver software may allow it to work like a scroll wheel, so you may be able to use it for shortcuts that use a scroll wheel.

Using Context Menus

Which dining experience is more elegant: making a trip to the buffet table or sitting back while a server brings you your drinks and your meal? Obviously, being served is more civilized than hunting and gathering. The same is true in Photoshop, where context menus can save you many trips to the menu bar.

A context menu pops up in the work area instead of from a menu bar, dialog box, or palette, putting relevant commands right under your mouse. The contents of the menu change depending on (as the name implies) its context—whatever it is you are clicking (**Figure 3.13**). If you use a multi-button mouse, you get a context menu by clicking with the right mouse button. If you're a Mac user with a single-button mouse or laptop trackpad, you can see a context menu by Ctrl+clicking.

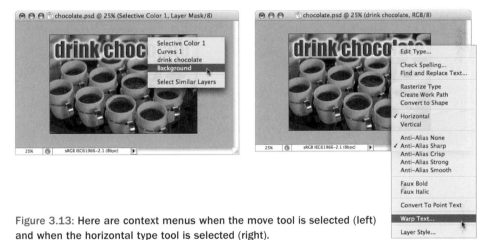

Figure 3.13: Here are context menus when the move tool is selected (left) and when the horizontal type tool is selected (right).

For Windows users, the right mouse button needs no introduction. (I say right mouse button, but of course if you're left-handed you've probably set up the secondary button to be the left mouse button.) If you're a Mac user who hasn't yet discovered the efficiency advantages of the right (secondary) mouse button, consider the following. Let's say you've selected an area of a document and you want to rotate the selection marquee. Normally, you'd have to go up to the Select menu and choose the Transform Selection command that's near the bottom of that menu. An easier, faster way is to choose Transform Selection from the context menu that's available when a selection is active. It's because of that convenience that I can't live without the right mouse button today, even though I spent all my early computer years using Apple's one-button mice.

Context menus really come into their own when you work on a large monitor. On a large monitor or on a multiple-monitor system, the distance from the middle of a document to the menu bar may be quite a long way. With context menus, you can keep the mouse where it is more of the time, which is important when you're painting or retouching.

If you aren't seeing the menu commands you expect, make sure you're clicking on the right object or area.

 TIP Don't forget to look for context menus in palettes, too. Not all palettes have context menus, but most of the palettes containing lists do (Layers, Paths, Channels, and so on). In palettes that have context menus, you'll find that you get different context menus depending on whether you click on a list item or in an empty area of the palette.

It's All in Your Mind

"There's got to be a better way." If you hear yourself uttering that phrase under your breath as you work, it's a sign that you should stop and take a closer look at what's slowing you down in Photoshop.

If you're a complete beginner at Photoshop, before you start optimizing your workflow it's more important to first know what your workflow is—to understand and master the tasks that form the core of your workflow. Once you've got that list down, you can start going down the list and identifying where you might be able to streamline your workflow using the keyboard shortcuts or modifier keys described in this chapter.

As you become more experienced, you might want to take a look at how you use your hands. Think about how often you switch between the keyboard and the mouse and consider adjusting which shortcuts you use based on that. For example, if you find yourself zooming in and out a lot and you have a mouse with a scroll wheel, think about using the scroll wheel to zoom so that you don't have to press shortcuts or change your current tool. On the other hand, if you mostly use a graphics tablet with a stylus and neither has a rotary control, you probably want to use the keyboard shortcuts for zooming. That's how you want to think in order to work out the right shortcuts for you. Achieving maximum efficiency in Photoshop has a lot to do with achieving the perfect mix of usage across the keyboard, your mouse or stylus, and your two hands.

CHAPTER FOUR

Getting Ahead with Presets and Saved Settings

LOOKING OVER THE PALETTES IN PHOTOSHOP can be kind of like looking out over the ocean. You see the surface, which looks nice enough, but if you could see under the surface you'd find wonders that reach all the way down through the murky depths. Like the ocean, the palettes look rather straightforward on the surface. Want to select a rectangular area? Grab the rectangular marquee tool from the Tools palette and drag it. Easy enough. But peek under the surface and you'll find that the rectangular marquee tool has a number of options. In fact, every tool in the Tools palette has at least one option; you see a tool's options in the aptly named options bar that runs across the top of the Photoshop work area.

From the point of view of flexibility, having lots of tool options is great—you can adapt the tools to many situations. The downside of having tools that are so configurable is that it can be a hassle to change between frequently used combinations of settings when there are so many settings to change and remember.

That's where presets and saved settings come in. With presets, you don't have to remember or write down all the settings that make up your favorite way to set up a tool—you simply save a preset for that configuration. Presets are even more valuable when you use the same tool in very different ways. For example, when you're retouching photos with one of the brush tools, a brush size that works well for a high-resolution image is too large for a low-resolution Web image. You can save two brush presets with brush sizes that are best for your particular Web and print image sizes and name them descriptively so that one click completely changes how the tool works.

Think about creating a preset whenever you've spent a bit of time crafting just the right settings for a tool. If you coordinate a design or production team, providing presets for tools may make it easier to maintain your organization's production standards. Photoshop also lets you save settings from dialog boxes, which work similarly to presets: You can save favorite settings to a file on disk and import them into a document or distribute them to others.

Photoshop already includes a number of presets that provide a great head start in working with many of the tools. You can also use the built-in presets as examples and starting points for your own presets. Adding presets to Photoshop is one of the ways in which you can personalize Photoshop, adapting it to your specific needs.

Think of this chapter as the scuba gear you can use to explore the deep riches of Photoshop presets. Time to go diving!

PRESETS AREN'T DEFAULTS

It's important to not confuse *presets* with *defaults*. A default is how a tool or feature works before you change any of its settings. A preset is a saved configuration that you can use to instantly reconfigure a tool or feature at any time.

Creating and Using Your Own Tool Presets

Let's build a tool preset—a preset that remembers how you set up a particular tool. A tool preset isn't the only kind of preset, but I cover the others in the next section, "Kinds of Presets."

For this example, suppose you're on a team that creates Web ads that use photos as background images, and you often need to crop images down to a standard banner size of 468 pixels wide by 60 pixels tall. To do this without a preset, you first select the crop tool. In the options bar, enter 468px for Width and 60px for Height. Finally, you drag the crop tool to set the crop rectangle and press Return or Enter to apply the crop.

If your workgroup crops hundreds of images to a few banner sizes throughout the year, you sure don't want everyone to be typing the width and height over and over. That's where a preset comes in. To create a preset for the 468 × 60-pixel banner size:

1. Select the crop tool.

2. On the options bar, specify every crop tool option you want to save in the preset. For this banner ad example, it's only necessary to enter 468px for the width and 60px for height. (You can also enter a resolution if you want to make sure the cropped images all conform to a resolution specification, but for the Web, pixel dimensions matter, and resolution doesn't.)

3. Click the Tool Presets picker at the left end of the options bar and click the Create New Tool Preset button (**Figure 4.1**).

4. Name the preset and click OK.

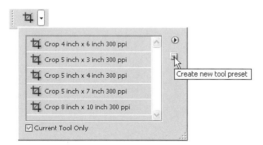

Figure 4.1

To use the preset, just click the Tool Presets picker and select the preset from the list.

Suppose that in addition to Web graphics, you often produce ads at 3 by 2 inches at 300 dpi. It's just as easy to create a preset for that size and resolution. Simply follow the preceding steps 1 through 4, but with one addition: Before you create the preset, also specify 300 dpi in the Resolution field (**Figure 4.2**).

Figure 4.2: A tool preset includes all values entered on the options bar, so creating a crop tool preset now would include the Width, Height, and Resolution values currently entered.

TIPS You can display the list of tool presets in different ways. Click the round menu button and choose from the list display commands. For example, you can display brush tool presets in six ways, including just the names, just the brush tip thumbnail, or a brush stroke sample.

If you want to reset the options bar to its defaults before creating a preset, click the Clear button on the options bar (not available for all tools).

Kinds of Presets

There are seven kinds of presets in Photoshop, but it's sometimes more helpful to think of them in two major categories: tool presets, and everything else. Tool presets are all found in the options bar, whereas the other six kinds also appear in other palettes, as I describe later in this section. Keeping that distinction in mind can help you look for a preset in the right place.

Brush Presets and Tool Presets for Brushes

A tool preset remembers how you set up the options bar for a tool in the Tools palette. Click the Tool Presets picker at the left end of the options bar to display a list of any tool presets available for the current tool. If you disable the Current Tool Only checkbox, the Tool Presets picker lists all tool presets for all tools.

Saving brush settings can be kind of confusing because brush configurations really exist on two levels. First there are brush presets, which live in the Brushes palette. When you save a brush, that brush remembers the settings you set up only within the Brushes palette. On top of that you have tool presets for brushes, which live in the options bar. A tool preset for brushes remembers the brush you selected and also includes the settings you set up in the options bar (**Figure 4.3**).

Brush presets aren't just for the brush tool itself. You can make brush presets for other tools that act as brushes, such as the Clone Stamp and History brushes. If you do extensive painting or retouching that involve tweaks to the options bar, you'll want to study brush presets more closely.

The Brushes palette itself is so deep that a complete description of all of its features is outside the scope of this book; you can find option-by-option descriptions in Photoshop Help. This topic focuses on how to use brushes as presets.

To create a brush preset:

1. In the Tools palette, select the brush tool you want to customize.

2. Click the Brushes tab in the palette well or choose Windows > Brushes.

3. If you want to use an existing brush preset as a starting point, select Brush Presets and then select a brush preset from the list. Your changes won't replace the preset you select.

4. Select Brush Tip Shape and specify settings on the right (**Figure 4.4**).

5. As needed, select any of the brush attributes below Brush Tip Shape on the left side and specify settings on the right.

6. After you've configured the brush the way you want, click the Create New Brush button at the bottom of the Brushes palette. Name the brush and click OK.

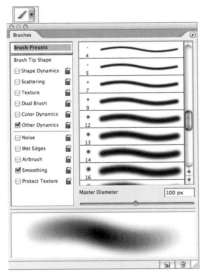

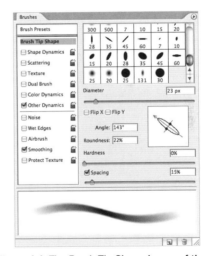

Figure 4.3: A tool preset for brushes remembers the combination of brush tool settings plus all settings on the options bar.

Figure 4.4: The Brush Tip Shape is one of the many settings you can save as part of a brush preset.

To create a tool preset for a brush:

1. In the Tools palette, select a brush tool.

2. In the options bar, click the Brush Preset picker (second from the left) to select the brush you want. If the brush you want isn't in the list, open the

Brushes palette, where you can create a new brush or edit the brushes in the list, and then make sure the brush you want is selected in the options bar.

3. Make sure all settings in the options bar are the way you want them to be in the tool preset.

4. In the options bar, click the Tool Presets picker and click the Create New Tool Preset button.

5. Name the tool preset and click OK.

To use a brush tool preset:

1. In the Tools palette, select the brush you want to use.

2. In the options bar, click the Tool Presets picker to see the Tool Presets list and select the preset you want to use.

 NOTES If the Brushes palette is dimmed, you probably selected a tool that only supports basic brush options. For example, the Healing Brush only uses the basic Brushes palette options because there isn't much point in having a calligraphic Healing Brush. You can still set basic brush options by clicking the Brush Preset picker in the options bar, next to the Tool Presets picker.

If your scratch disk space is limited, you may want to minimize the number of brush presets you keep with a document. You can use the Preset Manager (Edit > Preset Manager) to delete brush presets you aren't using. Tool presets for brushes don't consume RAM.

Swatch Presets (Swatches)

A swatch preset is a saved color specification. You've probably heard of *swatches*; that's actually just another, shorter way of saying *swatch presets*. They live in the Swatches palette, as you've probably noticed. Swatches help you specify colors consistently, either within your own document or across a workgroup if you distribute your swatches to others.

The swatches you see aren't saved with individual documents, but with Photoshop settings in general. If you customize the Swatches palette, those changes stay in effect for any document you have open. Any document you open takes on the swatches currently in effect in Photoshop, which may not be the same as the swatches that were available the last time you edited that document. The colors in your document won't change, however.

To create a swatch preset:

1. Set the foreground color using either the color picker in the Tools palette or the Color palette (**Figure 4.5**).

2. In the Swatches palette, click the Create New Swatch of Foreground Color button (**Figure 4.6**).

To use a swatch preset, just select a swatch.

Figure 4.5

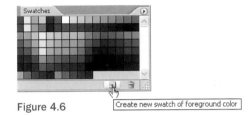

Figure 4.6

Create new swatch of foreground color

Tool Presets for Gradients

Remember how brush configurations exist at two levels? That's true for *gradients* as well. You'll find that the options bar for the gradient tool contains both a list of gradient presets and a list of tool presets for the gradient tool.

To create a tool preset for the gradient tool:

1. In the Tools palette, select the gradient tool.

2. In the options bar, click the gradient picker arrow (**Figure 4.7**) to select the gradient you want. If the gradient you want isn't in the list, click the gradient itself to open the Gradient Editor, where you can create a new gradient or edit the gradient presets in the list. (Because this topic focuses on presets, we won't go into the ins and outs of the Gradient Editor here.)

Tool Presets picker ——

—— Gradient picker

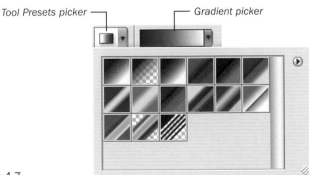

Figure 4.7

3. Make sure the settings in the options bar are the way you want them to be in the tool preset.

4. In the options bar, click the Tool Presets picker and click the Create New Tool Preset button.

5. Name the tool preset and click OK.

To use a gradient preset:

1. In the Tools palette, select the gradient tool.

2. In the options bar, click the Tool Presets picker to see the Tool Presets list and select the preset you want to use.

Layer Styles and Layer Style Presets

A layer style is a visual effect, like the drop shadows, strokes, and fills you apply using the Layers palette or the Layer Style dialog box. Many cool Photoshop effects are actually made up of stacked layer styles, and you can save any combination of layer styles as a one-click layer style preset. Layer styles live in the Styles palette (Window > Styles). Photoshop comes with many layer styles built in, so you can use the Styles palette to easily try them out or to use as starting points for your own layer styles.

To create a layer style preset:

1. In the Layers palette, select a layer to use just as an example to set up the layer style preset. The example layer should be about the size of the layers you'll typically use with the layer style you're creating.

2. Set up all of the layer styles you want to include in the layer style preset (**Figure 4.8**).

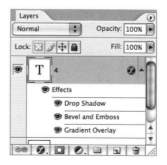

Figure 4.8

3. In the Styles palette, click the Create New Style button (**Figure 4.9**).

To use a layer style preset, select a layer and click a layer style in the Styles palette.

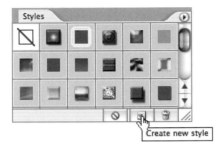

Figure 4.9

As with brushes and gradients, there are two levels going on here, so I just want to summarize the distinction again, just to be clear. A layer style is only a single instance, whereas a layer style preset can include a combination of multiple layer styles. A layer style preset can still be useful for a single instance of a layer style if you want to apply that layer style with specific settings (**Figure 4.10**).

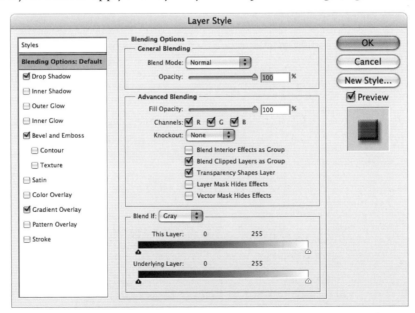

Figure 4.10: Layer styles are listed in the Layer Style dialog box, whereas layer style presets (saved layer style combinations) are listed in the Styles palette in Figure 4.9.

Pattern Presets

A *pattern* is an image that Photoshop remembers as a tile. You can make a pattern out of any selection or image. When you apply a pattern to a layer, the pattern fills the layer by repeating itself over and over. Pattern presets are often called just *patterns*. You'll encounter patterns in the Edit > Fill dialog box or in the Pattern adjustment layer.

To create a pattern preset:

1. Select a layer or use the rectangular marquee tool to select an area of a layer.

2. Choose Edit > Define Pattern.

3. Name the pattern and click OK (**Figure 4.11**).

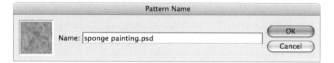

Figure 4.11

To use a pattern preset:

1. If you want to apply the pattern to a specific area, select that area first.

2. In the Layers palette, click the Create New Fill or Adjustment Layer button and choose Pattern Fill.

3. Click the pattern preset button (**Figure 4.12**), select a pattern, specify options, and click OK.

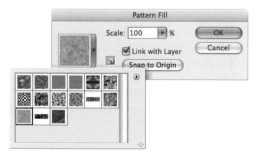

Figure 4.12

TIPS   You can also apply patterns by using the Edit > Fill command or by using the brush tool.

To fine-tune a pattern so that it doesn't look so much like a tile, try the Pattern Maker. Select the layer you want to use as a pattern and choose Filter > Pattern Maker.

 NOTE   Patterns consume scratch disk space, so if your scratch disk space is limited, minimize the number of patterns you use. Some of the built-in layer styles use patterns, and those patterns also take up RAM.

Contour Presets

You use *contours* to customize the bevel effects that you apply to layers. Contours appear in the Layer Style dialog box (**Figure 4.13**). If it isn't obvious how the contour shape translates into the final bevel, think of the contour as a cross-section—what the bevel's silhouette would look like if you sliced it off and looked at it from the end.

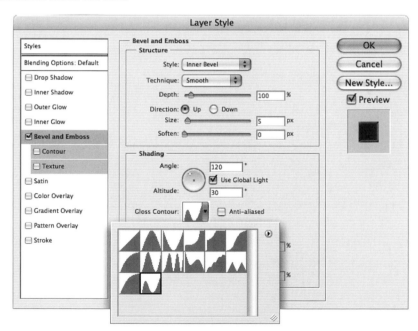

Figure 4.13: **Gloss Contour effects in the Contour picker customize the shape of an edge.**

To create a contour preset:

1. Select a layer.

2. In the Layers palette, click the Add a Layer Style button and choose a layer style in the list below Blending Options (**Figure 4.14**).

3. Click the Contour or Gloss Contour picker (the arrow, not the thumbnail) to see the available contours and then select the contour you want to use as a starting point (see Figure 4.13), such as bevel and emboss. If you don't see a Contour or Gloss Contour picker, select a different style along the left side of the Layer Style dialog box and make sure the one you don't want is unchecked.

4. Click the contour or gloss contour thumbnail (not the picker arrow) to open the Contour Editor dialog box (**Figure 4.15**).

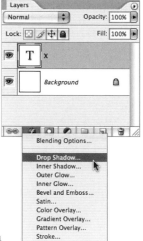

Figure 4.14   Figure 4.15

5. Shape the contour path by dragging the points on the curve. If points don't exist where you need them, click the path to add a point. To remove a point, drag it off the editor graph.

6. Click the New button, name the contour, and click OK.

7. Click OK to close the Contour Editor dialog box. The contour is now available to all layer styles.

8. If you were only creating a contour and you don't want to apply the selected effect to the selected layer, you can click Cancel until you return to the document window. Otherwise, continue applying layer styles to the selected layer and when you're done, click OK.

 TIP   As you edit a contour, you can preview the effect of your changes if the selected layer is visible in the document window.

Although contours are vector paths, you can't draw them with the pen tool or exchange them with Adobe Illustrator CS2. That's not a big loss, because they're usually simple enough to shape right there in the Contour Editor dialog box.

Custom Shapes and Tool Presets for Shapes

Shapes are vector-based paths drawn using shape tools or the pen tool. Unlike the pixel-based graphics you usually edit in Photoshop, shapes are resolution-independent, like the shapes you'd create in drawing programs like Illustrator. You can use shapes as masks or convert them to selections (**Figure 4.16**). When you want to create an area that involves flawlessly straight lines or perfectly smooth curves, it's often easier and faster to draw and edit its outline using a shape tool or the pen tool than it is to use other methods like the lasso tool.

Figure 4.16: Starting with a shape (left), click the Load Path as a Selection button in the Paths palette (center) to convert the shape to a selection (right).

Most of the shape tools are basic, such as the usual rectangle, rounded rectangle, ellipse, polygon, and line tools you've seen in countless other programs. If you need a vector shape other than those, such as a business logo, you can use the pen tool to draw a *custom shape*. You can save custom shapes in the options bar for later use, and Photoshop comes with some predefined custom shapes such as arrows and common symbols.

Shapes have two kinds of presets, just like the brush tools and gradients. You can save a custom shape, which will appear on the Custom Shape picker next to the standard shapes. You can also save a tool preset for shapes; as you probably guessed by now, a tool preset for a shape saves both the selected shape tool and all of the options bar settings for that tool. This can be very confusing, because you can have a custom shape that isn't part of a shape tool preset, or a shape tool preset that doesn't use a custom shape! Don't worry about such mental mazes; just remember the difference between creating custom shapes and creating tool presets for shapes.

 NOTE   You see the Custom Shape picker in the options bar only when the custom shape tool is selected.

To create a custom shape:

1. In the Tools palette, select the pen tool or any shape tool.

2. In the options bar, make sure the Shape Layers button is selected (**Figure 4.17**).

3. Draw a shape.

4. In the Layers palette, select the shape layer's vector mask (**Figure 4.18**).

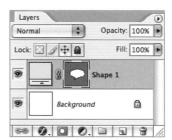

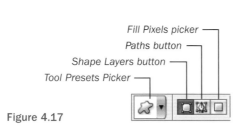

Fill Pixels picker ——
Paths button ——
Shape Layers button ——
Tool Presets Picker ——

Figure 4.17   Figure 4.18

5. Choose Edit > Define Custom Shape.

6. Name the shape and click OK. You can now select your new custom shape from the Custom Shape picker on the options bar when the custom shape tool is selected (**Figure 4.19**). This is kind of tricky—you often won't see the Custom Shape picker because it only appears when the custom shape tool is selected. Just remember to select the custom shape tool.

 TIP   You can use a shape in Adobe Illustrator as a custom shape in Photoshop. In Illustrator, select the shape and choose Edit > Copy. Switch to Photoshop and choose Edit > Paste. In the Paste dialog box that appears, select Shape Layer and click OK. With the new shape layer's vector mask selected, you can choose Edit > Define Custom Shape.

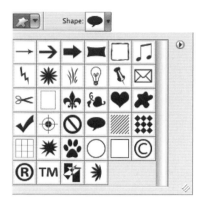

Figure 4.19

To create a tool preset for any shape tool:

1. In the Tools palette, select any shape tool.

2. Make sure the settings in the options bar are the way you want them to be in the new tool preset.

3. In the options bar, click the Tool Presets picker and click the Create New Tool Preset button.

4. Name the tool preset and click OK.

 TIPS Think about using custom shapes whenever you want to create simple graphics or masks, such as a company logo or a standard graphic symbol.

One advantage of a shape is that enlarging a shape doesn't result in jaggy edges, like those you get when you scale up a bitmap. However, when the document is exported or printed, the shape is converted into a bitmap at the resolution of the document as stated in the Image > Image Size dialog box. Shapes remain resolution-independent only when you save as a Photoshop PDF file.

 NOTE Custom shapes aren't the same as saved paths. Custom shapes live in the Shape picker in the options bar for shape tools for all documents, whereas saved paths live in the Paths palette for a single document. You use the first three icons on the left side of the shape tool options bar to determine whether a custom shape is added as a shape layer, a path, or as filled pixels on the current layer. Saved paths don't affect a layer until you convert the path to a selection.

INCLUDING MULTIPLE PATHS IN A CUSTOM SHAPE PRESET

You might have a logo or other complex vector-based symbol that you'd like to save for quick access in Photoshop. If you want more than one path to be part of the custom shape preset, there are a few things you should do before adding more paths to the original path.

1. In the Layers palette, select the shape layer's vector mask.

2. In the options bar, make sure the Paths button is selected and select one of the path area buttons in the group of four buttons beyond the shape buttons in the options bar. That controls whether multiple paths overlap or cut holes in each other (**Figure 4.20**).

3. Draw additional paths or shapes, and they should be added to the existing custom shape. If you already have an Adobe Illustrator version of the vector shape, you can paste it in.

4. When you're done, remember to save it as a custom shape, as described in the section "Custom Shapes and Tool Presets for Shapes" in this chapter.

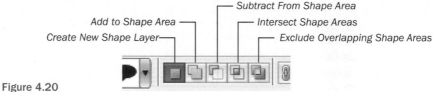

Figure 4.20

NOTE   You can't really edit presets. If you want to make changes to a preset, you have to start from the existing preset, modify it, add it as a new preset, and delete the old one.

Viewing All Tool Presets at Once

By default, the Tool Presets picker on the options bar lists only the presets for the tool selected in the Tools palette. If you'd rather see all presets for all tools, disable the Current Tool Only checkbox at the bottom of the Tool Presets list (**Figure 4.21**). Showing presets for all tools can be useful if you want to change to a different tool and preset with just one click; otherwise you have to have the right tool selected before you can pick the preset you want. On the other hand, if you have a long list of presets, you might be able to find a preset more quickly if you narrow down the list by enabling Current Tool Only.

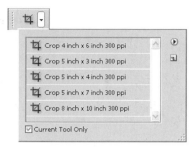

Figure 4.21: **Disable the Current Tool Only checkbox to list tool presets for all tools.**

If you become a total preset junkie, you can display the Tool Presets lists as a palette (**Figure 4.22**). Click the Tool Presets tab in the palette well or choose Windows > Tool Presets. In the Tool Presets palette, tool presets are always visible and you can position the palette anywhere on the screen—no need to go to the options bar. If you always want to use tools with specific presets, you could conceivably go as far as using the Tool Presets list as your primary way of switching tools, even hiding the Tools palette if you don't really use it.

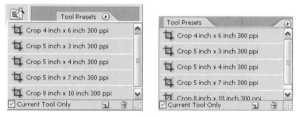

Figure 4.22: **The Tool Presets list viewed in the palette well (left), and then dragged out of the palette well to become the Tool Presets palette (right).**

TIP   Save your frequently used type specifications as tool presets for the type tools. Photoshop doesn't have paragraph or character styles, so you can use tool presets to store combinations options bar settings such as font, type size, and paragraph alignment.

Viewing and Managing All Presets at Once

Performing overall administration of your presets throughout Photoshop can be a bit of a challenge if you're trying to do it by going from palette to palette, because presets are spread out all over the place. Although the Tool Presets palette lists only tool presets, the Preset Manager (**Figure 4.23**) lists all presets of all types in one place, while also giving you the ability to rename and delete presets, save them to disk as files, and load them from disk. Saving presets to disk is useful for things like distributing standard presets throughout a workgroup, or simply storing backup copies of presets separately from Photoshop—a good idea in case you need to reinstall or upgrade Photoshop.

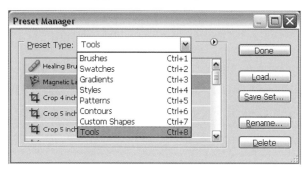

Figure 4.23: **You can manage all presets in the Preset Manager dialog box.**

To open the Preset Manager, choose Edit > Presets Manager. The Preset Manager command is also available on the palette menu for any presets palette. If you see presets in a dialog box, the Preset Manager command is in the menu that you get when you click the triangle button.

Some types of presets are easier to view as names (like tool presets), and others are easier to view graphically (like brushes). To change how the Preset Manager dialog box lists presets, click the pop-up menu icon and choose the way you want to list presets.

In the Preset Manager you see a column of buttons along the right side of the dialog box: Load, Save Set, Rename, and Delete. You can use those buttons to control which presets are stored inside and outside the document:

- To change the name of a preset, select a preset and click Rename.

- To delete a preset, select a preset and click Delete.

- To save presets as a file on disk, select presets, click Save Set, enter a descriptive name, and click OK.

- To import presets from a file on disk, click Load, select the presets file, and click Load.

TIPS In the Tool Presets list or palette, you can manage individual presets with a context menu. Context-click on a preset and you'll see the New Tool Preset, Rename Tool Preset, and Delete Tool Preset commands.

You can manage presets using the pop-up menu that appears with a preset list. For example, if you click the palette menu for the Styles palette, you see the Reset Styles, Load Styles, Save Styles, and Replace Styles commands. If you're looking at a list of presets in a place other than a palette, you can view the menu by clicking the round button with the triangle in it—for example, when you click the Tool Presets picker in the options bar.

In the Preset Manager dialog box, you can switch among preset types by using keyboard shortcuts. You can see the shortcuts in the pop-up menu at the top of the Preset Manager dialog box.

RESTORING DEFAULT PRESETS

If you want to reset Photoshop presets back to their state out of the box, you can't do it in the Preset Manager. Instead, go to the preset list for each type of preset and choose the Default command at the bottom of the preset menu list. For example, to reset swatches, click the Swatches palette menu and choose Default Swatches. If you're not sure where preset lists are stored, see the section "Kinds of Presets" earlier in this chapter.

Using Adobe PDF Presets

Adobe PDF (Portable Document Format) has been hailed as a way to solve the problem of exchanging files with people who don't have the same software that you do. As PDF has matured, Adobe has extended the format to meet more of the specifications required to send a file quickly over the Internet and to print a file reliably on a press—two opposing goals. Ironically, although PDF was invented to simplify document exchange, there are so many possible ways to set up a PDF that you can easily create a PDF that's wrong for its intended use. You can make a PDF that's too big for the Web, yet lacks necessary information for a press. To help keep PDF simple, Adobe developed presets for exporting PDF files and have standardized those presets across the Adobe Creative Suite, which includes Photoshop.

To see the Adobe PDF presets, choose Edit > Adobe PDF Presets.

You only need to pay attention to Adobe PDF presets if you save a Photoshop file in Photoshop PDF format (**Figure 4.24**). Photoshop PDF is an option in the Format pop-up menu in the Save As dialog box when you choose File > Save As, or when you use the PDF Presentation command to convert multiple image files into a multiple-page document or a PDF presentation. If you usually save images in Photoshop (PSD), TIFF, or JPEG (JPG) formats, you probably won't need to deal with PDF presets very often. If you're not sure if you need to use the Photoshop PDF format, see the section "Saving Flexible Files" in Chapter 15.

Figure 4.24: **The Photoshop PDF format option is available in the Save As dialog box.**

About the Built-In Adobe PDF Presets

When you use Photoshop PDF format, chances are you'll simply be able to use one of the built-in presets. Adobe carefully designed presets that would work well for their intended uses. Note, however, that these presets are designed primarily for output from page-layout programs where documents include lots of text and graphics; these presets are included in Photoshop mostly for consistency with other Adobe Creative Suite products. Here's a brief overview of the built-in Adobe PDF presets:

■ **High Quality Print.** This preset is intended for desktop printing, proofing, or review. It isn't intended for color press output—don't confuse this preset with the Press Quality preset. It can be good for PDF presentations if you need better image quality than you'd get from the Smallest File Size preset.

■ **PDF/X-1a:2001.** Don't be intimidated by the cryptic name. PDF/X-1a is an ISO (International Standards Organization) standard for CMYK press output. Some media organizations now specify PDF/X-1a as the standard format for submissions such as ads. If you aren't familiar with PDF/X-1a, just think of it this way: If your clients aren't asking for it, you don't need to worry about it; if your clients are asking for it, all you need to do is save a copy of your Photoshop file with this preset selected and it will conform to the standard.

- **PDF/X-3:2002.** This preset exists for the same reasons as PDF/X-1a, but where PDF/X-1a is a pure, traditional CMYK standard, PDF/X-3 allows RGB and color-managed files. Again, you only need to pay attention to this preset if you're required to submit files in the PDF/X-3 format, and all you need to do to comply is save a copy of your Photoshop file with this preset selected.

- **Press Quality.** If you're producing a Photoshop PDF file that's going straight to press for CMYK output, select this preset. Note, however, that in many work-flows, Photoshop files are saved as Photoshop or TIFF files and placed into a page-layout document (such as those you create with Adobe InDesign) before output to press. Chances are you don't need to use this preset unless you really are preparing a Photoshop PDF file that will be output to press separations without being included in a page-layout document.

- **Smallest File Size.** This preset may be useful if you're saving a Photoshop PDF document in order to send it over the Internet for a PDF-based draft review. (Photoshop PDF files work well in review cycles that use the collaborative review features of Adobe Acrobat.) To reach a small file size, this preset drasti-cally compresses images, reducing them to draft quality. Never use the Smallest File Size preset for final high-resolution color output.

Creating Custom Adobe PDF Presets

If your workgroup uses Photoshop PDF extensively, you may decide that you'd like to customize an Adobe PDF preset. Before you do, though, check the built-in presets carefully to see if any of them is already suitable for your needs. Adobe tried to cover the most common print and online uses of PDF when it created the built-in presets. Also, if you have a reason to save Photoshop PDF files instead of in the more typical Photoshop or TIFF formats, chances are it's because your recipient requires certain Adobe PDF settings. Find out which Adobe PDF preset your recipient wants you to specify, or if they've created their own Adobe PDF preset that you need to load. For example, you may be sending a PDF ad to one of the many major magazines that requires ads to be submitted in the PDF/X-1a standard, and because Photoshop already includes a built-in preset for that standard, you won't need to create your own preset.

In the event that you do need to create your own Adobe PDF preset, I'll quickly walk you through the panels.

To examine Adobe PDF presets:

1. Choose Edit > Adobe PDF Presets.

2. Select a preset in the Presets list (**Figure 4.25**).

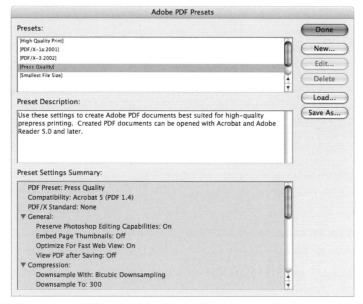

Figure 4.25: **The Adobe PDF Presets in the Adobe PDF Presets dialog box are already tuned and tested for common types of output.**

3. Read the Preset Description and Preset Settings Summary.

To create an Adobe PDF preset:

1. In the Adobe PDF Presets dialog box, examine the existing presets and select the one that's closest to the preset you want to create.

2. Click New.

3. In the Preset field, enter a preset name.

4. If the preset must conform to a specific PDF standard, choose it from the Standard pop-up menu. To maintain compatibility with the standard you choose, changing the standard may change which options are available in the Edit PDF Preset dialog box.

5. Select each panel in turn, specify options, and click OK when you're done. For an overview of the options, see the topic "Options in the Edit PDF Preset Dialog Box."

 NOTE   You can't edit any of the built-in PDF presets (the presets in square brackets) If you want to create a variation on a built-in PDF preset, use a built-in preset as a starting point by selecting it before you click the New button.

Options in the Edit PDF Preset Dialog Box

The Adobe Photoshop Help file contains quite a bit of detail about the options in the Edit PDF Preset dialog box (just search for *pdf presets* in Photoshop Help), so in this topic I focus on how to decide which option you need. I don't cover the Summary panel because all it does is give you a one-stop overview of the settings for that PDF preset.

Don't be surprised that I don't go into a great amount of detail in this section. So many of the options involved in customizing a preset are concepts that are used in other areas of Photoshop already, such as compression and color management—this isn't the place to discuss those concepts fully. If you want to create a preset and you don't understand all of the compression options, starting from the preset that's closest to the type of output you're targeting should set you up with reasonably appropriate compression settings.

Standard and Compatibility Pop-up Menus

The Standard and Compatibility pop-up menus at the top of the Edit PDF Preset dialog box control which options are available in the other panels of the dialog box (**Figure 4.26**):

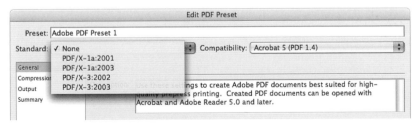

Figure 4.26: The Standard and Compatibility pop-up menus in the Edit PDF Preset dialog box let you conform a PDF preset to the technical requirements of those receiving your PDF files.

- **Standard.** You can select from the PDF/X standards supported by Photoshop. Remember, these standards exist to simplify prepress output. If you're sending PDF files to someone who requires a PDF/X standard, choose it; if not, it's better to choose None.

- **Compatibility.** Choosing a later version of PDF can allow better support of transparency and smaller files. However, the PDF/X standards require PDF 1.3 compatibility. The differences among PDF versions are described in detail in the Photoshop Help topic "Adobe PDF Compatibility Levels."

General Panel

The options in the General panel (**Figure 4.27**) are those that don't fit in the other panels:

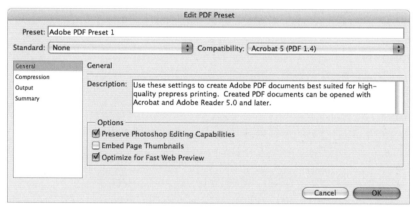

Figure 4.27: The General panel in the Edit PDF Preset dialog box provides basic options for a PDF preset.

- **Preserve Photoshop Editing Capabilities.** To allow a Photoshop PDF to be fully editable in Photoshop, including layers and text, enable this checkbox. If it's disabled, make sure you keep a copy of the original Photoshop file.

- **Embed Page Thumbnails.** All this does is generate a preview thumbnail of the document for Open and Save dialog boxes. It doesn't affect output. If you view a Photoshop PDF in Acrobat, Acrobat can generate a page thumbnail preview too.

- **Optimize for Fast Web Preview.** This doesn't affect file size or download speed of a Photoshop PDF on the Web—if you enable it, a multi-page PDF displaying in a Web browser will become visible before it completely loads, so you spend less time looking at a blank window. It probably won't make any difference for a single-page Photoshop PDF, but it could make a difference if you create a PDF presentation or contact sheets for Web viewing, because those are typically multiple-page files.

Compression Panel

You can find detailed descriptions of the settings in the Compression panel (**Figure 4.28**) in the Photoshop Help file (the topic is "Compression and Downsampling Options for Adobe PDF"), but frankly, you may not need to worry about them to that degree of detail. Compression settings depend on the output you want, and because Adobe already created very good built-in presets based on press, desktop printing and Internet output, you can get the settings in this panel to be close to ideal if you simply select the preset that most closely matches your output before you click the New button to create your preset. If you then want to fine-tune the settings further, you can study the detailed descriptions of each individual option in the Help file. Here are a few quick pointers on the choices:

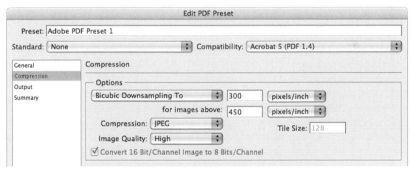

Figure 4.28: The Compression panel in the Edit PDF Preset dialog box lets you fine-tune the balance between quality and file size.

■ In general, the choices in the Compression panel are a tradeoff between quality and file size. If you choose settings that generate higher quality, the PDF file size is larger. Test your preset to find the right balance.

■ Downsampling can save space. If you're compressing photographs, Bicubic is probably the best method. If you're compressing art with solid colors, try options other than Bicubic. Your resolution should be consistent with the type of output: 300 dpi or more for press, 150 dpi for general desktop printing, and 100 dpi or below for Web or e-mail.

■ In the Compression pop-up menu, JPEG and JPEG2000 are better for photographs, and ZIP is better for solid-color art.

■ If some options aren't available, try changing the settings in the Standard and Compatibility pop-up menus. Older versions of the PDF standard don't support options like JPEG2000.

Output Panel

Like compression, the correct settings for the Output panel (**Figure 4.29**) are highly dependent on the output, so once again you'll probably get close to the ideal settings if you simply base your new preset on the existing preset that's closest to the type of output for which the PDF file is ultimately headed. The options in the Color section have to do with color management, so you should change them only if you already have a good working knowledge of color management and color conversion.

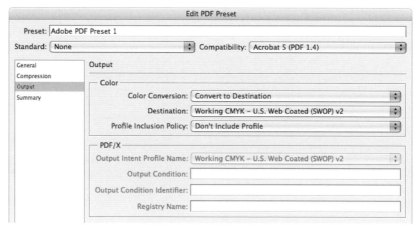

Figure 4.29: **The Output panel in the Edit PDF Preset dialog box provides options for specific output conditions.**

The PDF/X section is available only when you've chosen a PDF/X standard from the Standard pop-up menu, and you can fill out the options in that section only in a way that conforms to the PDF/X standard you chose.

 TIP   If you often use the PDF Presentation command, you might consider creating an Adobe PDF preset that has higher quality than the Smallest File Size preset but generates a smaller file size than the High Quality Print preset.

Loading and Saving Settings

Many dialog boxes or menus in Photoshop include Load and Save buttons or commands. The dialog box buttons are great for remembering settings for a feature that doesn't support presets.

In a dialog box, use the Load button to import settings from a file on disk. For example, if you're preparing to submit ads to a magazine, the magazine may have sent you an Adobe PDF Presets file; you can import those presets by using the Load button in the Adobe PDF Presets dialog box.

In a dialog box, use the Save button to save your presets to a file on disk so that you can back them up or send them to colleagues. Others can use the Load button to import presets you send to them.

To save settings to disk:

1. Click the Save button or choose a Save command (**Figure 4.30**). If you don't see a Save button or command, that feature may not allow saved settings.

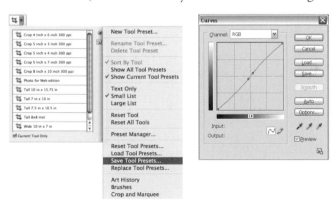

Figure 4.30

2. Specify a name for the settings file. Be careful to preserve the filename extension; different types of settings files use different filename extensions.

3. If Photoshop displays your Documents (Mac OS X) or My Documents (Windows XP) folder, specify a location for the settings file. If Photoshop displays a specific folder, it's usually better to leave the location alone; see the nearby sidebar "Where to Store Presets."

4. Click Save.

To load dialog box settings from a settings file, simply click the Load button or choose a Load command, select the settings file you want to import, and click Load.

WHERE TO STORE PRESETS

Photoshop keeps some custom settings in special folders. When you click the Save button, pay attention to the folder where the dialog box opens by default. If the custom setting you're saving belongs in a certain folder, Photoshop usually opens that folder in the Save dialog box. For example, when you click Save in the Proof Setup dialog box, the folder that appears in the Save dialog box by default is the Proofing folder (**Figure 4.31**). When Photoshop displays the View > Proof Setup submenu, it looks in that folder for proof settings to list on the submenu. If you click the Save button and you see your usual default documents folder (Documents on Mac OS X or My Documents on Windows) (**Figure 4.32**), that means that where you save the file isn't critical. For example, you can store Curves dialog box settings anywhere you want.

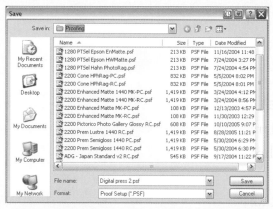

Figure 4.31: **When saving a proof condition preset, Photoshop defaults to the Proofing folder.**

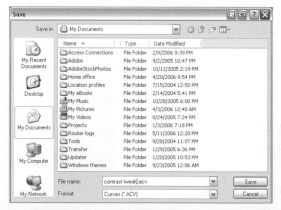

Figure 4.32: **When saving a Curves preset, Photoshop displays the user documents folder, indicating no special folder for the preset.**

CHAPTER FIVE

Creating How-To Tutorials and Tips

WHEN YOU'RE LEARNING A NEW PROGRAM, reaching for the manual is a time-honored tradition. But if you don't have the manual, where do you turn? With Photoshop, the answer is easy: the Help menu. The Help > Photoshop Help command contains the entire contents of the printed manual and more, and in addition, further down in the Help menu are how-to tutorials that can guide you through common tasks.

If you coordinate a workgroup or teach a class, you can add your own how-to topics to the Help menu of your copies of Photoshop. As long as you have a basic knowledge of HTML, adding your own tutorials to the Photoshop Help menu is quick and easy. Others can also install your custom topics by simply dropping them into a special folder and restarting Photoshop.

In this chapter, I show you a how-to so that you can see how it works, and then I walk you through making your own how-to.

What's the Idea Behind How-To Topics?

So what does a how-to do that the Help file doesn't do? The answer is that the Help file (and the User Guide, which contains the same content) is reference oriented: Its table of contents is organized from the point of view of commands and features, not the actual tasks you need to do. But if you're new to Photoshop, you may not know which feature Photoshop provides for a certain task. In this way, the how-to topics built into Photoshop can help you get started.

By writing your own how-to topics, you can make Photoshop more directly relevant to your colleagues or students by creating topics that are immediately related to common tasks at your organization or school. Your how-to topics can be as deep as a complete tutorial or as simple as a list of links to helpful topics on the Web.

Using a How-To Topic

Before you make your own how-to topics, it's a good idea to see how the existing ones work. Photoshop actually has two kinds of how-to topics. The first kind opens up in the Adobe Help Center and looks just like the rest of the Help files. The second kind opens up in your default Web browser; you find these at the bottom of the Help menu. When you create your own how-to, it appears with the browser-based how-to topics at the bottom of the Help menu. Let's try one of each kind.

First, let's look at the kind of topic that opens in the Adobe Help Center. In Photoshop, choose Help > How to Paint and Draw > To Customize a Brush. The Adobe Help Center opens to the topic about brush options (**Figure 5.1**).

Now let's look at the other kind of how-to. In Photoshop, choose Help > How to Create How Tos. Your default Web browser opens and displays a page covering that topic (**Figure 5.2**). When you make your own how-to topics, they'll open in the default Web browser just like this topic did.

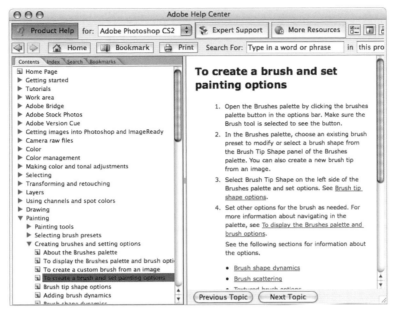

Figure 5.1: **A built-in how-to topic opens in the Adobe Help Center.**

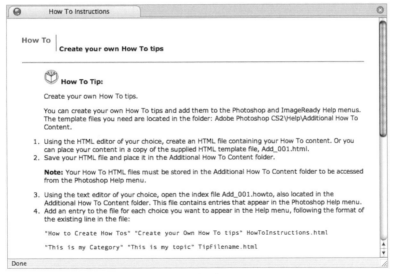

Figure 5.2: **A custom how-to topic opens in a Web browser.**

Making Your Own How-To Topic

Aside from basic computer skills, the only skill required to create your own how-to is knowledge of Hypertext Markup Language (HTML). Knowledge of Cascading Style Sheets (CSS) is also helpful, but not required.

To write your own how-to, you need to create at least two files: an HTML file containing your instructions, and a file that links to your HTML file from the Help menu in Photoshop. Both files are stored in a folder called Additional How To Content, which is stored inside the Help folder inside the Adobe Photoshop CS2 application folder on your computer. Adobe includes an example file in that folder, called HowToInstructions.html. It's a useful document to refer to, but it doesn't walk you through an example. If you don't know how to code in HTML using a text editor, you can use a graphical Web page editor such as Macromedia Dreamweaver or GoLive.

To see how this works with a specific example, let's say I'm the production manager of an online news site that has specific requirements for publishing a photo alongside a news story on the Web. We have a small staff, so on some breaking stories we allow reporters to upload their own photos. Because of this, we decide that every machine should have detailed instructions about preparing a photo for the Web site. I come up with a how-to topic, and in the following steps, I create the topic and add it to the Help menu in Photoshop.

 NOTE   In the Web image-processing example, I kept the image-processing steps simple for clarity. If you're actually processing images for the Web, the best procedure for your workflow may be different or may involve more steps.

To add a how-to topic to the Photoshop Help menu:

1. Write the topic you want to add. If you are using a Web page editor, you can prepare the topic directly in that program (**Figure 5.3**). I'm using Dreamweaver.

2. Save the topic as an HTML file, using an HTML filename extension. In my example, the filename is WebPrep.html.

3. On the desktop, go to the Adobe Photoshop CS2 application folder and open the following folder (**Figure 5.4**):

```
Adobe Photoshop CS2/Help/additional how to content/
```

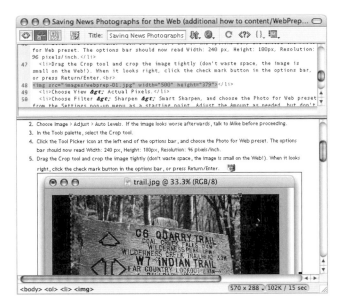

Figure 5.3

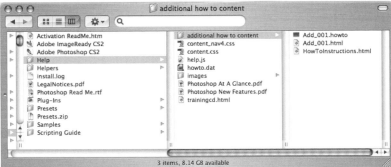

Figure 5.4

4. Use a text editor to open the file Add_001.howto. (You probably don't want to double-click the file—its filename extension isn't standard for a text file, so it may open in a program you didn't expect, or it may not open at all.)

5. Add a new line that contains three elements: the name of the submenu where you want to add the new topic, the name of the new topic as you want it to appear in the menu, and the actual filename of the topic (**Figure 5.5**). I added the line for my new topic like this:

```
"Department Standards" "Prepare an Image for the Web" WebPrep.html
```

■   Department Standards is the name of my new submenu.

Figure 5.5

- Prepare an Image for the Web is the name of the command I'm adding to the submenu.

- WebPrep.html is the filename of the document I want Photoshop to open when someone chooses Prepare a Photo for the Web command.

6. Save and close the file Add_001.howto. Some text editors save Rich Text Format (RTF) by default, like TextEdit on Mac OS X and WordPad on Windows—don't use RTF. Make sure you save the file in text-only format while preserving the .howto filename extension.

7. Copy your HTML how-to topic file into the Additional How To Content folder (**Figure 5.6**). Don't forget to also copy any linked images or other local content that your HTML file refers to. This example uses screenshots contained in an Images folder that is also copied into the folder.

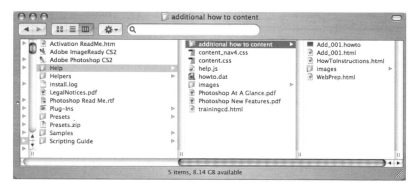

Figure 5.6

8. Start Photoshop (or if Photoshop is running, quit and relaunch it). Photoshop updates the Help menu only when it launches.

9. Test your new topic. See if it shows up under the Help menu in Photoshop (**Figure 5.7**). Make sure your submenu displays properly and that choosing a topic command opens it properly in your default Web browser (**Figure 5.8**).

Figure 5.7

Figure 5.8

NOTE   You can include images, movies, and Flash content in the how-to topic, as long as they are compatible with the Web browsers on the computers where you'll install your topic. You can store the images in the same folder as the topic or in another folder on the machine or over the network—the only thing that matters is that the machine has access to the images.

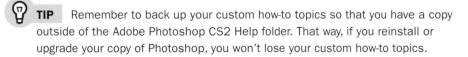

TIP   Remember to back up your custom how-to topics so that you have a copy outside of the Adobe Photoshop CS2 Help folder. That way, if you reinstall or upgrade your copy of Photoshop, you won't lose your custom how-to topics.

Distributing How-To Topics

As you've seen, how-to topics are stored in the Additional How To Content folder. To distribute the how-to topics you've created, all you have to do is make copies of the files you added to that folder. Then you can e-mail the copies to other people or store them on a server for later downloading by others. Anyone who wants to use your how-to topics must store them in the Additional How To Content folder on their own computers and then restart Photoshop if needed. Remember to bring along any linked images you may have used.

CHAPTER SIX

Working with Adobe Bridge

ADOBE BRIDGE IS A SOMETIMES UNDER-APPRECIATED assistant in the quest for more efficiency. When Bridge first appeared in Adobe Creative Suite CS2, some people took one look at it, decided it was yet another image browser, and never opened it again. And that's too bad, because Bridge is actually a powerful tool for managing massive numbers of files at once.

One way to understand Bridge is to realize the difference between working with one document and working with many documents. Many people are used to working with Photoshop like this: Find an image, open an image, work on it, save and close it. Things change when you work on large, image-intensive projects such as magazines and catalogs, where you can save a lot of time if you have the ability to locate a specific image quickly, or apply the same change to any number of images.

You may think that those concerns don't apply to you if you aren't a production artist. Ah, but what about that cool new digital camera you just bought? With a digital camera, it's easy to shoot hundreds of images before you realize you've done it. You can accumulate images far faster than was practical with a film camera, and as your collection grows, you begin to face the challenges of processing large numbers of photos and finding a specific photo—exactly the problems Adobe Bridge is designed to help you solve.

How Can Adobe Bridge Help?

To get a handle on why Adobe Bridge is useful, it helps to understand what Bridge does beyond simply browsing for images in the folders on your desktop. After all, you can approximate the general look of Bridge by opening a folder on your desktop and setting it to large icon view. Bridge goes well beyond that superficial comparison, so let's take a quick look at what Bridge can do:

■ **Organize and find graphics files.** Bridge can locate files based on *metadata*, the additional data you can add to a file. For example, when you take a digital photo, the camera saves an image file that includes the time, date, and exposure information. In Bridge, you can attach more information to that photo, such as keywords, names, a caption, and a copyright notice. Once all that's entered, you can use Bridge to retrieve photos using that metadata. For example, you can search for all photos containing the keyword *canoe* that were taken on May 18, 2006.

■ **Select multiple files for editing.** In Bridge, you can select multiple photos and pass them directly to Photoshop for batch processes. If you use Adobe Camera Raw, you can edit Raw files from Bridge without opening Photoshop, which can save RAM.

■ **Select the best files for editing.** You can use Bridge to rate and label files. By rating files using the 5-star system in Bridge, you can keep track of your best (and, if you like, worst) images. By attaching color labels to files, you can mark and select different groups of files while still keeping them together in a single folder.

■ **Open files in a program of your choice.** Once you've used Bridge to select the files you want to edit, you can open them in another program using all the usual methods, including double-clicking and drag-and-drop.

■ **Buy Adobe Stock Photos.** On the surface, Adobe Stock Photos might look like an occasional convenience, but they do offer a few efficiency enhancements:

Adobe Stock Photos aggregates images from multiple stock houses, so when you do need to find a photo for a project, Adobe Stock Photos represent one-stop shopping for that task. Also, Adobe Stock Photos are fully integrated with Photoshop and Creative Suite 2. Adobe Stock Photos contain built-in metadata, and Bridge, Photoshop, and other Creative Suite applications can indicate whether a stock image is a comp (sample) or purchased.

TAKE IT TO THE BRIDGE (AND BACK)

Adobe designed Bridge to be integrated with Photoshop (and other Adobe Creative Suite programs). That's why you'll find multiple ways of opening Bridge. Consider this as an opportunity to pick a way to open Bridge that best matches how you like to work or best matches the situation at hand.

When you have a document selected in Bridge, you can open that image in Photoshop by choosing File > Return to Adobe Photoshop CS2 or by pressing its keyboard short-cut. You can also drag the document from Bridge to Photoshop (to the Photoshop Dock icon on Mac OS X, or to the Photoshop application workspace in Windows XP). Finally, you can context-click a document in Bridge and choose the Open With command to specify which program you want to use to open the document.

Going the other way, you can start from a document that's open in Photoshop and view it in Bridge by clicking the Go to Bridge icon in the options bar (**Figure 6.1**), or by choosing File > Close and Go to Bridge.

If you become addicted to the workflow enhancements of Adobe Bridge, you may find a couple of other tips helpful. Consider adding Bridge to your Dock (Mac OS X) or taskbar (Windows XP) so that you can easily start and switch to Bridge. You can also set Bridge to open whenever you open Photoshop by enabling Automatically Launch Bridge in the General Preferences dialog box of Photoshop.

Figure 6.1: The Go to Bridge button, next to the palette well in the Photoshop options bar.

Making Bridge Equal to Your Tasks

Although Adobe Bridge browser windows are useful just the way they first appear, they're quite configurable. Feel free to change the way the window looks so that it best serves the task you're trying to accomplish. If more than one browser window would be useful to you, choose File > New Folder to open additional browser windows to view different folders, or even to view different views of the same folder. If these Bridge concepts don't sound familiar to you, read on for ways that Bridge can benefit your workflow.

Touring the Bridge Work Area

You'll use Bridge more efficiently if you're familiar with the main areas of a browser window. The main area of a browser window is a view of a folder on disk and the files and folders inside it.

Being able to look at a list of files and folders isn't that special; you can do that using your normal desktop, after all. What Bridge brings to the party is the ability to connect your files and folders directly to features that let you process those files efficiently.

Let's take a look at where those features are in the Bridge work area (**Figure 6.2**):

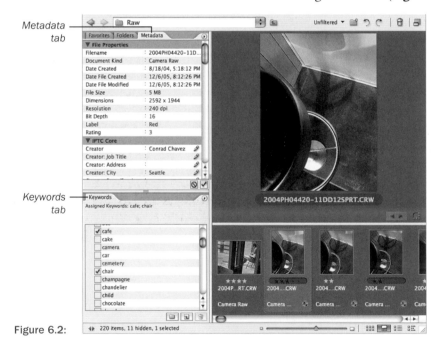

Metadata tab

Keywords tab

Figure 6.2:

- In the Label menu, you can rate selected files and assign colored labels to them.

- In the Tools menu, you can apply a range of processes to the selected files. While you can apply Tools menu commands to one file, they're really intended as *batch processes*—commands that accelerate your work by processing a large number of selected files, such as an entire photo shoot. The Tools menu is one place where Bridge integrates heavily with Photoshop and also with Adobe Illustrator and Adobe InDesign, because some of the commands send selected files straight to those programs, and in addition, process the files using specific Photoshop or Illustrator features or actions. For example, you can use Bridge to select 20 files and through the Tools menu have Photoshop create a contact sheet from all 20 files.

- In the Metadata tab, you can annotate files with information such as a copyright notice or caption.

- In the Keywords tab, you can annotate files with keywords, which you can later use when searching for files.

Because the first step in using Bridge is selecting a specific folder or file, a browser window gives you several ways to view the folder or file you want to see:

- To view a folder or file that's buried deep within many other folders, use the tree view in the Folders tab to dig quickly through many levels of a disk.

- If the folder or file you want is already visible on the desktop, just drag the folder or file icon onto the Bridge Dock icon on Mac OS X, or to the Bridge application workspace in Windows XP. The icon you drag opens in a new browser window.

- If you recently viewed a folder in Bridge, look for its name in the pop-up menu at the top of a browser window, in the section of the menu marked Recent Folders.

- If you know you'll want to see a particular folder often in the future, select it and choose File > Add Favorites. After that, you'll be able to see it in the Favorites tab, or in the Favorites section of the pop-up menu at the top of a browser window.

Optimizing a Bridge Window

Once you've got the right folder in view, you might want to adjust the browser window you're using to view the folder, to make it work better for the task at hand. Luckily, Bridge makes it easy to adjust its windows.

A good place to start is to choose Window > Workspace and choose a command from the Workspace submenu:

- ■ To see thumbnails of files in a folder, choose Light Table (**Figure 6.3**,). This command is a quick way to get a visual overview of folder contents by hiding everything except file thumbnails.

Figure 6.3

- ■ To get to a folder quickly, choose File Navigator (**Figure 6.4**). This view displays just the Favorites tab, the Folders tab, and file thumbnails.

Figure 6.4

■   To concentrate on entering or viewing image metadata, choose Metadata Focus (**Figure 6.5**). This view displays the Favorites, Metadata, and Keywords tabs along with the file thumbnails.

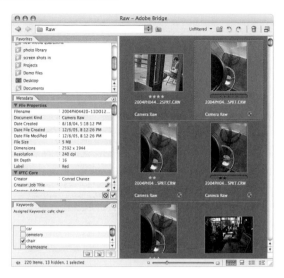

Figure 6.5

■   To inspect individual files visually, choose Filmstrip Focus (**Figure 6.6**). This view displays only files, but the twist is that it displays a large preview of the currently selected file.

Figure 6.6

I'm about to tell you how to fine-tune these views, but I wanted to point out the Workspace menu choices first because they are already task optimized and are therefore a good starting point for your own window customizations.

When you want to adjust a browser window, and the built-in workspaces don't quite get you there, you've got these options:

■ Choose a command from the View menu (except for the first two, Compact Mode and Slide Show). The second section of the View menu changes how files and folders display, without changing the panel arrangement. The third section of the View menu controls which panels are visible.

■ Manually arrange the parts of a browser window by dragging its dividers and by dragging tabs from one browser window pane to another.

By controlling both the displayed features and the arrangement of tabs and panes, you can reconfigure a browser window to fit the different phases of your workflow.

 TIP   If you want to see more file and folder thumbnails in a browser window but you don't want to make them any smaller, choose View > Show Thumbnail Only to hide the text under the thumbnails. This is a good solution if you can easily tell files apart by their thumbnails.

Saving Your Own Bridge Workspace

One of the most efficient decisions you can make in Bridge is to save your most useful workspaces. When you save a workspace, it's added to the Window > Workspace submenu, so you'll be able to change workspaces instantly as you change what it is you're doing with your files.

 NOTE   A Bridge workspace sets the configuration of the frontmost browser window and can't save a layout of multiple windows.

To save a workspace:

1. Set up a browser window just the way you like it (**Figure 6.7**).

2. Choose Workspace > Save Workspace.

3. Enter a name for your workspace (**Figure 6.8**).

Figure 6.7

Figure 6.8

4. If you want, choose a keyboard shortcut from the available function keys in the pop-up menu.

5. If you want the workspace to use a particular position and size on your monitor, enable Save Window Location as Part of Workspace.

6. Click Save.

To use a saved workspace, just choose its name from the Window > Workspace submenu or, better yet, press its keyboard shortcut if you set one up.

 TIP If the yellow tool tips are in your way when you mouse over thumbnails, turn them off by disabling the Show Tooltips option in the General pane of the Bridge Preferences dialog box.

Seeing Bigger File Previews

Sometimes you want to see a file larger than its Bridge thumbnail size. Bridge offers several ways to do this; use the method that works best for your workflow:

■ The Filmstrip view (View > As Filmstrip) displays a large view of the currently selected file and a single strip of thumbnails. This view displays a file at actual size or fits it within the available space, whichever is smaller. If you want to zoom in further, you have to open the file in Photoshop or another program; however, if a camera file is in a supported Raw format you can zoom in further using Camera Raw (see third bullet).

■ In a browser window, the Preview tab can display a larger view of a file. I don't use the Preview tab very much because you have to set aside enough space to make the Preview tab significantly larger than the thumbnail of the file—I prefer to use that space to display more metadata or keywords instead.

■ If you want to zoom in on a camera file that's in Raw format, choose File > Open in Camera Raw. In Camera Raw, you can use the zoom tool to magnify the image up to 400%.

 TIP   You can make more room for the large preview by reducing the size of the thumbnail filmstrip. Do this by enabling the Show Thumbnail Only command (View > Show Thumbnail Only) to get rid of the text under the thumbnails and by making the tab pane narrower.

Using Multiple Bridge Windows

You're not limited to a single browser window, and that's a good thing. Similar to the folder windows on your desktop, you can open additional browser windows so that you can compare folder contents and drag and drop files between folders. To open a new browser window, choose File > New Window.

If you frequently need to return to a particular folder, save yourself a lot of unnecessary back-and-forth navigation by leaving that folder open in one browser window and opening a second browser window to view other folders. Similarly, when you run the Edit > Find command, enable the Show Find Results in a New Browser Window checkbox so that you don't have to lose the state of the folder where you performed a search, such as the scroll position and any active selections (**Figure 6.9**).

Figure 6.9: **Showing find results in a new browser window.**

A less obvious but valuable reason to have multiple windows is to see different views of a single folder. For example, you might be looking at a folder containing 150 images from a photo shoot and you're entering keywords. Maybe you're trying to remember the names of people in a photo, and you remember that some of their names are already entered in another part of the shoot. You can leave one browser window set to the image you're currently editing and open another browser window for the same folder so you can select the image you want to refer to while you're editing the first image.

Multiple views of the same folder have other helpful uses. One window can show a folder sorted by name, while another window shows the same folder sorted by date. Or a different set of files can be selected in each window (**Figure 6.10**), so that you can send each set of selected files to different Photoshop actions.

Figure 6.10: **Two windows of the same folder, but with different selections in each window.**

One annoyance of Bridge is that it doesn't have any features for automatically arranging multiple windows—there aren't any Tile, Arrange, or Cascade commands, and you don't even get a list of open windows! You can sort of get around this by taking advantage of the fact that a saved workspace remembers the position of a browser window. For example, I sometimes like to have two browser windows take up an equal amount of space on the left and right sides of my monitor. I saved a workspace for each half of the monitor, and so I can instantly resize and slide a browser window to the left or right side of the screen by pressing the keyboard shortcut for my left side or right side workspace.

There are so many uses for multiple windows that you'll inevitably come across a situation where multiple windows save the day.

 TIPS   Because Bridge doesn't provide a list of open windows, it's a good idea to memorize your operating system's keyboard shortcuts for flipping through a stack of open windows within a program. On Mac OS X, the shortcut is Command-` (backward accent); on Windows, it's Ctrl-Tab.

When you move files you've edited with Adobe Camera Raw, Bridge moves any XMP files associated with the Raw files. Sounds trivial, but it means a lot if you work with Raw files, because other programs leave XMP files behind when you use them to move Raw files to a different folder. Moving XMP files with Raw files means you don't lose your Adobe Camera Raw edits when you move Raw files.

USING BRIDGE TO WATCH A FOLDER

Bridge is great for watching files arrive in a folder. For example, if you're processing digital camera photos or scanning image after image, open a browser window for the folder where you save your files. As they arrive, you can watch them fill the browser window one by one. Filmstrip view is good for this purpose, because you can quickly check each file with a large preview, using the arrow keys to go from image to image.

If you work with multiple computers or are networked with colleagues, you can have a browser window watch a drop folder where files are saved from other computers, so that you can see what's arriving.

This technique works best on a fast computer, because Bridge does require some CPU time to build previews. If you want your processing to proceed as quickly as possible, you may want to avoid pointing Bridge to the folder of completed files until all processing is complete.

NOTE   Be careful when you drag files and folders to Bridge—it matters where you drop them. If you drop a file or folder onto the Bridge program icon (Mac OS X) or program window (Windows), Bridge opens a new browser window for that folder. If you drop a file or folder into a browser window, Bridge moves it into the folder displays in the window. If you aren't careful, you might move a folder you meant to view!

Annotating Files in Bulk

In Bridge you can annotate images by adding information such as a star rating, keywords, and other metadata so that retrieving those files in the future is easier and faster. Every bit of metadata you add to an image is information you don't have to remember, because the metadata travels with the image.

Using metadata also liberates images from inflexible folder structures. For example, if you have a photo of a bear in the woods in Washington state, do you store the photo in a folder named Bears, a Woods folder, or a Washington state folder? You can't store it in all three folders at once, and if you decided to make three copies of the image, you'd quickly tire of managing (and updating) duplicate files. Metadata solves this problem: If you annotate the image with the keywords *bear*, *woods*, and *Washington state*, it doesn't really matter where you store the image—if you use a program like Bridge that can search on keywords, you can store the image in any folder you like, perhaps in a folder for the shoot or the date of the shoot. You certainly aren't limited to using Bridge to search by metadata; digital asset managers such as iView Media Pro do so, too. If you aren't already annotating your files, you can see how doing so can greatly improve your efficiency.

Before you can annotate multiple files in Bridge, let's review where you can apply different types of annotations:

- Rate files from one to five stars using commands on the Label menu or by clicking along the rating scale that appears under a selected image (**Figure 6.11**). The rating scale also appears in Adobe Camera Raw.

- Enter IPTC-standard metadata (except keywords) in the Metadata tab, or in the File Info dialog box (File > File Info).

- Enter keywords in the Keywords panel or in the File Info dialog box.

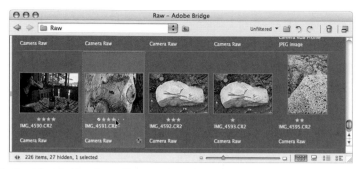

Figure 6.11: **Dragging in the star rating area to set a rating.**

- Label files using commands in the Label menu.

Now let's look at some ways you can annotate many files quickly.

With any annotating method, clearly you'll get more done faster if you perform multiple selections as often as possible. For example, if you have a folder full of landscape photos and you want to annotate all rock images with the keyword *rock*, select as many rock images as you can and then enable the *rock* keyword checkbox in the Keywords tab (**Figure 6.12**). If the keyword you want to apply doesn't exist, click the New Keyword button at the bottom of the Keyword tab (**Figure 6.13**), name the new keyword, and press Enter or Return.

When a folder contains more images than you can see at once in a browser window, don't obsess about selecting every last image containing a rock before applying the keyword—there's more of a chance that you'll make a selection mistake that applies the wrong metadata to some images. Instead, you might want to select and tag images a screenful at a time.

If you need to apply the same group of keywords to many images throughout a shoot, create a keyword set. Click the New Keyword Set button at the bottom of the Keyword tab, name the new keyword set, and then with the set selected, choose New Keyword to add each keyword to the set. To apply all keywords in the set, enable the checkbox next to the name of the keyword set (**Figure 6.14**). There's no problem with having the same keyword in different keyword sets, and you can drag a keyword from one set to another. You can also use keyword sets to organize your keywords when the list gets long.

Figure 6.12: **Applying a keyword to multiple selected images.**

Figure 6.13: **Clicking the New Keyword button.**

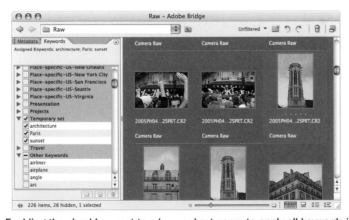

Figure 6.14: **Enabling the checkbox next to a keyword set name to apply all keywords in the set.**

Some types of metadata, such as a copyright notice, apply to every one of your images. In that case, you want to choose Edit > Select All and then apply the metadata so that it applies to all images in the folder. Whenever you apply metadata to a large number of images, it may take a while for Bridge to record the changes to them all—you can check progress in the status bar at the bottom-left corner of a browser window.

You may want to apply several metadata fields at once, such as the country and city where images were shot, to many or all images in a folder. That can go much faster if you use a metadata template. See the sidebar "Using Metadata Templates."

 TIPS   When rating images or applying labels, don't forget to take advantage of the rating and label keyboard shortcuts in the Label menu. If you want to be able to rate or label images by pressing just a number key, disable the Require the Command/Ctrl Key to Apple Labels and Ratings preference in the Labels panel of Bridge preferences.

If you're using Mac OS X 10.4 or later, you can use the Spotlight search feature to search for image metadata. For example, if your disk contains images you tagged with the keyword Boston, entering Boston into Spotlight retrieves those images.

The File Info dialog box (File > File Info) appears in both Bridge and Photoshop, so if you have an image open in Photoshop and you want to edit its metadata, you don't need to switch to Bridge to edit that image's metadata. However, you must use Bridge if you want to edit multiple files.

At times, Bridge may tell you that metadata can't be edited. Sometimes that's because of metadata standards that make some types of data read-only, such as the capture date from a digital camera. If you're using Bridge to edit metadata that you believe should be editable, but Bridge doesn't let you, see if the image is open in Photoshop or another program, because only one program is allowed to edit a file at a time. In Bridge, a small document icon appears below a thumbnail if that file is open.

USING METADATA TEMPLATES

There may be metadata groups that you want to apply to a large number of images. For example, you may want to enter the country, state, and city where images were shot, or your name, address, and other contact information. Instead of laboriously entering all of that data line by line, you can create a metadata template:

1. Select an image that you want to use as an example to create the template.

2. Choose File > File Info and, using the panes in the File Info dialog box, enter the metadata you want to include in the template. Any metadata that you don't want to include should be blank.

3. In the File Info dialog box, click the round menu button in the top right corner and choose Save Metadata Template. Name the template and click Save.

To apply the metadata template, select one or more files in a browser window, click the menu button in the Metadata tab, and choose your template from the Append Metadata or Replace Metadata submenu. Append Metadata inserts metadata from the template only where the same metadata is blank in the selected image, whereas Replace Metadata replaces any existing metadata whether or not the same metadata already exists in the file.

If you want to share metadata templates with colleagues, note that the menu button in the File Info dialog box contains the command Show Templates. Choosing that command opens the Adobe support files folder and selects the XMP folder within it. Inside the XMP folder is the Metadata Templates folder, which contains the metadata templates themselves.

Batch Processing and Automating with Bridge

The most valuable use of Adobe Bridge may be to simplify processing large numbers of images. In previous versions of Photoshop, you could certainly batch-process images in a folder, but the process was rather clumsy and inflexible compared to the workflows possible with Bridge. Bridge integrates and simplifies the tasks of annotating, selecting, opening, and processing files.

To take full advantage of batch processing, you'll want to make sure you also understand how to annotate files (see the section "Annotating Files in Bulk") and how to select and open multiple files (see Chapter 7).

Once you've selected files in a Bridge browser window, you can batch-process them using the commands on the Tools menu (**Figure 6.15**). The Tools menu is more powerful than it looks, because you can extend it using scripts and plug-ins that provide a direct line to Photoshop and other Adobe Creative Suite products.

Figure 6.15: **Commands on the Tools menu.**

- Batch Rename, the first command on the Tools menu, is a Bridge feature that's more than just a way to rename files. The Batch Rename dialog box is designed so that you can easily make your files' new names conform automatically to a given file-naming standard. For example, if you prefer to name all of your images using the date shot, sequence number, and ISO rating, you can use the Batch Rename feature to rename files from their original digital camera names to your standard naming convention. You can read more about the Batch Rename command in the section "Renaming Many Files at Once."

- Version Cue tracks versions of files you edit, so that you can return to earlier or alternate versions without having to come up with your own way of tracking changes.

- The Photoshop Services and Photoshop submenus on the Tools menu integrate directly with Photoshop and are some of the most useful commands in the Tools menu. Photoshop Services sends your images to online vendors for prints, books, and other output products. The Photoshop submenu links up with batch operations you may recognize from Photoshop, such as Contact Sheet II. The Image Processor command in the Photoshop submenu is a one-stop shop for converting, resizing, and compressing any number of images, and you should check it out before creating your own actions. For complete control you can use the Batch command in the Photoshop submenu; you can use the Batch command to process selected images through any action available in Photoshop including actions you've designed yourself.

- If you write your own scripts, you can add them to the Tools menu. I cover scripting in Chapter 19.

Renaming Many Files at Once

The Batch Rename dialog box is a powerful way to rename an entire folder of files and is relatively straightforward to use. The key area in the Batch Rename dialog box is the New Filenames section, where you string together building blocks for your new filenames.

The files you rename with the Batch Rename command must be in the same browser window. That doesn't mean they have to be in the same folder—you can run Batch Rename on files in Find results or in a collection, which can contain files from different folders.

To rename many files:

1. In a Bridge browser window, make sure the files are in the sequence you want so that they will be numbered properly. If they aren't in the right order, arrange them by choosing a sort order from the View > Sort submenu, or rearrange them manually by dragging.

2. Select the files to rename. (If you don't select any files, Bridge will rename all files in the folder.) Choose Tools > Batch Rename (**Figure 6.16**).

Figure 6.16

3. Click the Copy to Other Folder radio button, click Browse, and set an empty destination folder so that you don't overwrite existing files.

4. In the New Filenames section, select an option for how files are to be renamed. For example, if you want the new filename to consist of the shot date and a sequence number, select Date and Time from the top pop-up menu, click the plus button to add a new naming option and select Sequence Number. For Sequence Number, enter the starting number and the number of digits. The Preview section at the bottom of the Batch Rename dialog box shows you how it's going to turn out.

5. In the Options section, you can choose to keep the original filename in the XMP metadata associated with the file, if the original filename has value. You can also specify the operating system compatibility for the new filenames.

6. When you're done, click Rename.

AVAIL YOURSELF OF DR. BROWN'S SERVICES

One of the more popular plug-ins for the Tools menu is Dr. Brown's Services, which cram all kinds of useful batch-processing goodness into well-organized dialog boxes. Dr. Brown's Services is a free product you can download from Photoshop guru Russell Brown's Web site: www.russellbrown.com. It's also a great example of how you can enhance the Tools menu with a script. As of this writing, Dr. Brown's Services includes these components:

■ Dr. Brown's Caption Maker, which builds captions from each image's metadata, while also optionally copying, resizing, and sharpening images (**Figure 6.18**).

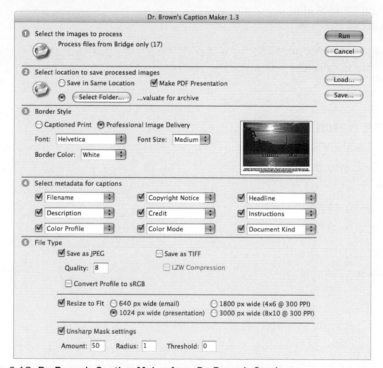

Figure 6.18: Dr. Brown's Caption Maker from Dr. Brown's Services.

■ Dr. Brown's 1-2-3 JPEG, which can save three different types of JPEG images in one pass. This is great when you want to convert a Raw, TIFF, or PDF master file to JPEG images suitable for high-, medium-, and low-resolution work such as print, presentation, and Web.

■ Dr. Brown's Merge-O-Matic, which combines selected images into frames of an animation.

■ Dr. Brown's Place-O-Matic, which creates a high-dynamic-range image from a single Raw file.

■ Dr. Brown's Auto Correct, which generates JPEG images from original files after applying automatic image correction.

■ Dr. Brown's Manual Correct, which generates JPEG images from original files after presenting a sequence of dialog boxes that guide you through basic image corrections.

■ Dr. Brown's Black and White, which generates black-and-white JPEG images from original files after giving you the opportunity to control the toning of the black-and-white image (such as sepia toning).

Because it includes so many useful batch processes, Dr. Brown's Services is a no-brainer to download, especially because you can't beat the price.

Sending Batch Jobs to Photoshop

You can use the Tools menu in Bridge to send selected images to Photoshop and apply Photoshop automation tasks to them. Although you can do this in Photoshop alone, you often save time by using Bridge to locate and select the files you want to process—especially when you can take advantage of Bridge's ability to find and collect files according to the metadata in your images.

If Photoshop isn't already open when you send a job to Photoshop from Bridge, Bridge opens Photoshop. Once Photoshop starts processing, you can close Bridge if you want to.

To send a batch job from Bridge to Photoshop:

1. In a single Bridge browser window, select the images you want to process. If you want to process all images in a folder, choose either Edit > Select All or Edit > Deselect All. (If one image is selected, that will be the only image sent to Photoshop; if no images are selected, it's assumed you want to process the whole folder.)

2. Choose a command from the Tools > Photoshop submenu. Your computer switches to Photoshop, and a dialog box appears for the feature you selected (**Figure 6.17**). From this point forward, Photoshop has control of the files.

3. Specify options in the dialog box and continue. (I describe the Batch dialog box in detail in Chapter 18.)

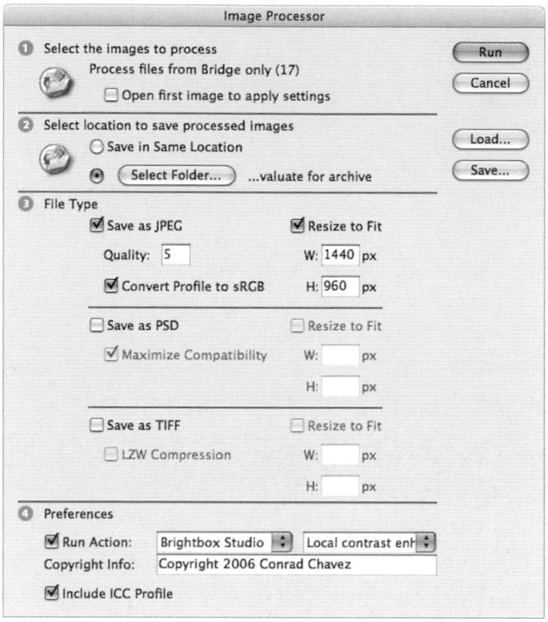

Figure 6.17

While Photoshop is busy processing images, you can't use Photoshop yourself. However, you can switch to any other program, including Bridge, and continue working. If you have another batch job that you want to send to Photoshop, you can start selecting files for it in Bridge, but you can't send any more batches to Photoshop until Photoshop is done with the previous batch job.

For more information and tips about Photoshop actions, see Chapter 17.

TIPS   If you want to stop a batch process, switch to Photoshop and press Esc. There may be a delay in stopping the process if it's in the middle of a lengthy processing task. If you are stopping a batch action, wait until the next image opens in Photoshop; if you cancel while an image is opening, Photoshop may simply try to open the next image.

Trying to make bulk edits to Raw camera files? See the section "Copying Camera Raw Settings" in Chapter 11.

When batch-processing files, avoid saving the processed files to the same folder as the original files. If by chance you make a mistake in the batch-processing settings, you won't be able to recover your original images if you saved over them with the new, processed images. Always set a destination folder where you can verify that the batch-processing operation went as expected; if there's a problem, you can throw out those images, adjust the batch-processing settings, and run the batch again.

Walking Through a Batch Process

Let's take a look at how you might tie together the ideas in this chapter. Suppose I'm approaching a handoff deadline for a book project, and I need to make sure all my images are in the CMYK color space of my publisher. I use Bridge to find out which files aren't ready yet and then send those straight through a Photoshop action. Here's how I do it:

1. In Photoshop, I prepared a CMYK conversion action in advance, so that it will be available when I run the batch process. (For information about creating actions, see Chapter 17.)

2. In Bridge, I navigate to the folder containing the images.

3. I decide to open a second window to monitor the folder that will receive the completed images (**Figure 6.19**).

Figure 6.19

4. Choose Edit > Find and enter the criteria (**Figure 6.20**). I want to find all images that are not CMYK, so I enter that criteria. No other folders are involved, so I leave the Look In menu at the current folder and don't enable Include All Subfolders.

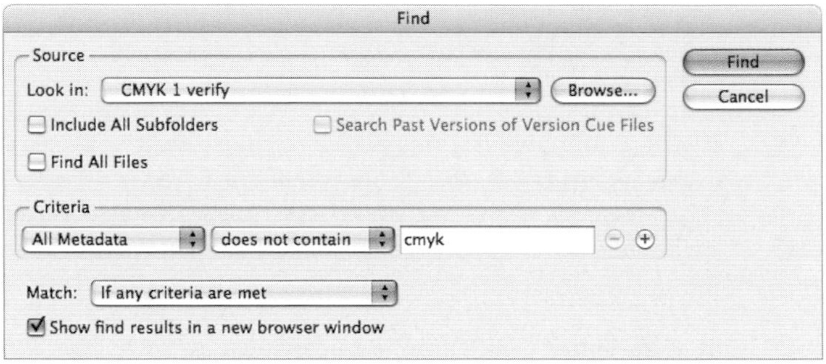

Figure 6.20

5. I want to see both my original window and the search results window, so I enable Show Find Results in a New Browser Window.

6. I click Find. In a new browser window, Bridge displays four files that aren't CMYK (**Figure 6.21**). The search is based on knowing that if a file is CMYK, the Color Mode metadata will say CMYK color.

Figure 6.21

7. I make sure none of the four files is selected (so that Bridge will send all files in the folder to Photoshop), and then I choose Tools > Photoshop > Batch. Photoshop opens and presents the Batch dialog box (**Figure 6.22**).

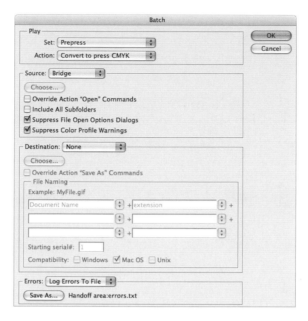

Figure 6.22

8. In the Batch dialog box in Photoshop, I select the action I created to convert images to CMYK TIFF images for my publisher and verify that the other Batch dialog box options are correct. Then I click OK, and Photoshop processes the files sent to it by Bridge. (The Destination is set to None, which allows the destination recorded in the action to take effect.)

9. I watch the destination folder (which I recorded into the action when I created it) and monitor the progress as Photoshop converts each file (**Figure 6.23**).

Figure 6.23

10. Now I can run a Find on the original folder, but this time finding all CMYK images so I can drag them into the folder with the files I just converted to CMYK. Now all of the files are converted to CMYK and in the same folder.

 TIPS Bridge works together with your desktop, so you can drag and drop files between a Bridge browser window to a normal Mac OS X or Windows folder window.

You don't have to leave Bridge to do basic file-management tasks. For example, there's a New Folder command under the File menu. You can also rename a file or folder; with a file or folder selected, press the spacebar, type the new name, and then press Return or Enter.

CHAPTER SEVEN

Opening the Right Files Quickly

Opening files doesn't seem like the most glamorous subject on earth, but if you're going to process large numbers of files, the one thing you don't want to do is open them one by one. In many cases, processing files efficiently doesn't start with opening the files—it starts earlier, by selecting the right files in the first place. For example, if you have a folder full of car images and you only want to select the Fords, it's going to go a lot faster if each of the Ford images is tagged with a *Ford* keyword. Instead of selecting files by looking for them visually and clicking them, you can then choose Edit > Find and set up a search for files where *Ford* appears in the keywords and process only those files. That's what this chapter is about: integrating the Find function in Adobe Bridge with the Open command in Photoshop.

Finding Files Fast

You may be used to using the Find command in a word processor to search text, and using the traditional Find command in an operating system to search file-names. The Find command in Adobe Bridge goes deeper than that. In addition to being able to search in more traditional ways, you can search *metadata* (key-words, shot data such as capture date, and so on) embedded in your images by you, your camera, or others. Taking advantage of the ability to search metadata in Bridge can help you select the right files more quickly. If you can retrieve the files you want using metadata alone, you can send those files directly from Bridge to Photoshop; see the section "Working with Adobe Bridge" in Chapter 6.

In the example below, my goal is to apply specific noise-reduction settings to all photos shot at ISO 1600 and that I rated higher than 2 stars from a shoot, so I decide to do a Find on *1600* in the metadata.

To find files:

1. In Adobe Bridge, choose Edit > Find (**Figure 7.1**).

Figure 7.1

2. In the Source section, specify the folder you want to search. (If you need to search more than one folder, set the Look In menu to a folder that contains all the folders you want to search and enable the Include All Subfolders checkbox.)

3. In the Criteria section, specify what you're looking for using the choices in the first pop-up menu. (If you're looking for criteria that isn't listed, such as ISO or color profile, choose All Metadata and enter it there.)

4. If you want to search using multiple criteria, click the plus button to add another criterion (**Figure 7.2**). To remove a criterion, click the minus button next to it.

5. Make sure the Match menu is set for the type of search you want.

Figure 7.2

6. It's a good idea to enable Show Find Results in a New Browser Window so that you can preserve the view settings and any selections you might have in the original browser window.

7. Click Find. The Find Results appear (**Figure 7.3**). In this example, the original folder has 147 items, and the Find Results window has just 62 items.

Figure 7.3

Use caution when searching on metadata. Bridge metadata searching is not sufficiently precise because not all metadata fields are listed individually. In the ISO search example just given, it isn't possible to search for *ISO 1600* because ISO is in a metadata label, not a value in the data itself, so it's necessary to search on *1600* within the general Metadata option in the Find dialog box. However, if a file uses the value 1600 in another metadata field, yet not in the ISO field, Bridge Find still picks up that file. Therefore, when you search using the Metadata option, it's a good idea to double-check your Find results using the Metadata tab.

 TIP   If the Find function doesn't seem to be finding files that are present, there may be a problem with the Bridge cache. First try doing a Find with the Find All Files checkbox enabled to make sure it isn't a problem with the way you're entering criteria; if Find All Files returns no files for a folder where there are files, then there is a problem. Choose Tools > Cache > Purge Cache for This Folder to rebuild the cache.

Saving Searches as Collections

If you perform the same search often, you can save that search as a *collection* so that it appears in the Collection section of the Favorites pane. A collection is based on the metadata in an image, so be aware that a collection can change if you change the metadata in your images—it's a saved search, not a static file list. For example, if you create a collection that retrieves all four-star images in a certain folder, and then you decide that some four-star images are actually three-star images, you'll see fewer images in that collection the next time you open it.

To create a collection:

1. Do a Find for the criteria you want in the collection.

2. In the Find Results window, click Save as Collection (**Figure 7.4**).

3. If you want the collection to run on the folder in which you originally created the collection, disable the Start Search From Current Folder checkbox (**Figure 7.5**). If the checkbox is enabled, the collection performs its search on the last folder you viewed in that browser window, not the folder you originally used for the selection.

4. Click Save.

Figure 7.4

Figure 7.5

To open a collection:

1. In the Favorites tab, or in the Favorites section of the pop-up menu at the top of a browser window, select Collections.

2. Double-click the collection you want to open.

Tuning Your Selections

Even after a search, you may want to process only some of the files in a browser window. If the files you want to process can't be isolated by their metadata, then you have to perform old-fashioned manual selection. Bridge has some ways to help you out here, too.

To begin with, the same methods you use to select multiple objects in other programs also work in Bridge. In Bridge, you can select a continuous range of files by clicking the first file you want to select and Shift-clicking the last file you want to select. You can add more individual files to a selection by Command-clicking/Ctrl-clicking them.

In addition, Bridge contains commands that can sometime be shortcuts to the selections you want. For example, if you want to select all files in a browser window except three, your first thought might be to choose Edit > Select All and then manually deselect the three files with the Command/Ctrl key. Nothing wrong with that, but in some cases you may find it easier to first select the three files you want to exclude, and then choose Edit > Invert Selection (**Figure 7.6**). The previously selected files become deselected, and the previously unselected files become selected. **Table 7.1** summarizes making selections in Bridge.

Figure 7.6: **Original selection before (left) and after (right) choosing Edit > Invert Selection.**

TABLE 7.1: Selection Techniques in a Bridge Browser Window

To...	...do this
Select all files	Choose Edit > Select All
Deselect all files	Choose Edit > Deselect All
Exchange selected and deselected files	Choose Edit > Invert Selection
Select a continuous range of files	Click the first file, then Shift-click the last file
Select a discontinuous range of files	Click the first file, then Command/Ctrl-click each file you want to add
Make a rectangular selection	Drag a selection rectangle around the thumbnails
Select all files containing labels	Choose Edit > Select Labeled
Select all files without labels	Choose Edit > Select Unlabeled

Opening Multiple Files

Opening multiple files from Bridge is much like opening individual files, but with a few "gotchas" to watch out for. The main potential problem is when you open multiple selected files in Bridge by double-clicking or pressing Enter or Return. When you use those two methods, Bridge opens the selected files using their default applications, which means they may not always open in the program you expect. Depending on which files you selected, you might see files opening in various programs at once.

For more control, open multiple files from Bridge by dragging them to the Dock icon (Mac OS X) or program workspace (Windows XP), or context-click the selected files to choose a program from the Open With submenu (**Figure 7.7**). Keep in mind that when you select multiple files of different file types, you might not be able to open all of them with the same program—the Open With submenu is a bit shorter in these cases, listing only the programs that can open all the selected file types.

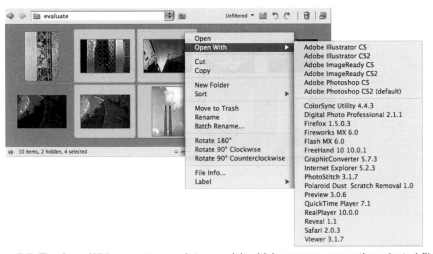

Figure 7.7: **The Open With context menu lets you pick which program opens the selected files.**

It's a good idea to think about whether it's necessary to open files at all. If you're working on just one file, it makes sense to open it. But if you're processing many the same way, you can let Bridge and Photoshop do the opening for you. If you open 20 files in Photoshop because you want to apply the same Curves adjustment to all 20, Photoshop must set aside enough RAM and disk space to hold all of them and all their layers and history states. If you design a Photoshop action that can apply your adjustment and run it as a batch action, Photoshop opens the files one at a time, and only needs memory for one open document at a time.

CHAPTER EIGHT

Positioning Precisely

PHOTOSHOP IS JUSTLY FAMOUS FOR ITS ABILITY not only to improve photographs, but also for its power and flexibility in combining photos, graphics, and type into smoothly unified composite art. If you frequently arrange Photoshop layers or selections in your work and want to position them more quickly and yet precisely, this is your chapter.

In this chapter, I talk about positioning layers visually, by dragging them around. If you want to position layers numerically, use the Edit > Free Transform command instead and enter position values into the options bar using the suggestions for entering and editing values precisely (see "Shortcuts for Entering Numbers and Text" in Chapter 3). Of course, if you really want total control over positioning layers as precisely and quickly as possible, get to know both the visual and numeric methods and use whichever one addresses your current situation more efficiently.

Tweaking Units of Measure

Before I actually start discussing how to position layers in Photoshop, it's good to talk about units of measure. Photoshop provides quite a range of them, and you can quickly switch to the one you want to use.

When the rulers or numeric entry fields are visible (choose View > Rulers if they aren't), you can context-click them to change the unit of measure (**Figure 8.1**). You don't have to use the same unit of measure for everything. You can set the rulers to display in inches, while setting fields in the options bar to their own units of measure that are different from each other and from the rulers'.

Figure 8.1: **Context-clicking to change units in rulers (left) and in the options bar fields (right).**

The Units and Rulers panel of the Preferences dialog box is another place where you can specify the unit of measure for rulers. Right below that is the Type option, where you can specify a unit of measure for type sizes. That makes it possible to lay out your document in inches while specifying type in points (**Figure 8.2**).

Figure 8.2: **Customize units of measure for the rulers and type in the Units and Rulers pane of the Preferences dialog box.**

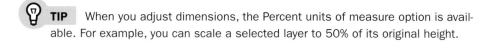

TIP   When you adjust dimensions, the Percent units of measure option is available. For example, you can scale a selected layer to 50% of its original height.

The Grid and Guides

To help you position layers, Photoshop can display a grid, and you can also add ruler guides independently of the grid. As in page-layout programs, you can use the grid and the guides together in a hierarchical relationship: You can use the grid to mark the overall structure and spatial rhythm of your layout, while using guides to mark major divisions in your composition (**Figure 8.3**). Both the grid and guides have a snap-to option so that you can use them not only as a visual reference but also to make layer edges snap to the grid or guides.

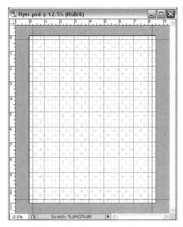

Figure 8.3: **Grid marking fundamental units of composition, and guides (red) marking printer margins in this example.**

Photoshop also includes an interesting feature called Smart Guides. With Smart Guides, instead of having to set up your own guides, the simple act of positioning layers creates temporary snap-to guides that follow layer edges as you reposition them (**Figure 8.4**). All grid and guide features are nonprinting and customizable.

Figure 8.4: **Dragging with Smart Guides on (left) displays the guides when edges are in perfect alignment (right).**

Do you need to use them all? Maybe not. Things can get crowded on screen when the grid, guides, and Smart Guides are all turned on. To use the right combination of layout features without crossing over into overkill, think of these features in this way:

■ If you're working on a design that's highly structured, you'll probably want to turn on the grid (View > Show Grid) and its snap-to feature (View > Snap to > Grid) so that all layers align to a regular ruler increment, such as every quarter inch. If your design is not so exact, you can leave the grid on but turn off the snap-to feature.

- If your design is based on major irregular divisions, then guides are more important than the grid. Drag guides out of the rulers, and when they're set up just right, lock the guides (View > Lock Guides).

- If your design is largely freeform, but you'd like layers to line up easily as you drag them near each other, Smart Guides (View > Show > Smart Guides) are probably the ticket.

- And of course, if your design is a mix of those types, you can freely mix the grid and guides and their snap-to settings.

Let's take a look at setting up and adjusting these features.

Setting Up the Grid

You control the grid in three places:

- To hide or show the grid, choose View > Show > Grid.

- To control grid appearance, adjust the options in the Grid section of the Guides, Grid & Slices panel in the Preferences dialog box. The options are pretty self-explanatory (**Figure 8.5**). You can customize the color by clicking the color swatch.

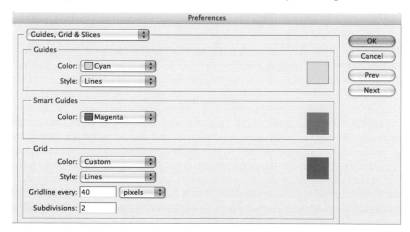

Figure 8.5: **Customize the grid using the Grid options in the Guides, Grid & Slices panel of the Preferences dialog box.**

■   To control the snap-to behavior of the grid, enable or disable the View > Snap to > Grid command.

Setting Up Guides

Here's a quick guide to guides:

■   To add a guide, drag one out of the horizontal or vertical ruler, position it on the canvas, and release the mouse.

■   To move a guide, first make sure that View > Lock Guides is disabled and then use the move tool to drag it somewhere else.

■   To delete a guide, first make sure that View > Lock Guides is disabled and then use the move tool to drag it out of the document.

■   To control the appearance of guides, adjust the options in the Guides section of the Guides, Grid & Slices panel in the Preferences dialog box (**Figure 8.6**).

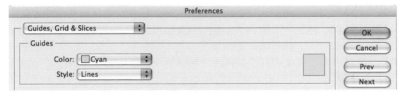

Figure 8.6: **Adjust the appearance of guides using the Guides options in the Guides, Grid & Slices panel of the Preferences dialog box.**

■   To toggle the snap-to behavior of the grid, enable or disable the View > Snap to > Guides command.

 TIP   Double-click a guide to open guide preferences rather than digging your way through the Preferences dialog box. This works only if View > Lock Guides is disabled.

Smart Guides and Snapping to Layer Edges

Smart Guides are wonderful because they're so low maintenance. You don't have to set them up manually except for turning them on. Smart Guides follow layer edges and centers. As you drag a layer, the Smart Guides appear whenever the edges or center of the layer you're dragging aligns perfectly with the edges or center of another layer. The two layers don't have to be close to each other.

It's often best to use Smart Guides (refer to Figure 8.4) in concert with the View > Snap to > Layers command. When you use Smart Guides, and Snap to Layers is off, you must drag a layer slowly and then let go when the Smart Guides appear, indicating that you've reached precise alignment. When Snap to Layers is on, you can be a bit more casual about it: You only need to drag a layer close enough to another snap-enabled object, and the layer's edges will snap to the other object precisely.

To control the appearance of Smart Guides, adjust the options in the Smart Guides section of the Guides, Grid & Slices panel in the Preferences dialog box (**Figure 8.7**).

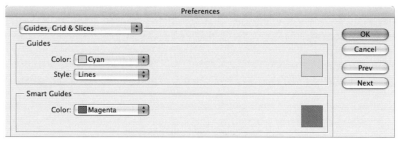

Figure 8.7: **Change the color of Smart Guides in the Guides, Grid & Slices panel of the Preferences dialog box.**

 TIPS   If you don't see Smart Guides appearing, drag the layer more slowly. Smart Guides are very precise, so if you drag one layer quickly past another, the Smart Guides may appear so briefly that you won't see them.

The more snap features you turn on, the more you should be mindful of possible interactions between them. Turning on all alignment features can be frustrating, because a layer can end up snapping to everything—the grid, guides, and other layers. One edge of the layer might snap to another layer's edge, making it difficult to snap the other side of the layer to a guide.

Aligning and Distributing Layers

When you're on a deadline and you've got many layers to line up, you don't have to drag them all into place. You can take advantage of the Align and Distribute commands. Photoshop then arranges the layers for you, instantly and precisely. Aligning layers lines them up along the same edge or along their centers (**Figure 8.8**). Distributing layers inserts an equal amount of space between them (**Figure 8.9**).

Figure 8.8: Text and button layers for a Web page design, before (left) and after (right) being aligned by their horizontal and vertical centers.

Figure 8.9: Three button layers (left) first aligned by their vertical centers (middle) and then distributed by their horizontal centers (right) to space them evenly.

To align or distribute layers:

1. Select the layers you want to align or distribute. If you're distributing layers, you must first select at least three layers (**Figure 8.10**).

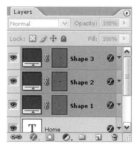

Figure 8.10

Both aligning and distributing rely on your ability to select the layers you want to align or distribute. Just use the same multiple-selection techniques that work elsewhere: In the Layers palette, Shift-click to select a continuous range of layers; or Command/Ctrl-click to select a discontinuous range of layers. If you have the Auto-Select Layers option enabled in the options bar for the move tool, you can simply Shift-click layers in the document window itself.

2. With the move tool selected, click an align or distribute button on the options bar (**Figure 8.11**). All of the alignment and distribution options are also available as commands in the Layer > Align or Layer > Distribute submenu.

Figure 8.11

TIP For more control over how layers align and distribute, use the rectangular marquee tool to drag a selection rectangle. If a selection marquee exists when you align layers, Photoshop aligns the layers within the edges of the selection marquee.

Positioning Example: a Web Page

If the features in this chapter seem a little academic, it might help to see a practical example of when and how you might use the precise visual positioning features in Photoshop. Suppose I'm going to mock up a Web page in Photoshop, and my mockup is due . . . well, as soon as possible, of course!

Setting Up a Grid

First I need to set up the overall structure of the page. I know I'm going to have a header, a body, and a footer.

1. I start the document by choosing File > New. In the New dialog box I choose 800 × 600 from the Preset pop-up menu and then click OK, creating a new document that's 800 pixels wide by 600 pixels tall (**Figure 8.12**).

2. I make sure that the View > Show > Grid command and the View > Snap to > Grid commands are enabled (**Figure 8.13**).

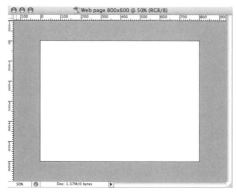

Figure 8.12

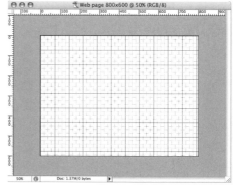

Figure 8.13

3. Because this is a Web page measured in pixels, I want the grid to have appropriate spacing, so I open the Guides, Grid & Slices panel in the Preferences dialog box.

4. In the Preferences dialog box, I set the Gridline Every option to 40 pixels (**Figure 8.14**). You want to specify a value that makes sense given your design; mine happens to be based on 20-pixel units, but entering 20 pixels would put too many dark gridlines on screen. You may also want to use a value that divides evenly into your canvas size; if I had set up a 1024×768-pixel document, I might have decided to set Gridline Every to 32 or 64 pixels. Notice that Photoshop updates the canvas as you change the grid values.

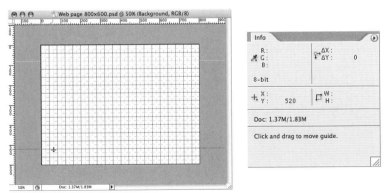

Figure 8.14

5. I set Subdivisions to 2 because dividing the major 40-pixel gridlines by two gives me the 20-pixel blocks I'm using for the foundation of my design. If I were working in inches, I would set subdivisions to 4 to create quarter-inch subdivisions or 8 to create eighth-inch subdivisions, for example. I click OK, and the grid is now set up.

6. I move on to adding the guides. I want the header and footer to be 80 pixels tall, so I drag a couple of guides out from the horizontal ruler and drop them at the 80 and 520 marks according to the vertical ruler. I like to monitor position using the Info palette; it updates as I drag so I always know where I am (**Figure 8.15**). Thanks to the snap-to-grid feature, the guides snap into place when I drag them close to a gridline.

Figure 8.15

Adding a Header and Footer

I want to add 80-pixel-tall bars across the top and bottom of the page to serve as the header and footer. Here's how I do it:

1. I select the rectangle tool (not the rectangular marquee tool) in the Tools palette and drag it across the top of the page (**Figure 8.16**), watching the width (W) and height (H) readouts in the Info palette to make sure I'm drawing each of them at the size I want (800 x 80 pixels). I set its color to yellow by double-clicking the shape layer thumbnail in the Layers palette, choosing a color in the color picker, and clicking OK.

2. I switch to the move tool and, with the header shape layer selected in the Layers palette, I Option/Alt-drag the header rectangle to make a copy that I move to the bottom of the page (**Figure 8.17**). Of course, with the snap-to-grid feature enabled, the new footer snaps precisely into place.

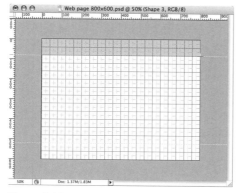

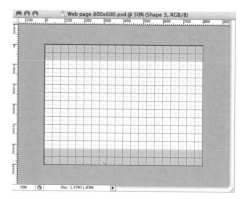

Figure 8.16

Figure 8.17

Adding a Navigation Bar

I want to add a navigation bar with a row of buttons, just below the header.

1. Using the rectangle tool again (this time by pressing its keyboard shortcut, the U key), I drag it just below the header rectangle and make it one minor gridline deep (20 pixels) (**Figure 8.18**). I edit the shape's yellow color by double-clicking the shape layer thumbnail in the Layers palette.

2. I select the horizontal type tool in the Tools palette and then click near the near the left edge of the yellow header. I type *Store* and press Enter (not Return) to apply the text. With the text layer selected in the Layers palette, I use the

Figure 8.18

options bar to set the font, size, and paragraph alignment (to Left Align Text). I switch to the move tool and press the arrow keys to nudge the type into place.

3. Now I want to mock up the buttons on the navigation bar. I press T as a shortcut to switch back to the horizontal type tool, and in an empty area of the page, I drag a rectangle 80 pixels wide by 20 pixels tall according to the Info palette. The snap-to grid feature makes this go quickly because the dimensions fall on the grid. I type the button text (**Figure 8.19**) and press Enter.

4. With the text layer selected in the Layers palette, I use the options bar to set the font, size, and paragraph alignment (to Center Text). Then I use the Character palette (Window > Character) to lower the Baseline Shift value so that the text is vertically centered in its text layer (**Figure 8.20**). I select the move tool, and then I drag and nudge the text into place on the navigation bar.

Figure 8.19

Figure 8.20

5. I want to add the other navigation bar buttons. At this point there are several equally good ways I can maintain precision visually, without numbers or calculations:

■   Using the move tool, I could Option+drag/Alt+drag the first text layer to the right and let the snap-to grid keep it aligned.

■   If I didn't want grid snap to be enabled, I could still use the move tool to Option+Shift+drag/Alt+Shift+drag the first text layer to the right to copy it (**Figure 8.21**) and then edit the content of the new text layer. The Option key copies, and the Shift key keeps the copy aligned with the original.

■   I could work without the grid but make sure that View > Show > Smart Guides is enabled. Then, using the move tool, I could Option+drag/Alt+drag the first text layer to the right and use the Smart Guides to keep the copy lined up with

Figure 8.21

Figure 8.22

the original. If View > Snap to > Layers is enabled, it's easy to Option+drag/ Alt+drag aligned copies without having to press Shift (**Figure 8.22**).

- Using the move tool, I could Option+drag/Alt+drag the first text layer to the right and not worry about perfect alignment right now (**Figure 8.23**). Later, I'd select the text layers and use the Align and Distribute buttons on the options bar to align the text layers and space them evenly (**Figure 8.24**).

Figure 8.23

Figure 8.24

The method you choose may depend on how many layers you're positioning. With just a few layers, it's easy enough to drag with modifier keys to copy (Option/Alt) and keep aligned (Shift). With many layers, it's typically less work to lay them out approximately and then use the Align and Distribute buttons or commands to fix everything in one swift move.

 TIPS   Because the Option/Alt key creates a copy when applying a transformation to a layer (such as moving it), you can also use the Option/Alt key to copy when you're entering a numeric value. Select a layer, choose Edit > Free Transform, type a new horizontal or vertical position into the options bar, and press Option+Return/ Option+Enter. In the navigation bar example, entering a new horizontal position and pressing Option+Return/Option+Enter copies the text layer and moves it horizontally, while maintaining its vertical position so that it's still aligned with the original.

Nudging with the arrow keys is an easy way to make small, precise position adjustments. With the move tool selected, pressing the Up Arrow and Down Arrow keys moves a layer vertically one pixel, and the left and right keys move a layer horizontally. Don't forget to combine nudge keys with modifiers—adding Shift amplifies the nudge to 10 pixels instead of just one, and adding Option/Alt copies the selected layer.

CHAPTER NINE

Smarter Selections

PAINTING IN PHOTOSHOP IS VERY STRAIGHTFORWARD. If you've got the Brush tool in hand, you just start painting. But for more exacting corrections or enhancements on specific areas of a Photoshop document, you need to select an area. The time-honored way to select an area is to drag the lasso tool around the area you want to select—that method goes all the way back to MacPaint in 1984—but Photoshop provides many alternatives that can be faster in various situations.

TIP   When using any of the selection tips in this chapter with a layered document, remember to first select the correct layer in the Layers palette.

Marquee and Lasso Tools

The time-honored way of selecting an area is the one you've probably tried in the low-end paint programs that come with many computers: drawing a selection marquee. Photoshop has four marquee tools (**Figure 9.1**) and three lasso tools (**Figure 9.2**). To help you pick out the right one, I summarize them in **Table 9.1**.

Figure 9.1: **Hold the mouse button on a marquee tool in the Tools palette to choose from all marquee tools.**

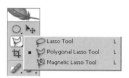

Figure 9.2: **Hold the mouse button on a lasso tool in the Tools palette to choose from all lasso tools.**

TABLE 9.1: Manual Selection Tools

To select...	...do this
A rectangular area	Drag the Rectangular Marquee tool
An elliptical area	Drag the Elliptical Marquee tool
An area that's only one pixel tall or wide	Drag the Single Row Marquee tool or Single Column Marquee tool
A freeform area	Drag the Lasso tool
A freeform area of straight lines	Drag the Polygonal Lasso tool

The single column and single row marquee tools can be useful for drawing borders and retouching scratches and other very thin defects in scanned photos.

Modifying Selections

When you use the rectangular marquee and elliptical marquee tools, some of the standard modifier keys I talked about earlier in the book can help you adapt the tools on the fly:

■   To constrain the rectangular marquee tool to a square and the elliptical marquee tool to a circle, add the Shift key.

- To draw a selection area from the center, add the Option/Alt key.

- To reposition a selection area as you draw it, add the spacebar.

After you create a selection, you can adjust its size, position, and angle by choosing Select > Transform Selection.

By combining the modifier keys and the Transform Selection command, you can quickly fit a selection to an area (**Figure 9.3**).

Figure 9.3: **The easiest way to draw a selection to match the hubcap is to Option+drag/Alt+drag from the center (left). The selection needs to be rotated to match the photo, and that's easily done using the Transform Selection command and dragging outside the transform box (right).**

 TIP   You can store a selection in a document by choosing Select > Save Selection. When you want to activate the selection, choose Select > Load Selection or Command/Ctrl+click the channel in the Channels palette.

Selecting Based on Tone or Color

When you're about to make a selection, ask yourself if the area you want to select is already visually distinct, like a single tone or color. If it is, save yourself time by using a tool that can create a selection from a tone or color, or create selections from channels or layer masks if they're already available in your document (**Figure 9.4**). I summarize these in **Table 9.2**.

Figure 9.4: **From left to right: A layer, a channel containing a saved selection, Command/Ctrl+clicking the channel in the Channels palette, the resulting selection, and the final graphic after one more step of adding a black solid color layer that automatically used the selection.**

TABLE 9.2: Selecting by Tone or Color

To select...	...do this
One area of a specific tone or color	Select the Magic Wand tool, adjust options bar, and click the tone or color you want
All areas of a tone or color value or range	Choose Select > Color Range
Based on an existing channel	In the Channels palette, Command/Ctrl-click the channel
Based on an existing layer mask	In the Layers palette, Command/Ctrl-click the layer mask
By letting Photoshop follow a high-contrast edge	Drag the Magnetic Lasso tool along an edge

Being able to create selections by tone or color gives you an important advantage: Instead of having to draw selections with marquee and lasso tools, you can create a selection with painting tools, which is sometimes easier. Just paint black into a channel and convert the channel to a selection. When you create a selection from a channel or layer mask, the selection is made from areas darker than 50% gray.

 TIP   The magnetic lasso tool lays down a path of points along an edge defined by contrasting tones or colors. If the points don't go where you want, press Delete to remove the most recent point and drag to guide the magnetic lasso along the edge.

USING THE COLOR RANGE DIALOG BOX

The Color Range dialog box (**Figure 9.5**) is powerful, but a little intimidating at first glance. Fortunately, there is a simple approach to using it. Start by choosing Select > Color Range, and follow these guidelines:

■ Click the Select pop-up menu to see if any of the presets is a shortcut to the tone or color value or range you want to select. If none of them is helpful, leave the Select pop-up menu set to Sampled Colors.

■ If you set the Select pop-up menu to Sampled Colors, use the eyedropper to click a tone or color in the document window. Sampled Colors is the default, so it may already be set for you.

■ If you want to extend the range of the selection to similar tones or colors, drag the Fuzziness slider.

■ If you're using the eyedropper and you want to add dissimilar tones or colors, such as selecting both red and blue areas, use the Add to Sample eyedropper to click the additional tones or colors in the document window. You can use the Subtract from Sample eyedropper to remove tones or colors from the selection.

■ The Selection Preview pop-up menu can give you a better idea of the current selection than the preview in the Color Range dialog box.

When you click OK, Photoshop creates a selection from the tones and colors you picked.

Figure 9.5: **In the Color Range dialog box (left), I used the eyedropper to click the orange door so that it would become a selection, previewed as white on black (right).**

 TIP   To soften a selection edge, choose Select > Feather.

Selecting by Drawing a Path

If you're trying to make a selection with smooth curves, but it isn't a circle or ellipse, drawing it with the lasso tool can be frustrating and tedious. The pen tool is the most precise way to create freeform curves, but it takes time to learn as well. If you're proficient using the pen tool, you may find it easier to draw a path with the pen tool first. Then convert the path to a selection by Command/Ctrl+clicking the path in the Paths palette (**Figure 9.6**).

Figure 9.6: **From left to right: A Pen tool path drawn around the subject, Command/Ctrl+clicking the path in the Paths palette, and the resulting selection.**

TIP   You can create a selection from an Adobe Illustrator path by copying and pasting the path into Photoshop.

Combining Selections

It's often easier to build a selection by drawing smaller selections and adding them onto each other. For example, if you want to select the shape of a cross, you don't need to draw the entire shape by hand; instead, use the rectangular marquee tool with the Add Selection button selected in the options bar (**Figure 9.7**) to draw two rectangles that merge together wherever they overlap. The other buttons on the options bar provide other ways to combine two shapes.

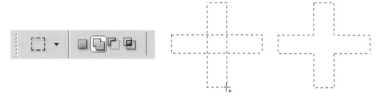

Figure 9.7: **From left to right: The Add button selected in the options bar for the rectangular marquee tool, dragging the first rectangular selection, and dragging the second selection that combines with the first because the Add button is selected.**

You can also control how selections combine by pressing modifier keys as you use a selection tool. Pressing the Shift key adds to an existing selection, like the Add to Selection button in the options bar. Pressing Option/Alt removes the area you're currently dragging from an existing selection, like the Subtract from Selection button in the options bar.

You can use the selection buttons and modifier keys to edit any type of selection. For example, you can use the Select > Color Range command to create an initial selection and then remove specific areas from the selection by Option/Alt-dragging the lasso tool through the selection.

CHAPTER TEN

Working Efficiently with Layers

AT THE MOST BASIC LEVEL OF IMAGE EDITING, you edit the pixels of an image. That's a straightforward way of working, but once you change the pixels, the ability to change your mind and keep your options open is limited. When you create a document that consists of discrete compositional elements, *layers* provide a way to maintain the independence of each element in a composition. Layers are like a stack of clear film with a different graphic on each piece of film. If you frequently combine multiple elements into a larger image, such as a digital collage, layers let you rearrange elements at any time without permanently erasing what's underneath. Layers also allow other kinds of data, such as type and smooth vector paths, to exist in a Photoshop document with pixel-based (*bitmap*) layers.

Creating Bitmap Layers

The most common type of layer is a *bitmap layer*—a layer consisting of pixels, such as a photograph or art you created with the brush tool. The most obvious way to create a bitmap layer is to click the Create a New Layer button in the Layers palette. (**Figure 10.1**).

Figure 10.1: **Click the Create a New Layer button in the Layers palette to create a new bitmap layer.**

You can also create a layer from any part of another layer. To do this:

1. Select a layer in the Layers palette.

2. If you want to make a layer from just a part of the selected layer, create a selection.

3. Choose Layer > New > Layer via Copy, or Layer > New > Layer via Cut. The new layer appears in the Layers palette. The Layer via Copy method leaves the original layer unchanged.

 TIP Frequent users of the Layer via Copy command use its keyboard shortcut Command/Ctrl+J, because it's faster than opening the Layer > New submenu. Layer via Cut is less popular because it removes data from the original layer, leaving a hole.

Selecting Layers

If you work with layers often, you may find yourself constantly moving the mouse over to the Layers palette to select layers. To save your wrist from all those trips across the screen, try some of these tips for easier layer selections:

■ With the move tool selected, enable Auto Select Layer in the options bar (**Figure 10.2**). With Auto Select Layer enabled, you don't need to go to the Layers palette to select a layer—just click any visible part of the layer. The Auto

Select Groups option adds the ability to select a layer group by clicking any layer in the group.

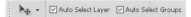

Figure 10.2: **When the Move tool is selected, the Auto Select Layer option appears in the options bar.**

- Whether or not you use Auto Select Layer, you can context-click a document and see a list of all layer content under the cursor. You can then select a layer by choosing a layer name from the context menu.

- Use keyboard shortcuts for the Layers palette. Option/Alt+[selects the next layer below, and Option/Alt+] selects the next layer above. When you use these keyboard shortcuts, it's a good idea to keep an eye on the Layers palette to make sure you've selected the correct layer.

 TIP   Be sure to take advantage of the many commands on the Layers palette menu, which you can see by clicking the round button in the upper-right corner of the Layers palette.

Adjustment Layers

Using an adjustment layer, you can edit adjustment layer settings at any time, as many times as you want, without reducing the quality of the original image. That's because an adjustment layer applies a change without permanently altering any of the underlying layers (**Figure 10.3**). All of this gives you great flexibility in trying out alternatives and changing your mind without too much hassle. Adjustment layer changes apply only when you create final output, such as saving a JPEG version or printing.

Figure 10.3: **An adjustment layer (left) stores its edits separately from the original layer, so you can hide the adjustment layer (right) to disable the edit.**

A useful side effect of having adjustments on their own layer is that you can duplicate the adjustment layer to make copies of the adjustments. For example, you can duplicate an adjustment layer to try out a slightly different version of an existing adjustment layer, or you can drag an adjustment layer into other documents that need the same adjustment, as I describe in Chapter 11.

To create an adjustment layer, click the Create New Fill or Adjustment Layer button in the Layers palette and choose the type of layer you want to add. You can also choose Layer > New Adjustment Layer and choose a layer type from the submenu.

To edit an adjustment layer, just double-click its thumbnail in the Layers palette. (Don't double-click the icons to the right of the thumbnail unless you want to edit layer mask options.)

DUPLICATING LAYERS

You duplicate all types of layers in the same way. To duplicate a layer in the same document, either drag the layer to the Create a New Layer icon in the Layers palette, or choose Layer > Duplicate Layer and make sure the same document is selected in the Document pop-up menu in the Duplicate Layer dialog box (**Figure 10.4**). Selecting another document name in the Document pop-up menu is a quick way to copy a layer to another document.

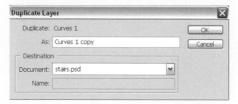

Figure 10.4: **In the Duplicate Layer dialog box, you can choose a destination document for a duplicate layer.**

Layer Groups

If you work with complex compositions involving many layers, the long list of layers in the Layers palette can become unwieldy. To simplify layer management, organize layers into groups (**Figure 10.5**). Layer groups are similar to the folders on your desktop; in fact, layer groups use folder icons.

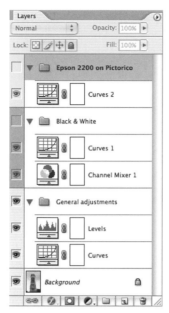

Figure 10.5: **Using layer groups, you can organize layers and move or hide multiple layers together.**

To create a layer group, click the Create a New Group button in the Layers palette and drag layers into it, or select the layers you want to group and choose New Group from Layers from the Layers palette menu.

 TIP   If you use layer masks and blending modes, it's good to know that you can apply a layer mask or blending mode to a layer group. It then applies to the entire group of layers.

Shape Layers

Although Photoshop does its best to preserve the quality of bitmap layers when you scale, rotate, and apply other transformations, shape layers retain their quality perfectly when you transform them. If you plan to work with solid-color graphics that you expect to manipulate before they reach their final form, think about using shape layers. I talk about creating and using shape layer presets in "Layer Styles and Layer Style Presets" in Chapter 4; here I describe a little more about shape layers themselves.

Unlike bitmap layers, a shape layer doesn't contain pixels—only *paths*, lines that remain smooth at any resolution. You add a shape layer to your document using any of the shape tools or the pen tool (**Figure 10.6**). If the shape you want doesn't already exist, and you are proficient with the pen and shape tools, you can draw the shape, select it, and choose Edit > Define Custom Shape to create the shape. You can also add a shape layer by copying and pasting a vector object from Adobe Illustrator.

Figure 10.6: **A shape layer (left and center) scales without losing sharpness (right).**

A shape layer takes on the default foreground color, but you can change it by double-clicking the shape layer thumbnail in the Layers palette. Once you've added a shape layer to your layout, you can edit the shape itself as you would a path by using the path selection tool, the direct selection tool, and the pen tool. Proficiency with those tools is required if you want to use shape layers effectively.

 TIP   Transformation commands work as well for shape layers and paths as they do for bitmap layers. When you look at the Edit menu when a path is selected, the Transform command and Free Transform submenu appear as the Transform Path command and the Free Transform Path submenu.

Smart Objects

Smart objects cleverly overcome a limitation of bitmap layers—the fact that bitmap layers lose detail when you repeatedly apply transformations such as scaling and rotation. Normally, when you transform a bitmap layer, the edited layer is rendered at the resolution of the document. For example, if you start with a bitmap layer that's 100 pixels tall by 100 pixels wide, and you scale it down by 50% of its original height and width and confirm the change, the resulting layer is only 50 pixels tall by 50 pixels tall. Because the size reduction turned a 10,000-pixel layer into a 2,500-pixel layer, 75% of the original layer data was tossed out when you scaled it down. If you change your mind later and scale up the layer, you can't restore the lost data. Smart objects avoid this problem because they don't throw out data when you transform. A scaled-down smart object looks exactly like a scaled-down bitmap layer, but behind the scenes, Photoshop remembers all of the data from the layer at its original size. If you later scale up the smart object, Photoshop goes back to the original data and renders the smart object at the resulting size. Using smart objects can make your Photoshop documents larger, because the document must store data that you may or may not need in the future.

The original content of a smart object doesn't have to be a bitmap layer. You can create a smart object from any content that exists as a layer in Photoshop, such as type or shapes. You can also create a smart object from multiple layers.

To create a smart object, select a layer or layers and choose Layer > Smart Objects > Group into New Smart Object. A smart object layer uses a special icon in the Layers palette (**Figure 10.7**). To edit a smart object, just double-click the layer icon in the Layers palette. To convert a smart object to a bitmap layer, choose Layer > Rasterize > Smart Object, or Layer > Smart Objects > Convert to Layer.

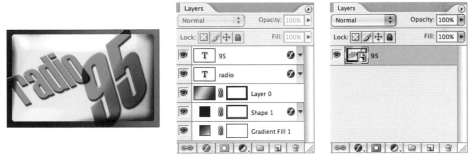

Figure 10.7: **A document's layers before (left and center) and after (right) being converted to a smart object. The document's appearance doesn't change, but its layer structure does.**

Because a smart object *refers* to original image data instead of *being* actual image data, smart objects also make it easier to maintain multiple copies of a layer. When you duplicate a smart object, all duplicates refer back to the layer on which the smart object is based. If you edit a smart object, all of the copies of the smart object also update. Combined with the alignment and distribution commands I cover in Chapter 8, smart objects are a great way to create step-and-repeat documents that are easy to update (**Figure 10.8**).

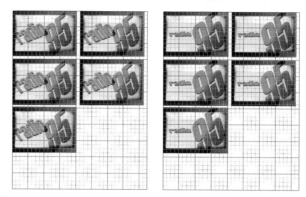

Figure 10.8: **Multiple copies of a smart object (left) all update at once after editing the contents of the smart object (right).**

Smart objects are such a useful idea that Adobe didn't stop there. When you use the File > Place command, you import a file as a smart object. Ordinarily, that saves you the step of converting a layer into a smart object. But if you place a Raw format file from a digital camera, it imports as a special kind of smart object: By double-clicking the camera Raw format smart object, Adobe Camera Raw opens so that you can edit the conversion of the Raw file at any time.

 TIPS   Many commands on the Layer menu are also available from the Layers palette menu, or by context-clicking a layer thumbnail, mask thumbnail, or layer name.

You can update a smart object by replacing it with an external file, by selecting the smart object layer and choosing Layer > Smart Object > Replace Contents. This is an efficient way to update many copies of a smart object at once, because all instances of the smart object update instantly. The new file is embedded (copied into the Photoshop document), not linked as in a page-layout program.

Layer Comps

Layers naturally make it easy to store and view different versions of a document, because you can copy layers to create variations on them. There's just one catch: Every time you want to evaluate whether you should use one layer or another, you must hide the first layer and show the second layer; then to switch back you must show the first layer and hide the second layer. If you want to compare design variations involving different combinations or arrangements of various layers in the document, it isn't practical to remember each combination or arrangement—in the past, it was necessary to save two separate documents containing each layer configuration.

Layer comps make it much easier to compare layer configurations. A layer comp can remember which layers are visible, where they are, and what layer style they use, making it possible for one document to store two or more different compositions based on the same layers (**Figure 10.9**).

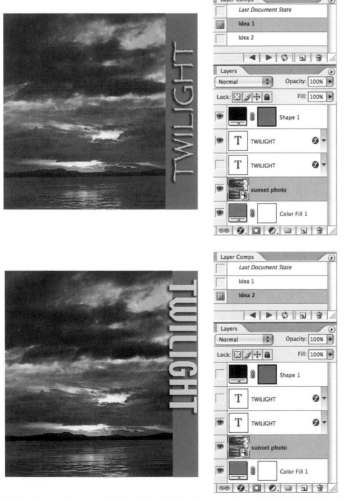

Figure 10.9: In the Layer Comps palette, *Idea 1* (top) remembers a different layer configuration than *Idea 2* (bottom).

To create a layer comp, use the Layers palette to set the visibility, position, and layer style of all layers and then click the Create a New Layer Comp button in the Layer Comps palette. By default, the Layer Comps palette is in the palette well at the right end of the options bar.

DOUBLE-CLICKING AND CONTEXT MENUS IN THE LAYERS PALETTE

Double-clicking or context-clicking on different parts of the Layers palette does different things depending on where you position the mouse pointer. This is good, because double-clicking leads to many different shortcuts. On the other hand, you need to know where to click to get what you want.

Use these double-click shortcuts in the Layers palette:

■ To open the Layer Style dialog box, double-click on a layer thumbnail or in the empty area to the right of the layer name.

■ To set layer mask display options, double-click a layer mask.

■ To rename a layer, double-click the layer name.

■ To open the Layer Properties dialog box, Option/Alt+double-click a layer thumbnail.

Context menus use similar areas of the Layers palette. You'll see different context menus when you click on the layer thumbnail, a mask thumbnail, or in the empty area to the right of the layer name.

CHAPTER ELEVEN

Correcting Many Images Quickly

IF YOU HAVE A LARGE NUMBER OF IMAGES to adjust in a short period of time, you're probably on the lookout for any possible way to speed that process. Having large batches to process is even more common now that digital cameras make it so easy and inexpensive to shoot hundreds of images in just a few hours. The Photoshop team is well aware of this challenge (after all, they own digital cameras, too), so in Photoshop CS2 it's easier than ever to correct one image and apply the corrections to any number of other similar images.

Transferring Adjustment Layers

In Chapter 10, I describe how an adjustment layer keeps changes separate from the original image. In addition to making it easy to edit or remove changes from an image, an adjustment layer gives you another advantage over a traditional dialog box: You can easily move the adjustment layer to another image. If you made a correction that should work well on other images you have, all you have to do is drag that adjustment layer to the other document window (**Figure 11.1**). The layer becomes part of the other document, and the adjustment layer's changes apply instantly.

Figure 11.1: Both images are originally color images, but I added a Hue/Saturation adjustment layer to the first image to give it a sepia tone by enabling the Colorize checkbox. To apply the same tone to the second image, I dragged the first image's adjustment layer from the Layers palette to the second image's document window.

Even when two images look identical, double-check the results after you copy one adjustment layer to another. Slight differences between the original images may require a minor change to the settings in the adjustment layer.

TIPS The most direct way to create an adjustment layer is not from the menus, but by clicking the Create New Fill or Adjustment Layer button in the Layers palette and choosing the type of adjustment you want to add.

Some dialog boxes don't have adjustment layers, but they do contain Save and Load buttons. The Save button exports dialog box settings to a file, and the Load button imports dialog box settings from a file. I talk about these buttons in more detail in "Loading and Saving Settings" in Chapter 4.

WHAT'S RAW FORMAT ALL ABOUT?

Shooting digital photos in *raw format* is increasingly popular for people who want to get the highest possible quality out of their images. Working with raw files is the digital equivalent of processing your own film — you get more involved in the technical details of image processing to wring every last bit of quality out of your images.

Although raw files require more disk space than JPEG files, many feel that the increased quality of the data in raw files is worth the larger file size. The size of raw files also becomes less of an issue as the capacity of image storage cards continues to grow and their cost continues to drop.

Because raw files are raw, they must be converted to a format that can be used for final output, such as Photoshop, TIFF, or JPEG. It's similar to how a film negative isn't usable until you make a positive version. Similar to negative film, there's no single right way to interpret raw data — you can adjust the conversion so that the converted file is technically and aesthetically the way you want it. Adobe Camera Raw software exists to perform the conversion and provides controls so that you can convert raw files in a way that works best for your output.

It's worth noting that there isn't one raw format. Because "raw" in this context means the data that comes straight off the camera sensor, every camera has its own raw format. Right now, software like Adobe Camera Raw must be updated every time a new camera comes out. The Digital Negative (DNG) format standardizes raw camera data into a universal format so that your software only has to support DNG, instead of having to support every camera out there. DNG is supported by an increasing number of software programs. If you want to convert your raw files to DNG, you can download the free Adobe DNG Converter, available from: www.adobe.com/dng/

Transferring Camera Raw Adjustments

Raw files are read-only, so you can't alter the original data. How, then, do you edit a raw file? In Adobe Camera Raw, the raw file processor that comes with Photoshop, edits to raw files are saved in data separate from the original image data. In that way, it's like an adjustment layer—which makes adjustments easy to save and easy to transfer to other raw images.

Multiple selections are the key to changing many raw images quickly. You can work on multiple images in Camera Raw by selecting more than one image in Adobe Bridge before opening Camera Raw. (I talk about multiple-file selections in Chapter 7.) Of the images you open in Camera Raw, you can then select one or more of those images. If more than one image is selected in Camera Raw when you make adjustments, Camera Raw changes all selected images. You can also use the techniques below to apply one image's adjustments to many other similar raw images.

Creating Camera Raw Presets

You can save Adobe Camera Raw settings as a preset. When you do this, the name of your preset appears in the Settings menu in the Camera Raw dialog box. Saving a preset is a good idea when you expect that your settings will be useful for many images in the future. For instance, I have a preset that applies certain noise reduction settings for images I shoot at ISO 1600.

To create a Camera Raw preset:

1. In the Camera Raw dialog box, apply all of the adjustments that you want to save in the preset.

2. Click the round button next to the Settings pop-up menu and choose Save Settings. Or, if you want the preset to alter specific settings but leave other settings unchanged, choose Save Settings Subset, enable the checkboxes for the settings you want to affect, and click Save (**Figure 11.2**).

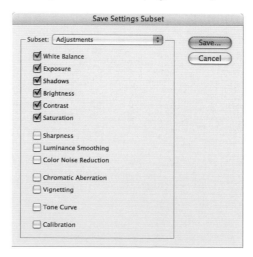

Figure 11.2

3. Name the settings file (leave the .XMP filename extension alone) and click Save.

To apply a Camera Raw preset, choose it from the Settings pop-up menu in the Camera Raw dialog box.

 TIP   You don't have to open Camera Raw to apply a preset. You can select one or more images in Adobe Bridge, choose Edit > Apply Camera Raw Settings, and choose a preset from the submenu.

Synchronizing Camera Raw Settings

When you open multiple images in Camera Raw, you can apply one image's settings to any other by *synchronizing* them. You can synchronize all of the settings, or just some of them.

To synchronize Camera Raw settings:

1. In the Camera Raw dialog box, select the image that has the settings you want to use as the source (**Figure 11.3**).

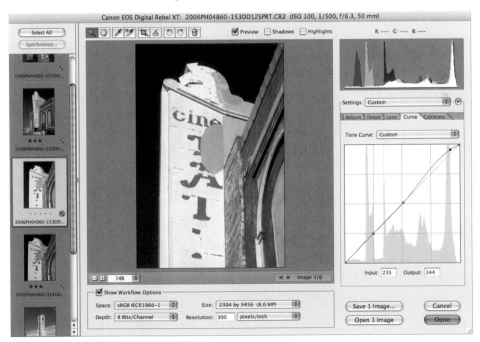

Figure 11.3

2. Select additional images by Shift+clicking (to select a continuous range of images), Command/Ctrl+clicking (to select a discontinuous range of images), or by clicking Select All. The source image appears with a dark outline so that you can distinguish it from the other selected images (**Figure 11.4**).

Figure 11.4

3. Click the Synchronize button.

4. In the Synchronize dialog box, specify which of the source image's settings you want to apply to the other selected images by enabling the checkboxes for them, or choose a preset from the Synchronize pop-up menu.

5. Click OK.

CHAPTER TWELVE

Accelerating Appearances with Layer Styles

PHOTOSHOP ISN'T JUST ABOUT PHOTOS, OF COURSE. Some graphic designers spend entire days using Photoshop not as a digital darkroom, but as a digital box of art supplies, creating illustrations, ads, fine art, and Web graphics.

Years ago, one way for Photoshop gurus to demonstrate their prowess was to create amazing drop shadows, bevels, and other 3D effects using complex channel manipulation sequences or stacks of layers. Then Photoshop added *layer styles*—popular effects pre-packaged into a convenient, one-step dialog box. For example, in early versions of Photoshop, you built a drop shadow by getting the silhouette of a layer, making a blurred shadow, and blending the shadow with the original layer. If you edited the original layer and its outer edge changed, you had to rebuild the shadow from scratch. Also, sometimes many layers were needed to create an effect, making the Layers palette harder to manage.

Today, all you have to do is apply the Drop Shadow layer style and tell it how big, how dark, and how opaque you want the shadow. A layer style belongs to a specific layer, and you can apply multiple layer styles to a layer, so you can use complex styles without cluttering the Layers palette. In addition, like adjustment layers, layer styles are nondestructive—layer styles aren't applied to the original layer data until you save in a flattened format or print, so you can edit an effect at any time. Layer styles are also live, so that you can change the content of a layer, and the effect updates itself to match. If you frequently use shadows, glowing auras, textures, sculpted edges, or any other similar effects, layer styles can save you a lot of time.

I don't cover each individual layer style feature, because that would take up an entire book on its own. To follow this book's theme of efficiency, in this chapter I cut through the details and subtleties of layer styles and instead give you ways to recognize when layer styles save you time and suggest quick and easy-to-remember ways to perform the more common layer style tasks.

When to Use Layer Styles

Get in the habit of checking out layer styles before building an effect manually, in case the effect is already available as a layer style. If your design will use any combination of the following effects (**Figure 12.1**), consider using a layer style:

- 3D effects, such as shadows, embossing, and rounded or beveled edges

- Textures, gradients, and patterns

- Colorizing or painting a stroke around an entire layer

Figure 12.1: **From left to right: Starting from a shape layer, I used layer styles to add the Drop Shadow, the Color Overlay effect, and the Stroke effect.**

Layer styles contain those attributes as building blocks which you can combine in many ways to create the effects you're looking for. Layer styles help you:

- Apply an effect without altering the original layer data.

- Edit, hide, or remove an effect from a layer at any time.

- Easily move or copy effects from one layer to another.

- Save effect settings as a layer style preset so you can apply it to any layer.

- Apply an effect to text.

Some layer styles duplicate or resemble the effects available in the Filter menu, but layer styles can sometimes be a better solution than a filter effect. Once you apply a filter to a layer, it's permanent. Layer styles are reversible, editable, and can be saved as layer style presets, making them more flexible and efficient. Although layer styles alter the edges and surface of a layer, layer styles don't alter the pixels themselves, so applying a filter may be a better solution when you want to process the pixels themselves. For example, if you want to emboss or add a texture, applying a layer style gives you more flexibility, but if you want to blur, sharpen, or add a brush stroke effect, you'll need to apply a filter.

Layer styles work just fine on bitmap layers, but shapes *and* layer styles are a powerful combination because you can edit both the shape and the layer style as many times as you want without lowering the quality of the effect or the layer (**Figure 12.2**). As you edit the shape, the layer style reshapes itself to match, so experimenting is painless. Type is made up of vector shapes, so you can edit type and the layer style updates accordingly (**Figure 12.3**).

Figure 12.2: **Starting from a shape layer (left), I applied a layer style that applied the Bevel and Emboss and Gradient Overlay effects (center). When I used the direct selection and pen tools to edit the shape, the layer style adjusted automatically (right).**

Figure 12.3: **For this Web page button, I applied the Outer Glow effect to the text (left). If I edit the text, the layer style automatically adjusts, because it applies to the entire type layer.**

TIP A layer comp can remember the layer style applied to a layer. When creating a layer comp (see Chapter 10), saving a layer style as part of the layer comp lets you use different layer comps to change the appearance of a layer, not just its visibility or position.

Adding a Layer Style to a Layer

If you've read this far into the book, you know that many features available in palettes also appear in the menus, and layer styles are no exception. You set up a layer style using the Layer Style dialog box. To open the Layer Style dialog box, do one of the following:

■ Double-click the area to the right of a layer name in the Layers palette (**Figure 12.4**).

Figure 12.4: **To add a layer style, double-click the empty area next to a layer name.**

■ Click the Add a Layer Style button in the Layers palette and choose an effect from the pop-up menu.

■ Choose Layer > Layer Style, and choose a layer style from the submenu.

Whichever way you choose, the Layer Style dialog box appears.

You can also apply a layer style preset, a predefined combination of layer style effects saved under a name. To apply a layer style preset, select a layer, open the Styles palette (Window > Styles), and click a style in the palette, bypassing the Layer Style dialog box. I talk about making layer style presets in Chapter 4.

 TIP   When a layer style is applied to a layer, you can see which effects are used in that layer style by clicking the triangle at the right end of the layer in the Layers palette.

Using the Layer Style Dialog Box

In the Layer Style dialog box, you see many panel headings running down the left side (**Figure 12.5**). You can use the checkboxes there to enable or disable any of the layer style effects. In each panel, controls are laid out similarly. To get the most out of layer styles, use the following approach to applying a layer style:

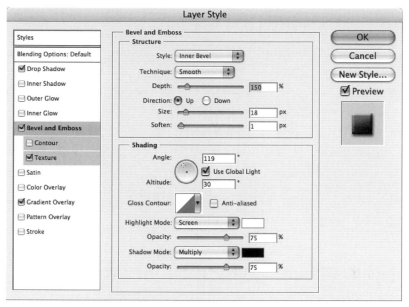

Figure 12.5: In the Layer Style dialog box, click a heading along the left side to change the effect controls in the center of the dialog box.

■ First check the Styles palette or the Styles panel of the Layer Style dialog box to see if the effect you want is already saved as a layer style preset. In the Layer Styles dialog box, you can see the Styles panel by clicking the Styles header at the top of the left column.

■ Some layer styles take advantage of the other presets available in the program. For example, many layer styles use contour presets, several use gradient presets, and others use pattern presets. If you're setting up a layer style that needs a preset that isn't already available, you may need to create it; see Chapter 4.

■ Use the center section of the Layer Style dialog box to set up layer style attributes.

■ Use the Preview checkbox to compare current Layer Style settings with the settings that were in effect before you opened the Layer Style dialog box.

Be careful—clicking a heading in the left column also enables an effect, so if you're experimenting it's a little too easy to enable more effects than you intended. If an effect isn't doing what you expect, double-check the heading checkboxes to make sure that the only effects enabled are the ones you want.

To edit a layer style, use the same methods you use to add a layer style. The easiest and fastest way is to double-click the layer style icon in the Layers palette. You can edit a layer style that you applied as a layer style preset, but it won't update the preset.

 TIPS Layer styles apply to the non-opaque area of a layer. For example, if you apply an emboss effect to a photograph, a layer style won't emboss anything in the photograph, only the outer rectangle of the entire photograph.

In layer styles, the Screen blending mode lightens underlying layers, so Screen is typically used for glow and highlight effects. The Multiply blending mode darkens underlying layers, so Multiply is typically used for shadows. If you want to make a glow act more like a shadow or vice versa, try changing the blending mode of an effect to the mode with the opposite behavior.

Applying a Layer Style to Other Layers

It's not unusual to come up with a great layer style on one layer and then apply the same effect to other layers. You can copy layer styles to other layers in three ways:

- Select a layer that uses the correct style, context-click the layer (Ctrl-click on Mac OS X or right-click on Windows) in the Layers palette and choose Copy Layer Style. Then select another layer, context-click the layer in the Layers palette, and choose Paste Layer Style. You can also choose Layer > Layer Style > Copy Layer Style or Paste Layer Style, but context-clicking is faster.

- In the Layers palette, Option/Alt+drag the layer style icon (**Figure 12.6**) from one layer to another. (If you drag the layer style icon without pressing Option/Alt, you'll move the layer style instead of copying it, which means you'll remove it from the source layer.)

- Double-click a layer that uses the correct style, and in the Layer Style dialog box click New Style. Name the style, specify whether the style should include effects and blending options. Click OK to close the New Style dialog box and click OK again to close the Layer Style dialog box. This creates a layer style preset that you can apply to any other layer using the Layer Style dialog box or the Styles palette.

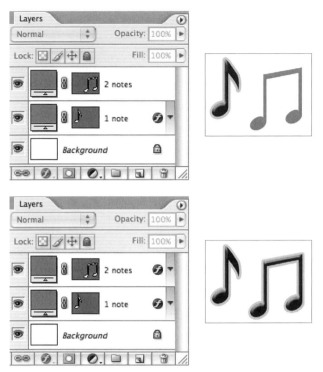

Figure 12.6: **To copy the single note's layer style to the two beamed notes, I Option/Alt+drag the layer style icon from the "1 note" layer to the "2 notes" layer.**

 TIP   Curious about the layer styles included with Photoshop and how the styles combine effects to achieve their looks? When a layer style is applied, open the Layer Style dialog box and select any checked heading. You'll see the exact settings that make up that effect.

Scaling a Layer Style

If you change the content of a layer that uses a layer style, in some cases the layer style settings may no longer be the right size for the content. For example, if you have a drop shadow that looks correct at 5 pixels wide on 48-point type, the shadow effect stays at 5 pixels wide if you change the type size to 24 points, causing the shadow to appear twice as wide as it should. Instead of adjusting the size of every layer style setting, you can simply scale the entire layer style.

To scale a layer style:

1. In the Layers palette, context-click on the layer style icon or a layer style itself.

2. From the context menu, choose Scale Effects (**Figure 12.7**). The command is way down at the bottom of the menu.

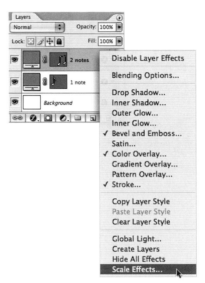

Figure 12.7

3. Adjust the scale percentage until the layer looks right and click OK.

You can also choose Layer > Layer Style > Scale Effects, but that's the longer way to get there.

CHAPTER THIRTEEN

Adding Transparency to Layers and Documents

TRANSPARENCY IS A BIT OF A GRAPHIC ARTS PARADOX, because the way you know it's working is when you can't see it. That's because transparency does its job not by occupying space, but by making space for something else. In Photoshop, you can apply transparency to an entire document so that it has a transparent background when you use the Photoshop document in a page-layout program such as Adobe InDesign, or on a Web page. Transparency also has an important use within a single Photoshop document: When you create a composition using multiple layers, transparency is what lets you see the layers behind the topmost layer. If transparency wasn't available, the entire top layer would be an opaque rectangle, and you wouldn't be able to see anything behind it.

Transparency isn't just for removing backgrounds or creating collages of different images. You can also use transparency to combine different versions of the same images, such as different exposures of a shot.

When you use transparency in this way, you combine images to show the best and hide the worst of each image. In this chapter I cover the essentials of transparency so that you can get the results you want as quickly as possible.

Seeing Transparency

As I mentioned, transparency works when you can't see it. That can make transparency a challenge to work with. For instance, how do you tell the difference between transparency and white? Photoshop solves that conundrum by displaying transparency as a checkerboard grid (**Figure 13.1**). You can adjust the size and color of the grid squares in the Transparency and Gamut panel of the Preferences dialog box (**Figure 13.2**). If you don't see the checkerboard pattern, it means the entire document area is opaque. Individual layers may have partial transparency, but when you put together all the layers, the entire document area is covered.

Figure 13.1: **The checkerboard indicates that an area is transparent on every layer in the document. White areas are opaque white.**

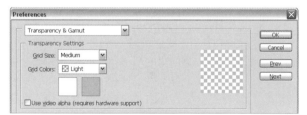

Figure 13.2: **You control how transparency displays in Photoshop by editing settings in the Transparency and Gamut panel of the Preferences dialog box.**

The *Background* layer, when present, plays a key role in document transparency. (That's the layer named Background in italics with a capital B, not just any layer that happens to be in the back of the layer stack.) When you start a new Photoshop document, you can set the default background to white, the current background color, or transparent. If you don't choose transparent, individual layers may use transparency, but the completely opaque background means that the final document won't have transparent areas.

The tricky part is that the default Background layer is not like other layers. It's opaque, locked in place, and you can't erase parts of it. If a document has a Background layer, and you want the document to have a transparent background, you can convert the opaque Background layer to a normal layer by Option/Alt+double-clicking it. As a normal layer, you can then use the techniques in this chapter (adjusting opacity, applying a mask, and so on) to create transparent areas on that layer. Or, if there isn't anything on that Background layer, you can simply delete it in the Layers palette by dragging it to the trash icon in the Layers palette. (You can delete the background only when at least one other layer exists.)

Choosing the Right Transparency Method

Not all transparency is alike. I've already talked about transparency at the document level and the layer level, but there are also many different ways to create transparency, and for certain types of output some techniques are more appropriate than others. For example, you might need GIF transparency for a Web page, but for a national magazine you might need a transparent PSD file or an EPS file with a clipping path. It's always best to start from your output goal to determine which technique to use. **Table 13.1**, next page, condenses the most common uses of transparency and what to do to get there. In the rest of this chapter I cover the ideas in Table 13.1 more specifically.

PERMANENT AND REVERSIBLE TRANSPARENCY

In the most general sense, there are two ways to make part of a layer transparent. You can apply a mask or blending mode, or you can simply erase parts of the layer. Whenever possible, an eraser tool (such as the background eraser) should be the last resort. It's better to use a mask or other method that doesn't involve erasing, because erasing is permanent. Once you erase layer content, you can't get it back unless a previous version of the layer exists in the History palette. In contrast, when you apply a mask, a blending mode, or another similar method, it's reversible. With masks, you can restore hidden areas by painting white into a mask instead of black. When you use an eraser tool, you can't change your mind later. If you want to preserve maximum flexibility in your workflow, use masks and avoid the eraser tools.

TABLE 13.1: Ways to Apply Transparency

To...	...do this
Make a painting tool partially transparent	Set the Opacity value in the options bar for the tool
Make an entire layer transparent	Set the Opacity value for that layer in the Layers palette
Make part of a layer transparent	Paint black in a layer mask, or draw a vector mask
Create transparency based on color combinations between layers	Apply a blending mode
Make a transparent document background for Adobe InDesign*	Remove opaque background layer, save as PSD
Make a clipping path	Draw a clipping path, save document as EPS or TIFF
Make a transparent document background for Web pages	Remove opaque background layer, save as PNG or GIF
Permanently delete areas of a layer	Paint a layer with the eraser or background eraser tool

* or other programs that can read transparency from a Photoshop-format document

 TIP   Opacity isn't just for creating transparency. For example, when you adjust the opacity of an adjustment layer, you reduce its effect on the underlying layers. Sometimes that's easier and faster than adjusting the controls in the adjustment layer's dialog box.

Setting Opacity

You find opacity controls all over Photoshop. An Opacity option is available for each layer and layer group, on the options bar for many painting and retouching tools, and is an option for effects such as layer styles (**Figure 13.3**). The prevalence of opacity controls in Photoshop means you can combine elements and effects with many subtle degrees of transparency among them.

Except for the Background layer, every new layer you add is transparent by default—when you add a new layer, you can see right through the entire layer

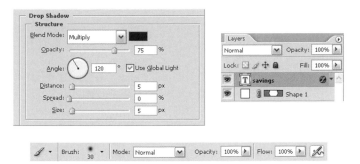

Figure 13.3: **Opacity is an option for effects (top left), layers (top right), and tools (bottom).**

until you start painting on it. When you set the opacity of a layer, you change the opacity of all non-transparent areas.

Within a document, there's a hierarchy to opacity affects how layers, tools, and features interact. Being aware of this hierarchy can help you untangle mysterious interactions between features. One of the most important concepts is that a layer sets the maximum opacity for everything on it. For example, if you set a layer to 100% opacity and paint on it using a brush set to 50% opacity, you get what you expect—pixels that are 50% opaque. But if you set a layer to 50% opacity and then paint on it using a brush set to 100% opacity, the painted pixels appear 50% opaque because they're limited by the opacity of their layer (**Figure 13.4**). Although the resulting pixels look the same in both examples, the difference is that you can raise the opacity of the layer in the second example to 100%, and then the pixels on them will become 100% opaque—because you painted those pixels with the brush tool set to 100% opacity.

Figure 13.4: **With layer opacity set to 50% (left), the brush stroke under the type appears 50% opaque (right) even though the tool itself was set to 100% opacity.**

Opacity is available in layer styles, filters, and other features. For example, Opacity is an option in the Drop Shadow layer style so that you can control the transparency of a drop shadow. Like tool opacity, opacity in layer styles and other features interacts with layer opacity.

TIPS   When an Opacity option is visible in the Layers palette or options bar, you can set opacity by typing number keys. Pressing 1 through 9 sets opacity to 10% through 90%, and pressing 0 (zero) sets opacity to 100%. For example, press 5 to set 50% opacity. To set a two-digit percentage, type two digits quickly; for example, type 42 to set 42% opacity. This tip is subject to the opacity hierarchy, so for example, if the Opacity option is visible both in the options bar for the brush tool and in the Layers palette, and you press 8, you set the opacity for the tool to 80%, not the layer. For the layer to pick up the shortcut, you need to select a tool, such as the rectangular marquee tool, that doesn't have an Opacity value.

If you use a pressure-sensitive graphics tablet and stylus, you can control tool opacity using stylus pressure. Just make sure the tool's Opacity Jitter is set to Pen Pressure in the Other Dynamics panel in the Brushes palette. If that sounds too complicated, just try out different brush presets; many of them are already designed to support stylus pressure.

Making Masks

While the Opacity value is easy to use and does exactly what it says, it affects an entire layer. When you want to make parts of a layer transparent, such as removing a background, the most flexible way is to add a mask to a layer. With a mask, black areas create layer transparency (hiding layer contents), white areas restore layer opacity (revealing layer contents), and gray areas are partially transparent, with darker areas being more transparent. This makes it easy for you to control transparency very precisely. In addition to letting you apply different degrees of transparency to various areas of a layer, using masks for transparency has other advantages:

- You can control transparency by painting black, white, and gray tones in a mask, using painting tools, fill commands, filters, and retouching features. For example, you can create a soft-edged vignette by painting a white ellipse into a black layer mask and applying a blur filter to the mask.

- You can change or remove the transparency at any time, without altering the original layer data. All you have to do is edit the mask or delete the mask. This has profound workflow advantages, because you're never stuck with your decisions—

if you need to recover an area you made transparent, just paint white back into that area of a mask.

■ You can create simple, hard-edged masks by adding a vector mask and drawing a shape into it.

 TIP To more easily remember whether to paint black or white in a mask, think of the phrase "Black conceals, white reveals."

As you've seen in the rest of the book, the real power of a feature in your workflow appears when you combine it with features in other areas of the program, like selections. Let's take a look at a quick example that draws upon features from all over Photoshop to help shape the mask. Suppose I have a layer with a background I want to remove. To do this, I would take the following steps:

1. On a layer that isn't the Background layer, I select the areas I want to keep visible. In this particular example, I use the Magic Wand and Lasso tools with modifier keys (see "Combining Selections" in Chapter 9) until all of the areas I want to keep are selected (**Figure 13.5**).

2. I click the Add Layer Mask button in the Layers palette. Because a selection is active, the new layer mask keeps the selection visible and hides everything else (**Figure 13.6**). If the resulting visible and hidden areas are the opposite of what you want, make sure the layer mask is selected in the Layers palette and choose Image > Adjustment > Invert to make hidden areas visible and visible areas hidden.

Figure 13.5

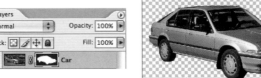

Figure 13.6

3. I select the layer mask, inspect the document, and edit the mask depending on what I see:

■ If I see additional areas that should be transparent, I paint black in that area of the mask.

■ If I see areas that were made transparent but they should be visible, I paint white in that area of the mask.

■ If the mask needs any other kind of cleanup, I Option/Alt+click the layer mask thumbnail to see only the mask while hiding the rest of the document. That makes it easy to see edges or stray black or white areas that need to be retouched with a brush tool set to black or white (**Figure 13.7**). Option/Alt+click again on the layer mask icon to display the document normally again.

Figure 13.7

 TIP   Layer masks can use the entire range of tones from black to white. To apply partial transparency to a layer, paint shades of gray in a layer mask—darker shades are more transparent. To see how this works, add a layer mask and fill it with a gradient from black to white.

To add a vector mask:

1. Select a layer in the Layers palette and choose Layer > Vector Mask > Reveal All.

2. Make sure the vector mask is selected.

3. Select a shape tool or the pen tool, make sure the Paths button is selected in the options bar, and draw the shape of the mask (**Figure 13.8**).

4. If needed, edit the path using the pen tool and the direct selection tool.

For a quick reference on how to add a mask and manipulate transparency with a mask, refer to **Table 13.2**.

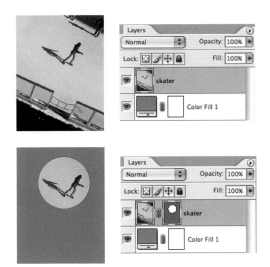

Figure 13.8

TABLE 13.2: Controlling Layer Transparency with Masks

To...	...do this
Add a layer mask that leaves the entire layer visible	Click the Add Layer Mask button in the Layers palette
Add a layer mask that hides the entire layer	Option/Alt+click the Add Layer Mask button in the Layers palette
Make an area completely opaque	Paint white on a layer mask
Make an area completely transparent	Paint black on a layer mask
Make an area more transparent	Darken the layer mask
Make an area more opaque	Lighten the layer mask
Disable/enable a layer mask	Shift+click a layer mask
Switch between showing document and layer mask only	Option/Alt+click a layer mask

 TIPS   Opacity, blending modes, and masks aren't just for layers. You can also apply them to layer groups.

You can't apply adjustment layers to a mask; they apply only to a layer itself. But you can apply masks to adjustment layers!

Using Blending Modes for Transparency Effects

Blending modes produce an effect by combining the colors of the current layer with the colors of underlying layers. Consider using blending modes when you've already tried setting opacity but wish the results had more or less contrast than you get by setting opacity alone. Blending modes can be difficult to understand, because what makes each mode different is that they use different mathematical formulas to compare a layer's colors with the layers behind it. Like opacity, blending modes are available for layers, painting tools, layer styles, and features like filters. In the Layers palette, blending modes appear on a pop-up menu next to the Opacity value. On the options bar, the blending modes pop-up menu is labeled Mode.

Although manipulating transparency isn't the main purpose of blending modes, applying various blending modes reveals underlying layers in different ways, creating the appearance of transparency (**Figure 13.9**). Because of this side effect, blending modes can be a quick and creative way of creating a transparency effect. (When blending modes aren't used to manipulate transparency, they're typically used for advanced image processing, as part of special techniques for color correction and sharpening.)

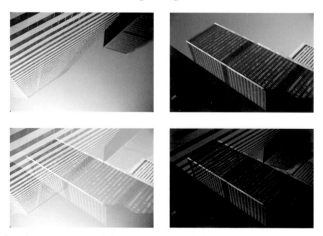

Figure 13.9: **Using the same two original images (top left and top right) as layers, I try two different transparency effects by simply changing the blending mode of the top layer to Screen (bottom left) and Linear Burn (right).**

It isn't easy to predict exactly which blending mode will produce the results you want, because of the math behind blending modes and the many ways in which different layers can affect the results. Still, you don't have to be an engineer to use blending modes—you can try two easy ways to quickly try them out: Simply cycle through them until you see the one you want or use guidelines to take an educated guess.

To cycle through blending modes, select one layer and press Shift+=. If the layer blending mode doesn't change, you're probably changing the blending mode of a brush tool in the options bar—choose a tool that doesn't use a blending mode before trying again.

To choose a blending mode through an educated guess, refer to **Table 13.3**, which summarizes what each blending mode does. You'll notice that blending modes fall into groups. Because it's not easy to predict how a blending mode will interact with different layer combinations, you can take a first pass by choosing a blending mode from the group that generally does what you're trying to do, and if it doesn't look right, try other blending modes in the same group. The differences between blending modes in the same group usually comes down to how much contrast they produce in tones and colors; for example, Vivid Light is similar to Pin Light but produces more intense colors.

Blending modes create the appearance of transparency, but they don't create areas that are actually transparent like areas created by a mask. If you want to create transparent areas for other programs, use layer masks or (if you must) erase areas of a layer.

TABLE 13.3: Choosing a Blending Mode

To...	...choose this blending mode
Reset a layer to use no blending mode	Normal
Darken a layer using underlying layers	Darken, Multiply, Color Burn, Linear Burn
Lighten a layer using underlying layers	Lighten, Screen, Color Dodge, Linear Dodge
Adjust contrast between layers	Overlay, Soft Light, Hard Light, Vivid Light, Linear Light, Pin Light, Hard Mix
Emphasize differences between layers	Difference, Exclusion
Use colors or tones from underlying layers	Hue, Saturation, Color, Luminosity

NOTE   The Behind and Clear blending modes appear only for painting tools and aren't available for layers.

 TIP   If you have a favorite blending mode, you can use a keyboard shortcut to apply it. To see a list of blending mode shortcuts, search Photoshop Help for "blending mode keys."

Making Transparent Backgrounds for Other Programs

Creating transparency for a document you'll use in another program is different than creating transparency for the layers within a Photoshop document. Layer transparency works fine within Photoshop, but when you use a document outside of Photoshop, the document must use a file format that stores transparency in a way that other programs recognize.

The format to choose depends on the final use of the document. For example, a Web page can't use a native Photoshop document; you must save a copy as a transparent PNG or GIF. Adobe InDesign recognizes transparency in Photoshop documents, so you don't need to change a thing before placing the document in an InDesign file. You can use **Table 13.4** as a quick reference for common types of transparent output, and I spell out the specifics after that.

TABLE 13.4: Creating Transparency for Other Programs

To preserve transparency for...	...do this
Adobe programs (print, video, Web)	Import as Photoshop document (no changes needed)*
QuarkXPress 7.0 or later	Import as Photoshop document (no changes needed)
Page-layout programs that don't support Photoshop transparency	Create clipping path; save as EPS or TIFF**
Non-Adobe Web design programs	Save as transparent PNG or GIF
Non-Adobe video-editing programs	Set up alpha channel, save as TIFF

* Verify that Photoshop transparency works with the version of the Adobe program you're using. Adobe Creative Suite 2 and Adobe Production Studio programs do support the Photoshop document format directly.
** Some page-layout programs may not read alpha channels in TIFF documents; in such a program try EPS with a clipping path instead.

Guidelines for Maintaining Transparency in Other Programs

Maintaining transparency is easier with newer programs and more challenging with older programs. That's because many newer programs recognize Photoshop transparency right away or recognize other standard ways of storing transparency. Older programs don't support Photoshop transparency or the newer, more efficient ways of storing transparency, making you do extra work to your Photoshop documents.

Your workflow is more likely to preserve transparent backgrounds in Photoshop documents if you use the following guidelines:

- Create new documents with a transparent background. When you choose File > New, choose Transparent from the Background Contents pop-up menu.

- All areas you want to remain transparent must really be transparent, not opaque white. The easiest way to check document transparency is to look for the checkerboard pattern that Photoshop uses to indicate transparency. If you see the checkerboard in all areas that you want to be transparent in other programs, the document is fine. If you see white instead, some layers may have unwanted opaque areas, or the document may include an opaque white, blank Background layer that you may need to remove.

- Store your master files as layered Photoshop documents. Don't flatten them or archive them in non-layered formats like JPEG. Most flattened files can't store transparency.

- If your master files aren't saved as 8-bit RGB documents (or 8-bit CMYK for press output), save copies using those specifications for use with most other programs. Other programs may not recognize transparency in Photoshop documents saved at other bit depths or color modes.

Creating a Transparent Background for Print

In recent years, Adobe has updated more of its programs to support Photoshop transparency directly, so that all you have to do is import an 8-bit Photoshop document, and all transparent areas of the Photoshop document are preserved. This is certainly true in Adobe InDesign CS2 and Adobe Illustrator CS2. In both programs, simply choose File > Place to import a Photoshop document, and if the Photoshop document has transparency, it appears that way on an InDesign or Illustrator page.

CREATING ALPHA CHANNELS FOR OTHER PROGRAMS

In a Photoshop document, an alpha channel is a channel that exists in addition to the color channels. For example, an RGB document contains red, green, and blue color channels, and any other channels are alpha channels. You might think of alpha channels as invisible layers, because they're aligned with document contents but aren't visible in final document output. They only affect the document when you convert them to a selection or when you use Photoshop or another program to act on the area marked by an alpha channel. Alpha channels are typically used for saving selections and marking document transparency for programs that use alpha channels for that purpose. Many print and video-editing programs rely on alpha channels to indicate which part of an imported file should be transparent, although most Adobe programs now use Photoshop transparency directly, so that you don't have to go through the following steps.

To use an alpha channel to create a transparent background for another program:

1. Select the background using any combination of selection tools.

2. Choose Selection > Save Selection.

3. In the Save Selection dialog box, make sure Document is the name of the current document, Channel is set to New, and Operation is set to New Channel (**Figure 13.10**).

4. Name the new alpha channel and click OK.

5. Choose File > Save As. In the Format pop-up menu, select the format required by the other program (TIFF is a typical format used with an alpha channel) and make sure Alpha Channels is enabled (**Figure 13.11**). Not all formats save alpha channels.

Some programs may not see the alpha channel right away; you may need to adjust a setting in the other program to tell it an alpha channel is available in the imported document. If you save the document with more than one alpha channel and you import the document into another program, you may need to choose which alpha channel to use.

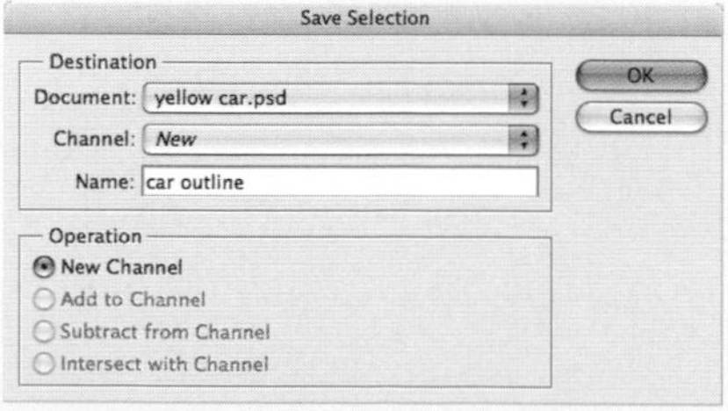

Figure 13.10

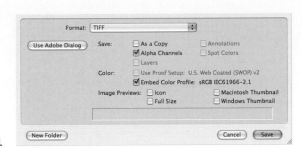

Figure 13.11

Older programs and non-Adobe programs may not recognize transparency in Photoshop documents. Older page-layout programs may recognize other ways to store transparency, such as alpha channels or clipping paths. Because alpha channels apply to more media than just print, I cover how to create them in the sidebar "Creating Alpha Channels for Other Programs." Clipping paths are typically used in print media only, so if you happen to be using a page-layout program that supports them, here's how to make one.

To save a document with a clipping path:

1. Create a path that marks off the area you want to make transparent (**Figure 13.12**). You can draw the path with the pen tool or you can select the background using any combination of selection tools and then convert the selection to a path (choose Make Work Path from the Paths palette menu, enter a Tolerance value, and click OK).

Figure 13.12

2. In the Paths palette, double-click the Work Path, name it, and click OK.

3. Choose Clipping Path from the Paths palette menu.

4. Name the path and click OK. (You typically don't need to enter a Flatness value unless there are output problems on an older output device.) The path name becomes outlined in the Paths palette (**Figure 13.13**).

Figure 13.13

5. Choose File > Save As. In the Format pop-up menu, choose one of the following formats:

- Choose Photoshop EPS, Photoshop PDF, or Photoshop DCS 1.0 or 2.0.

- If you're going to import the file into Adobe InDesign or Adobe PageMaker 5.0 or later, you can choose TIFF format.

6. Specify other save options as needed and click Save.

7. Import the file into the other program (**Figure 13.14**).

Figure 13.14

Creating a Transparent Background for the Web

As it is with print, Adobe makes things easier for you if you use Adobe GoLive CS2, the Web-site editor that comes with Adobe Creative Suite CS2. With Adobe GoLive, you don't have to convert a Photoshop document to a Web-friendly format; GoLive does it for you when you import the Photoshop document. It seems like more steps at first glance, but it's actually less work.

To use a Photoshop document with a transparent background in GoLive:

1. Prepare a Photoshop document with a transparent background.

2. In GoLive, open the Web page that will contain the Photoshop file and click the Layout tab at the top of the document window.

3. Drag the Photoshop document from the desktop to the GoLive document window.

4. In the Save for Web dialog box that appears, choose one of the presets for GIF or PNG and make sure the Transparency checkbox is enabled. Transparent areas appear as a checkerboard pattern (**Figure 13.15**). When you're ready, click Save to generate the transparent, Web-optimized file.

The optimized graphic appears on the page with its transparent background, so that the background of the page shows through the graphic (**Figure 13.16**).

Figure 13.15   Figure 13.16

> **NOTE** If you imported a Photoshop document containing multiple layers, GoLive imports each layer individually and recomposes them on the layout; simply repeat step 4 for each layer.

If you want to use a Photoshop document on a Web page and preserve background transparency, and you aren't using Adobe GoLive, you need to save a copy of your Photoshop document in either of the two formats that supports transparency on the Web: PNG (Portable Network Graphics format) or GIF (Graphics Interchange Format). The popular JPEG format doesn't support transparency.

To save a Web graphic with a transparent background:

1. Open a Photoshop document with a transparent background.

2. Choose File > Save for Web.

3. In the Save for Web dialog box, choose one of the presets for GIF or PNG. Transparent areas should appear as a checkerboard pattern.

4. Specify other options and click Save.

5. Import the saved PNG or GIF document into the other program.

> **TIP** In the Save for Web dialog box, if the image has a white or solid-color background that you haven't removed, you can make that color transparent. Choose a GIF preset, select the eyedropper tool, click the color that should be transparent, and then in the Color Table tab, click the Maps Selected Color to Transparent button (the button that looks like the transparency checkerboard, first in the row under the color table).

Creating a Transparent Background for Video Editing

If you're using Adobe video-editing programs such as those in the Adobe Production Studio, you can simply use Photoshop documents without conversion. Adobe Production Studio programs read the transparency in Photoshop documents without any adjustment necessary. It may still be necessary for you to set the Photoshop document to pixel dimensions and a color space that are appropriate for video, but you won't have to change its file format.

Most non-Adobe video software expects document transparency to appear in the form of an alpha channel (see the sidebar "Creating Alpha Channels for Other Programs"). Check the documentation for the video software you use to find out which file formats it supports for transparency and save your graphics from Photoshop in that format. For video programs, it's common to support formats such as TIFF and Photoshop with an alpha channel; native Photoshop transparency may not be supported.

Other than those considerations, as long as you've followed the suggestions in "Guidelines for Maintaining Transparency in Other Programs" and "Creating Alpha Channels for Other Programs," the transparency should transfer.

CHAPTER FOURTEEN

Rewriting History

Many programs have an undo feature, and some programs provide unlimited undo as long as a document remains open. Photoshop turns undo into a resource by providing the History palette, which keeps a list of recent undo steps. Not only can you return the document to any of the undo steps (called *history states*), but you can also use any history state as a source of content that you can paint into any other history state, essentially letting you mix versions freely.

Undoing and Redoing

Many programs have separate Edit > Undo and Edit > Redo commands. Photoshop's take on undo is slightly different. In Photoshop, the Edit > Undo command turns into Edit > Redo after you edit the document in any way, so using the command (or its shortcut Command/Ctrl+Z) only switches between the current and previous states of the document. This sometimes leaves new users of Photoshop wondering if Photoshop has only one undo step.

If you look just below the Undo command on the Edit menu, you see two more commands: Step Forward and Step Backward (**Figure 14.1**). These are the commands that let you move further back in the undo stack. The tricky thing is that you have to use this second set of commands (and shortcuts) if you want to undo more than just the last thing you did. In other words, if you want to try a quick before/after comparison with the Undo command, you simply press Command/Ctrl+Z a couple of times; but if you want to undo the last five edits, you press Shift+Command+Z /Shift+Ctrl+Z five times.

Figure 14.1: **The Undo command toggles between your last two edits. The Step Forward and Step Backward commands move up and down the history states in the History palette.**

The undo commands are set up this way in Photoshop because of the History palette, which I talk about in the rest of this chapter. The History palette keeps a list of edits, which means you can use the Step Forward and Step Backwards commands to "walk" up and down the history states. The beauty of this arrangement is that if you don't want to deal with the History palette just yet, you can use the Edit menu for both multiple undo and to undo/redo the most recent edit.

WHY LIMITED UNDO?

Photoshop doesn't have unlimited undo, and there's a good reason for that. A large Photoshop document requires a lot of memory to store every state of every layer. If you work with large files, such as those typically produced by today's digital SLR cameras, and you add layers to them, the history states can become so large that you wouldn't have space to store them all in RAM. For this reason, Photoshop stores history states on your scratch disk (that's your startup disk if you haven't changed it in the Plug-ins & Scratch Disks panel of the Preferences dialog box), and is set to a limit of 20 history states by default. Limiting the number of history states limits the amount of disk space consumed by Photoshop scratch files on your hard disk. If you've got a nice Photoshop system with one or more large external hard disks that are dedicated Photoshop scratch disks (see Chapter 1), you can increase the number of history states Photoshop remembers by changing the History States value in the General panel of the Preferences dialog box.

Using the History Palette Productively

On the surface, the History palette looks like a simple list of your most recent edits, but the History palette is much deeper than it looks. You can use the History palette not only to back out of mistakes, but also as a temporary idea book where you can store different iterations of a document and recombine their best parts.

To begin with, let's map out the History palette. When you open a document, the History palette appears divided into two sections (**Figure 14.2**). The lower section lists history states; you'll see it grow as you edit the document. The upper section lists history snapshots, which I get to later.

Figure 14.2: **The top of the History palette stores snapshots, and the bottom stores history states.**

The list of history states grows longer until it reaches the History States number specified in the General panel of the Preferences dialog box (see the nearby sidebar "Why Limited Undo?"). When the number of history states exceeds the History States setting, Photoshop removes the oldest history state. Only actual edits add a history state; changes that don't affect the document contents, such as scrolling the window, don't create a history state.

Going Back in Time

One of the most productive ways to use history states is to paint from one history state to another. This is useful when one of the history states contains content that you'd like to combine with the current iteration of the document. For example, suppose I colorize a photo, but then I decide I want to restore the original color to just a portion of the photo. To get the best of both worlds, I can use the history brush tool to paint in only the areas that need to be cleaned up.

 TIP   You can undo the File > Revert command, because choosing Revert creates a history state.

To use the history brush tool:

1. Edit the document until at least two history states exist (its original state and any edited state) (**Figure 14.3**).

Figure 14.3

2. In the History palette, click in the column to the left of the history state you want to use as the source for the history brush tool. The history brush source icon appears in the left column next to the history state.

3. Select the history state you want to use as the destination by clicking the name of this history state, not in the left column (**Figure 14.4**).

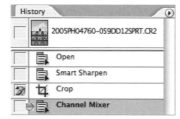

Figure 14.4

4. Select the history brush tool in the Tools palette.

5. Paint the areas where you want to add content from the source history state (**Figure 14.5**).

Figure 14.5

Using Snapshots to Preserve History States

There may be times when you recognize that a particular history state would be useful in the future, and you don't want to lose that history state as new states are added. You can retain a history state by creating a *snapshot*.

To create a snapshot, select a history state in the History palette and click the Create New Snapshot button at the bottom of the History palette.

History states and snapshots are best used for keeping iterations of a document that involve alternate sets of edits that can't be stored any other way, because there's one catch: History states and snapshots belong to the current editing session only. Once you close the document, they're gone. If you want to maintain different versions of a document across sessions, you might look into using Adobe Version Cue, which comes with Adobe Creative Suite 2. If you simply want to save alternate layer configurations with a document, you can do that using a layer comp (see Chapter 10).

Here's an example of how I use snapshots. I sometimes convert color photos to black-and-white using the Channel Mixer, but I can't predict which way will work out the best for a particular photo. So, I created an action that runs the image through several methods and keeps snapshots of each method. I can then decide which one to keep. I don't cover actions until Chapter 17, but what I want to show here is how you can make snapshots and choose from them.

To use history snapshots:

1. Edit the document until the document reaches the point where you'd like to make a snapshot of it.

(If you're wondering how I am doing the black-and-white conversions in this procedure, I use the advanced method of opening the Channel Mixer dialog box, entering different percentages for Red, Green, and Blue, and enabling the Monochrome checkbox. This provides more control than simply converting to grayscale. You can apply Channel Mixer as an adjustment layer from the Layers palette.)

2. Click the Create New Snapshot button at the bottom of the History palette (**Figure 14.6**). (To name the snapshot as you create it, or to control how layers are handled in the snapshot, Option/Alt+click the Create New Snapshot button instead.)

Figure 14.6

3. Edit the document again until you create another iteration you want to preserve and then click the Create New Snapshot button again. In this case, I double-clicked the Channel Mixer adjustment layer and changed the values.

4. Repeat steps 2 and 3 until you've created the possibilities you want to choose from.

5. In the History palette, select each snapshot to compare them. When you decide which one you want, leave it selected (**Figure 14.7**). Photoshop uses the selected history state as the new starting point for history states.

6. If you no longer need the other snapshots, you can delete them from the History palette by dragging them to the Delete (trash) icon at the bottom of the History palette.

Like history states, history snapshots are stored on your Photoshop scratch disk during an editing session. The size of your scratch disk limits how many snapshots you can store, and the size and complexity of the document determines the size of each snapshot.

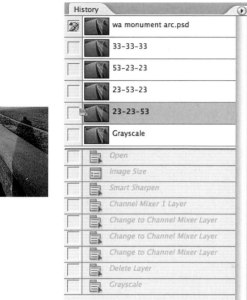

Figure 14.7

 TIPS By default, the History palette creates a history state as soon as you open a document. As long as the History palette contains that snapshot, you can always go back to that document state even if you've saved changes since you originally opened the document.

You can save a history state as a new document when you like a history state but you don't want to replace the current state of the document. Select the history state and click the Create New Document from Current State button, which is the first button at the bottom of the History palette.

Setting History Palette Options

You can fine-tune the operation of the History palette by choosing History Options from the History palette menu. In the History Options dialog box (**Figure 14.8**), three options affect how many states and snapshots are created: Automatically

Figure 14.8: You can change the behavior of the History palette using the History Options dialog box.

Create First Snapshot (that is, when you open the document), Automatically Create New Snapshot When Saving, and Make Layer Visibility Changes Undoable. The reason they aren't all on by default is that many more history states would be created, which means that the History palette wouldn't remember back as far before it started dumping the oldest history state. It's reasonable to enable these options if you've increased the number of History States in the General panel of the Preferences dialog box (see "Why Limited Undo?").

If you enable the Show New Snapshot Dialog Box by Default checkbox, clicking the Create New Snapshot button will act as if you Option/Alt+clicked it.

If you enable the Allow Non-Linear History checkbox, when you back up a few history states and branch off in another direction the History palette remembers the old branch of your edits. Again, this option is more practical if you have the disk space to increase the number of history states you can store; otherwise, it may not be able to remember much of each branch.

Keeping a History Log

Although there's no way to keep history states and snapshots after you close a document, you can keep a record of what you did, and it's called the *history log*. The history log is text that records your edits, but you can only read it. You can't play it back or reload it. You can use the history log to track your edits down to the settings you used in dialog boxes, and you can use that to manually reproduce the edits made to the file.

The history log was originally added to Photoshop so that judges and juries in court cases could have a precise record of how a digital photo presented in court as evidence differs from the original photo (for example, if a crime scene photo was brightened for clarity). If you set up the history log in a way that's appropriate for your work, it can be a valuable tool for documenting and analyzing your own processes and techniques.

If you want to keep a history log, enable the History Log checkbox in the General panel of the Preferences dialog box (**Figure 14.9**). You can choose whether you want to save a log with each file (select Metadata) or maintain a central log for all files (Text File). You can also use the Edit Log Items pop-up menu to set the level of detail for the log.

Figure 14.9: Enable and customize the history log in the General panel of the Preferences dialog box.

Keep in mind that if you increase the history log's level of detail, the history log can record minutiae like the folder paths and names of files you open, and the text you enter on text layers. If you choose to store the history log in metadata, it travels wherever the image travels. For example, if you type "My Stupid Boss" on a text layer because you're just playing around, and then you delete the text, the original text entry is still in the log. If you store the log in the image metadata, and your boss views the file in Adobe Bridge which can display the metadata, your boss may come across the log entry containing that text. If you or your organization has an interest in restricting certain information, you may not want detailed editing records to travel with the file. You might limit the level of detail or choose to store the log in a text file on your own machine, rather than keeping the log in the file's metadata.

CHAPTER FIFTEEN

Saving Documents Productively

FOR THE MOST PART, THE UNSTOPPABLE MARCH of more powerful computers and software is a wonderful thing. However, some parts of the workflow have become more complicated. Not too many years ago, most of the photographs handled by computers were headed for a press, and that means they were probably saved in TIFF format in the CMYK color mode at 8 bits per channel. Once you saved a document to that format, you were done, and the document could be pulled out and reused later without much fuss.

With the rise of the Web and digital video, suddenly computers started filling up with RGB photographs at screen resolution in all kinds of formats, and there was often some degree of file-format confusion when print and on-screen media professionals exchanged files. The color mode and file format that worked best in one medium could create disastrous results in another medium.

Now, options abound all over the industry. You can store digital photographs at 8, 16, or even 32 bits of color per channel, in the CMYK, RGB, or even Lab color mode, and as a Raw, TIFF, JPEG, or layered Photoshop file format . . . and those are just a sampling of the actual range of possibilities. You might even wonder which RGB color space you want to use: sRGB, Adobe RGB, ProPhoto RGB or yet another?

Fortunately, there is a way to simplify this technological Tower of Babel. It all comes down to how much quality you want to maintain, how much disk space you want to use up, the amount of power in your computer, and most importantly, the kinds of output where your Photoshop documents must look their best.

Saving a Master Document for Flexibility

Images you use for professional projects typically start from high-quality source material, such as digital-camera photos containing several megapixels, or a high-resolution scan of film or a print. As you adjust and refine the image in Photoshop, you might pile on the layers, masks, and channels, increasing the file size. When the time comes to hand off the document, and it needs to be in a different format, you convert the document to the required final format and you're done. For example, if you were preparing images in the CMYK color mode for press, you might simply archive the CMYK files used on the project.

However, preparing a document for a specific medium can remove much of the flexibility in the original document, often flattening layers or reducing the range of colors. For example, if you save an RGB document in CMYK color mode for press, you lose ranges of colors that can't be reproduced in CMYK. That's fine if the document will only be used on press in the future, but it restricts the color quality of the document if you later want to make an RGB version of the document for the Web or television. If you do expect to use a document for multiple media, it's better to maintain a master Photoshop document that isn't specifically tied to any medium. (Of course, if you always work in one medium, or if you are doing a one-time project where the content is unlikely to be reused, you may not be concerned with the ability to reuse Photoshop documents for different media or future projects, and therefore maintaining a master document might not be a top priority.)

If you do want to save a Photoshop document that's ready for all kinds of future uses, I'd recommend saving a master document that includes:

■ **The largest dimensions you expect the document to need in the future.**
Typically, this can simply be the resolution of the source document. In other
words, if you use an 8-megapixel camera to produce a 200 x 300-pixel portrait
for a Web page, and you think the same portrait will probably be needed for
next year's printed annual report, you definitely want to hang onto the original
8-megapixel document.

■ **Layers and masks.** Preserving layers lets you alter the composition for a future
use. Preserving masks lets you maintain the transparency of a layer in case you
want to use a layer over a different background in the future or restore areas of
a layer that are currently hidden by the mask. It's OK to merge layers that you
don't think you'll need to rework in the future, but avoid flattening the entire
document unless it's required.

■ **The largest color space you expect the document to need in the future.**
For most uses, the choice comes down to sRGB or Adobe RGB, while demanding
photographers may archive using ProPhoto RGB. For the rundown on color
spaces, see the nearby sidebar "What's the Right Color Space?"

■ **The highest bit depth you expect the document to need in the future.** For
images that are properly corrected for tone and color, 8 bits is quite enough. If
you expect an image's tones or color to be reworked significantly in the future,
you can choose to archive a 16-bit or higher version of the image—but only
if the image started out at that bit depth or higher. For example, if an image
started out as an 8-bit JPEG, you'll gain nothing from converting it to 16 bits.

■ **Type, effects, and vector shapes.** It's a good idea to preserve these layers
because you can edit them at any time without reducing their sharpness or quality.
For example, you can edit the text in a type layer at any time in the future. If you flattened or rasterized the type into the document as pixels (by flattening the document
or choosing Layer > Rasterize > Type), there's no practical way to change the text.

You'll use this master document as a fully editable source file. When you need
to reuse the Photoshop document in another medium down the road, simply
save a copy of the document at the required specifications for that medium,
resizing, flattening, and converting its color mode and color space as needed.

As you read the rest of this chapter, keep the ideas of a media-independent master and a media-specific final document in mind, because that concept drives
many of the choices I cover.

WHAT'S THE RIGHT COLOR SPACE?

Color space—the range of color available to an image—is widely misunderstood. The situation isn't helped by the number of color space choices for RGB alone (sRGB, Adobe RGB, and ProPhoto RGB to name just a few). Without getting into a book-length discussion of color management, I try to set things straight here.

One myth is that you have to choose one color space and stick with it forever, and that leads to endless arguments about whether a space like Adobe RGB or ProPhoto RGB is better than sRGB. The fact is that you can use different color spaces for capture, editing, and output. It's certainly easier to pick the color space closest to the range of colors of your final output and use that all the time, but that's most practical if you're going to stick with one kind of output all the time. For example, if you only prepare images for press, it's both sensible and simple to edit and hand off final files in the CMYK color space of your press. However, if you maintain master files that you convert to both print and Web media, you'll probably want to use a color space large enough to contain most of the colors you use in all the media for which you prepare images, such as Adobe RGB. (Avoid the temptation of choosing very large color spaces like ProPhoto RGB unless you have a very good handle on color management and 16-bit editing.)

It isn't necessary to convert all documents to the Photoshop working space (specified in Edit > Color Settings) before you edit. When documents come from different sources, it sometimes makes sense to leave them in their original color spaces while you edit as long as those are device-independent (not media-specific) color spaces like Adobe RGB or sRGB. Photoshop can maintain the individual color space of any documents you open, so that's not an obstacle. (Contrary to popular belief, the Photoshop working space setting in the Color Settings dialog box only comes into play when you open an image that *isn't* already tagged with a color space profile and automatic conversion is on in Color Settings.) You can work in any reasonable color space, and when it's time to prepare the media-specific versions, you can convert to the appropriate color space. For example, you can edit files that arrive in Adobe RGB and sRGB in their original color spaces, and when it's time to create the final images you convert all of them to the final CMYK color space. Or, when it's time to create the final images for the Web you can convert them all to sRGB.

How can Photoshop keep all this straight? If you maintain a properly configured color-management system, with accurate profiles installed for your monitor and printer and embedded in your images, Photoshop and other color-managed programs can use the profiles to reconcile color differences among documents so that they're displayed consistently and so that conversions are predictable. I know color management is a scary term to many, but if you can reach the point where you understand it, the effort is well worth it. For a complete and effective explanation of color management, I recommend the book *Real World Color Management* by Bruce Fraser, Chris Murphy, and Fred Bunting (Peachpit Press).

Saving for Specific Media

It would be nice if we could simply hand off a Photoshop master document to everybody, but that's not always possible. You're often required to provide a simplified document to exacting specifications based on the final medium. Such a document becomes the opposite of a Photoshop master document. Instead of carrying all possible data for any kind of output, you tune the document perfectly for one specific kind of output. You might constrain the image to a specific color mode, file format, and resolution, and you might be required to flatten layers. **Table 15.1** lists some typical output specifications for popular media, but for your own projects you'll want to confirm the exact production specifications of your particular job.

Table 15.1 represents specifications that mainly apply to programs that don't read Photoshop documents directly. Most Adobe Creative Suite and Adobe Production Studio programs can open or import 8-bit Photoshop documents without modification, saving you the trouble of converting to another format or having to read this section; see "Using Photoshop with Adobe Creative Suite."

TABLE 15.1: Sample Document Specifications for Different Media

Medium	Typical final specifications
Press	CMYK TIFF or EPS document at 300 dpi
World Wide Web	sRGB document in JPEG, PNG, or GIF format at the required pixel dimensions (resolution doesn't matter)
Digital video (standard definition)	sRGB document at the required pixel dimensions, typically 720 × 480 pixels but depends on video format
Digital video (high definition)	sRGB document at the required pixel dimensions, up to 1920 × 1080 pixels

Conforming a Photoshop document to media-specific settings can sometimes take you all over Photoshop. **Table 15.2** is a handy cheat sheet for where to go in Photoshop to change the most common document specifications that need to be changed for a specific medium.

TABLE 15.2: How to Make Changes for Media Compatibility

To change this...	...do this
Dimensions and resolution	Choose Image > Image Size
Color mode (RGB to CMYK)	Image > Mode > CMYK Color
Color space (convert to a profile)	Edit > Convert to Profile
Bit depth	Image > Mode > 8 Bits/Channel
Layers to a flattened document	Layer > Flatten Image

 TIP   If you often perform the same sequence of steps to prepare a master document for a specific medium, turn those steps into an action or script; see Chapters 17 and 19.

BIT DEPTH: HOW MUCH DOES IT MATTER?

You might hear about 8-bit and 16-bit images, and claims of higher bit depths are used to help sell hardware and software. Should you be using a higher bit depth for your master document or media-specific document? You can think of bit depth as being analogous to resolution, but instead of describing how many pixels an image has, bit depth describes how many separate levels of tone or color a pixel can store in each color channel (such as the red channel in an RGB image). Although 16-bit images can provide advantages for the capture and editing phase, 8 bits per pixel is still the standard for exchanging completed files for print, Web, and most video media, and most images are still edited in 8-bit color. There's no advantage to converting from 8- to 16-bit color. If you prefer to edit in 16-bit color, keep in mind that you'll probably need to convert your images to 8-bit color if you're handing them off to someone else.

16-bit color gives you additional flexibility in editing by helping prevent visible steps (banding) in tones and colors, but only if the original image was a high-quality capture at 16 bits per channel. (A badly captured 16-bit image is simply 16 bits of garbage.) 16-bit images require much more processing power, RAM, and disk space than 8-bit images, and you gain no color benefits without a calibrated monitor, so you don't want to use 16-bit color without a good reason. If the source image is well captured, and you can make tone or color corrections with just a few adjustments, you may not need to use 16-bit images at all. And if you're just starting out, 8-bit color is the easy choice because it's widely used and supported.

16-bit color is suitable for those who have specific quality requirements and the equipment and skills to support 16-bit editing throughout their workflow. If the use of 16-bit color is something of a niche, then who uses 32-bit color, which Photoshop CS2 supports? There are some high-end uses where the ability to store 32 bits per channel of tone and color actually helps, such as astronomy, Hollywood and game industry special effects, and high-end landscape and architectural photography.

Using the Save as a Copy Feature

The Save as a Copy checkbox in the Save As dialog box is intended to keep you from losing data, but it's a common source of confusion. And sometimes the Save as a Copy comes on all by itself, which adds to the confusion. The key to avoiding confusion is to understand its reason for being.

The Save as a Copy checkbox is there because of the conflicting requirements of master and media-specific documents that I've been talking about. For example, suppose you're preparing an image that needs to be delivered as a JPEG document. While building the document, you save the image in Photoshop format so that you can take full advantage of features like layers, vector type and shapes, and alpha channels. When it's time to hand off the final JPEG, you choose File > Save As and choose JPEG from the Format pop-up menu (**Figure 15.1**). When you do this, all of the Save option checkboxes become dimmed, and the Save as a Copy checkbox becomes dimmed and enabled. The reason Photoshop does this is to prevent you from replacing the current, full-featured Photoshop document with a JPEG document that can't store all of the Photoshop features you used. In the past, it was too easy to save over your full-featured document with a version that was no more than a flattened document containing only pixels, removing the flexibility of the master document. Whenever you choose a Save As format that can't store all of the features listed in the Save options of the Save As dialog box, Photoshop requires that you save as a copy.

Figure 15.1: In the Save As dialog box, saving a layered, annotated Photoshop document in JPEG format causes Save As a Copy to become enabled and dimmed.

Save as a Copy also becomes enabled if you save in Photoshop or TIFF format but disable any of the Save checkboxes, because once again, you're about to create a document with fewer editing capabilities than your master document.

An important effect of the Save as a Copy feature is that the document you save is not the document that remains open. If you want to work on a document that was saved using Save as a Copy, you must open it separately. The document that's open after you Save as a Copy is the master document you originally opened, and any changes you make to it don't appear in the Save as a Copy version. That's because the Save as a Copy version is like a spinoff of the master document, which makes perfect sense if you were using Save As to create a simplified, media-specific version of the master document.

Playing Nice with Other Programs

Buried in the File Handling panel of the Preferences dialog box is a setting called Maximize PSD and PSB Compatibility (**Figure 15.2**). Not everyone knows what it's actually for, and a lot of people turn it off after realizing that it makes Photoshop documents take up more disk space. Many believe that it's there so that older versions of Photoshop can read the document, but there's more to it than that.

Many other programs claim to be able to read Photoshop files, but not all of them understand all of the possible kinds of Photoshop documents. Some programs can only read Photoshop files that are flattened. Others can't read Photoshop documents in 16-bit color, that are layered, or that use the Lab color mode. The Maximize PSD and PSB Compatibility option exists to get around this problem.

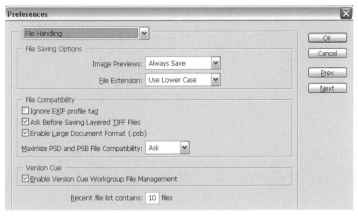

Figure 15.2: **The Maximize PSD and PSB Compatibility checkbox makes it possible for other applications to read feature-rich Photoshop documents, such as layered documents.**

It embeds a composite (flattened) version of the Photoshop document along with the usual Photoshop layers and other non-pixel data—that's why the document gets bigger. When a program opens or imports a Photoshop document that includes features it doesn't recognize, the program can fall back to the friendly composite version embedded in the document.

If you rarely view Photoshop documents with other programs, you might choose to disable Maximize PSD and PSB Compatibility and save some disk space. However, the more you handle Photoshop documents with other programs, especially non-Adobe programs, the more you want to enable that option. Remember that non-Adobe programs that handle Photoshop documents directly can include graphics-viewing utilities that come with your computer such as Apple Preview, page-layout software, video-production software, and digital-asset managers. Disabling Maximize PSD and PSB Compatibility may limit your ability to preview Photoshop documents in some Adobe programs. I keep it on because large hard disks are affordable.

CHAPTER SIXTEEN

Printing Right the First Time

YOU CAN PRINT FROM PHOTOSHOP the way you print from any other program—just choose File > Print and send it on through. However, if you print that way, you may not be getting the best print quality that Photoshop can achieve. By changing your print workflow just slightly, you gain much more control over how Photoshop prints color and positions the document on the paper.

You can use Photoshop to anticipate how a document will print. Some of the most common printing mistakes are having a document print at the wrong size or position on the page, and having printed colors appear incorrect. Photoshop contains features that can address both of these challenges. Since I started using the techniques in this chapter, I've been pleased at how much better I can predict how an image will end up on paper, and how much less paper and ink I consume through trial and error.

Previewing Print Size

Is your document at the correct print size? Photoshop gives you different ways to check:

- To see a pop-up graphic that graphically represents how the document size relates to the paper size and the printable area of that paper size, click the status bar in in the bottom-left corner of a document window (**Figure 16.1**). In the pop-up graphic, the outer rectangle represents the paper size. The gray area represents the unprintable margin areas as defined by the printer driver. The box with an X inside represents the document.

- To see and change document dimensions, choose Image > Image Size (**Figure 16.2**). In the Image Size dialog box, you'll want to change the dimensions that matter for your output. For print, you typically disable the Resample Image checkbox and edit the Document Size, while for onscreen work you typically enable the Resample Image checkbox and edit the Pixel Dimensions.

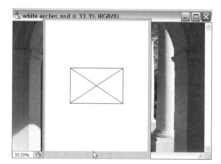

Figure 16.1: **To preview how the current document dimensions fit on the selected printer and paper size, click the status bar.**

Figure 16.2: **The Image Size dialog box shows you the document's physical dimensions (such as inches), its pixel dimensions, and resolution.**

- To see a larger version of the same elements as the status bar pop-up, but with control over size and position, choose File > Print with Preview (**Figure 16.3**). The Print with Preview dialog box contains a *proxy*, a thumbnail representation of the document that you can manipulate.

- To zoom the document window to match the physical size of the document when printed, choose View > Print Size. The Print Size command works correctly only after you enter the resolution of your monitor in the Screen Resolution value in the Units & Rulers panel of the Preferences dialog box (**Figure 16.4**).

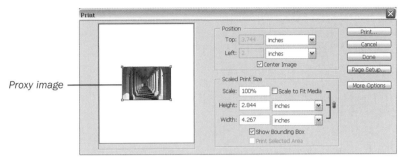

Proxy image

Figure 16.3: The Print with Preview command displays a dialog box that you can use to resize or reposition an image on the page.

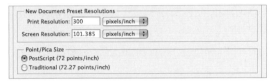

Figure 16.4: The View > Print Size command is accurate only if you enter the actual physical resolution of your monitor for Screen Resolution in the Units & Rulers panel of the Preferences dialog box.

By resolution, I mean the pixels per inch that you get after you divide the number of horizontal pixels on your monitor by the width of your monitor image (in inches). For example, my laptop screen has 1280 pixels and is 12.625 (12⅝) inches wide, and that works out to 101.385 pixels per inch. When you enter the correct resolution and you view at Print Size, the on-screen rulers (View > Rulers) should match an actual ruler that you hold up to the screen.

If the print preview in the status bar or in the Print with Preview dialog box doesn't seem to be the correct size, it means that either the printer settings or document dimensions are entered incorrectly. Here's what to do:

- If the page size or page margins don't look right, choose File > Page Setup and make sure all of the settings are correct—most importantly, the selected printer and the selected paper size (**Figure 16.5**). You may see incorrect previews when the wrong printer and paper size are selected, because the range and names of available page sizes can differ among printers. In addition, two different printers may be capable of different printable areas on the same paper size. Because the selected printer can change from document to document, make a habit of checking the Page Setup dialog box before you print or preview printing, especially if you work with more than one printer. Notice that the Print with Preview dialog box shows a larger margin on the bottom of the page in Figure 16.3 compared to Figure 16.5, because different Page Setup settings are enabled for each figure.

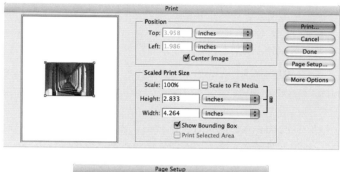

Figure 16.5: **The dimensions displayed in the Print with Preview dialog box (top) represent the relationship of the Image Size dialog box (see Figure 16.2) to the settings in the Page Setup dialog box (bottom).**

It's also important to know that when you're looking at the Page Setup dialog box, you're looking at options that are provided by your printer driver software, not by Photoshop. Because printer driver software is designed by each printer manufacturer individually, you may see different options when you change the selected printer, or options may be presented in a different arrangement. If you don't see an option that you expect to find in the Page Setup dialog box, first try every button and menu available, and if you still can't find it, ask the printer manufacturer.

■ If the document size doesn't look right, choose Image > Image Size and correct the values. Photoshop uses the values in the Image Size dialog box for the actual output dimensions of the document and as the default size for the print preview graphics. If you get it right in Image Size, you won't have to change it again in Print with Preview.

■   To change the position of an image on the page, choose File > Print with Preview and adjust the Position values or drag the proxy of the image. If all Position values are dimmed, or you can't drag the document proxy, disable the Scale to Fit Media checkbox and enable the Show Bounding Box checkbox. If the Top and Left position values are still dimmed, disable the Center Image checkbox.

That troubleshooting advice also applies after a document prints at the wrong size and position. However, if you use the print preview features properly, you should be able to anticipate size and position problems before you print, which can hopefully prevent a lot of wasted paper and ink.

 TIPS   Don't be concerned if the colors in the proxy image in the Print with Preview dialog box don't look right. The Print with Preview dialog box isn't color-managed, so don't use it to predict how colors will print. To preview color output on screen, use soft-proofing instead (see "Previewing Print Colors by Soft-Proofing").

If you have a habit of pressing the Command/Ctrl+P shortcut to print, and you like the Print with Preview dialog box, choose Edit > Keyboard Shortcuts (Chapter 2) to make Command/Ctrl+P the shortcut for the File > Print with Preview command.

If you're in the Print with Preview dialog box, and it doesn't look right, just click the Page Setup button—no need to close the Print with Preview dialog box.

To print multiple images on one sheet of paper, choose File > Automate > Picture Package.

Previewing Print Colors by Soft-Proofing

You can anticipate and avoid the most dramatic color printing surprises by taking advantage of *soft-proofing* (simulating printed colors) in Photoshop. Soft-proofing takes knowledge about your monitor and your final print conditions and adjusts the monitor image to display only the color range available under the targeted printing conditions—the device, the inks, the paper, and the print settings. What about the display you normally see? The normal monitor display in Photoshop and most other programs represents the full range of colors in the file itself, not how the colors are limited by particular printing conditions like CMYK inks on uncoated paper. That's why you often see a mismatch between colors onscreen and in print from the same file.

Before you can soft-proof successfully, your system must be using an accurate color profile of your monitor, and you must also have an accurate color profile of your final printing conditions. You create an accurate monitor profile using monitor calibration hardware (the PANTONE Huey is a simple, affordable device of this type). You typically get an accurate print profile by obtaining it from your output service provider. It's also possible for you to use a calibration product to create your own printer profile but that is usually best done by trained professionals. Photoshop includes some profiles, and your printer driver probably came with some, too, but those are generalized profiles that don't represent the actual behavior of specific devices such as the printer on your desk.

The simplest way to soft-proof is to choose View > Proof Setup and, from the Proof Setup submenu, choose the preset that matches the output condition you want to preview, if you have one. If you don't see a preset for your printing conditions on the Proof Setup submenu, you can add one by doing the following:

1. Choose View > Proof Setup > Custom.

2. In the Customize Proof Condition dialog box, choose your device's profile from the Device to Simulate pop-up menu (**Figure 16.6**).

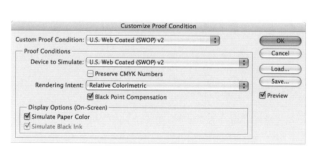

Figure 16.6

If you don't see your device's profile there, exit Photoshop and add the profile to your system. On Mac OS X, copy the profile to:

/Library/ColorSync/Profiles

On Windows XP, simply right-click the profile and choose Install Profile.

After you install the profile, restart Photoshop and start again at step 1.

3. Typically, you'll want to disable Preserve RGB (or CMYK) Numbers, set Rendering Intent to Relative Colorimetric, enable Black Point Compensation, and enable both Display Options. If you're previewing how your document will print at a service provider, double-check with them to make sure these settings accurately represent their output conditions.

4. Click Save and name the preset descriptively.

5. Now you can choose your printing condition from the View > Proof Setup submenu. Don't be alarmed if the image display appears slightly color-shifted and has a narrower range between black and white—the display is previewing the paper color and range of tones and colors those inks and paper can handle (**Figure 16.7**).

Figure 16.7

6. Fine-tune the image while viewing the soft-proof of the simulated final output.

If shadows are blocking up in the soft-proof, you can typically lift shadow detail back up into a zone that's easier for the printing conditions to reproduce by choosing Image > Adjustments > Shadow/Highlight and using a Shadow value above 0 (try starting at 10%, and don't go overboard) (**Figure 16.8**).

You can quickly switch between normal display and soft-proofing by enabling and disabling the View > Proof Colors command (Command/Ctrl+Y). You can also choose Window > Arrange > New Window for (document name) and enable Proof Colors in that window while leaving Proof Colors disabled in the original window.

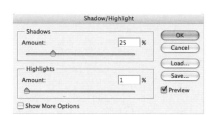

Figure 16.8

The best possible results from soft-proofing require a high-quality monitor, precise customized profiles for both the monitor and the final printing conditions, and properly chosen settings for color management. Because most users can't afford all that, for most users soft-proofing serves more as a guide to possible trouble areas in the final print. I use soft-proofing to catch the most obvious problems and fix them before I start consuming time and paper on test prints. Because I can solve more problems before I actually start making test prints, I don't have to make as many test prints.

 TIPS   On Mac OS X, don't click the Preview button in the Print dialog box. The Preview button is intended for programs that don't have their own preview function. When in Photoshop, preview document output using the Print with Preview and soft-proofing features in Photoshop.

Although I use the word "print" in the title of this section, you can also soft-proof how your Web graphics will appear on Mac OS X and Windows computers. Choose View > Proof Setup > Macintosh RGB or Windows RGB. In fact, you can soft-proof any output for which you have an accurate output profile, by saving a customized proof condition.

CHAPTER SEVENTEEN

Saving Time with Actions

WHEN YOU USE PHOTOSHOP TO PRODUCE LARGE NUMBERS of images to precise specifications, sooner or later you realize that you're doing certain tasks over and over. Repetitive tasks are both a warning sign and an opportunity. They're a warning sign because repetitive tasks are boring, causing your attention to wane; and they aren't good for your body either, as repetitive stress injuries show us.

Photoshop turns repetitive tasks into an opportunity, because you can use Photoshop to record and build automated sequences called *actions*. When you use actions, you turn the disadvantages of repetitive tasks into advantages. Instead of having to strain your attention span as you reproduce the same series of ten production steps on the 31st of 50 images, Photoshop does the ten production steps reliably and without question. Instead of performing time-consuming navigation through dialog boxes and palettes, you sit back and let Photoshop fly through the steps as fast as it can, and the only repetitive action for your wrist will be to raise your cup of coffee for another sip.

In this chapter, I talk about creating actions and running them on the current image. To run an action on multiple images (batch processing), see Chapter 18.

Loading Actions

You can begin using actions even if you've never made any of your own, because Photoshop already includes many actions. You see them in the Default Actions folder that appears in the Actions palette by default. You can add more built-in actions by choosing a built-in action set from the bottom of the Actions palette menu (Commands, Frames, and so on) (**Figure 17.1**); if you choose one, you add another actions folder to the Actions palette.

Figure 17.1: **The commands on the Actions palette menu play a major role in managing actions. Additional built-in action sets are available at the bottom of the palette menu.**

If you want to add actions that you've downloaded or obtained from Web sites, colleagues, or friends, choose Load Actions from the Actions palette menu, select the action set (it may have a .atn filename extension), and click Load.

On the Actions palette menu, you can also choose Replace Actions, which removes all existing actions from the Actions palette and then loads the action set you select. Choose Reset Actions to restore the Actions palette to its default state.

TIP   On Mac OS X, you can load an action set file into Photoshop by double-clicking the file outside of Photoshop.

Running Actions

The most basic way to run an action is to select its name in the Actions palette, and then click the Play Selection button at the bottom of the Actions palette (**Figure 17.2**). However, there are other ways to run actions that may sometimes be more useful, such as the following:

- To play just one step, double-click the empty area to the right of a step name.

- To start an action from one of the steps in the middle, select the step where you want to begin playing back the action and click the Play button; the action plays from that step to the end.

- To run an action in one click, choose Button Mode from the Actions palette menu (**Figure 17.3**).

Figure 17.2: **Click the Play Selection button to run an action.**

Figure 17.3: **When the Actions palette is in button mode, you can run an action by clicking once, and you can see the function key shortcuts.**

- If an action has a function key shortcut, press its shortcut. You can see function key shortcuts when the Actions palette is in button mode or by double-clicking the name of an action if button mode is not enabled.

- To exclude some steps from being run as part of an action, click the expansion triangle to the left of an action name, and then disable the check mark for the steps you want to exclude.

- To be able to specify dialog box options for a step when running an action, enable the Toggle Dialog On/Off button for that step in the second column of the Actions palette.

 TIP   When you see "(Selection)" in the name of a built-in action, that means you must make a selection before running the action.

Planning an Action

Before you record your own actions, it's a good idea to write a rough outline of the steps you're going to record, and refer to the list as you record. Although you can edit actions later, recording too many mistakes makes it harder to edit the action because you'll have to figure out which steps to keep and which to delete or edit.

In my example, I want to:

1. Open a document.

2. Resize the image to my desired pixel dimensions for the Web. I don't use Image > Image Size to do this, because the Image Size command doesn't treat horizontal and vertical images the same way. However, the File > Automate > Fit Image command does, so that's my answer.

3. Sharpen the image at an amount that looks good on the Web. I use the Filter > Sharpen > Smart Sharpen command for that.

4. Save the final image as a JPEG document at specific optimization settings. I want the image to include metadata; File > Save for Web doesn't do that but File > Save As does, so I plan to use the Save As command to create the JPEG.

You can see why I'd like to create an action out of this sequence, and I use it as the example in the next section, "Creating Actions." Although I'm perfectly capable of performing all those steps, I may not remember to do all of them at the correct settings every single time. With an action, I know they will all be done, precisely, every time. Actions aren't just about time savings and convenience; they're also about precise repeatability.

TIP Many actions are built to create effects, but an action may not always be the best way to create an effect. In some cases, your goal may be served better by using a feature such as a preset or a layer style. For example, a layer style is reversible.

Creating Actions

You can create your own action simply by recording it. In many cases, it's best to first record a "rough draft" of an action, and then fine-tune it after it's recorded. To show you how this works, I'll build an action for something I do often: preparing an image for the Web. You might ask if that's too simple of a task to turn into an action, but doing a good job of sending an image to the Web involves more than just choosing Save for Web. I often need to convert images from many different sources, which means they may not be at the right size or color space for the Web. The action I use can take all kinds of images and conform them to my Web specifications.

To record a new action:

1. If you want to create a new action set for the action, click the Create New Set button at the bottom of the Actions palette (**Figure 17.4**), name the set, and click OK.

2. In the Actions palette, select an action set to contain the new action.

3. Click the Create New Action button (**Figure 17.4**).

4. Name the action, and click OK (**Figure 17.5**).

Create New Set —————————————— Create New Action

Figure 17.4

Figure 17.5

5. Click the Begin Recording button.

6. Perform the steps required to complete the action. (Some things you do in Photoshop can't be recorded, such as brush strokes or path drawing. See the next section, "What You Can and Can't Record.")

As you record an action, it's a good idea to keep an eye on the Actions palette to make sure steps are added as you expect. If you do something and it isn't added to the action, you may have done something that isn't recordable, or the document is already in the state you're trying to apply (for example, choosing Image > Mode > CMYK Color has no effect if the document is already in CMYK mode). You can still add commands that aren't recordable by using the Insert Menu Item command; see the next section.

7. When you complete all the steps you want to record, click the Stop Playing/ Recording button (**Figure 17.6**). You don't have to record the entire action at once; you can stop and start recording as needed.

Figure 17.6

 TIPS   If you make a minor mistake while recording an action, you usually don't have to start over. It's easy to edit actions, so keep going if possible and just edit the incorrect step later (see the upcoming section, "Editing Actions.")

Photoshop saves actions only when you exit the program. If Photoshop were to crash, you'd lose any actions you made in the current session. (This is also true for preferences.) If you've recorded or edited actions that required a lot of work to create, exit Photoshop purely to ensure the actions are saved, or remember to save the action set by choosing Save Actions from the Actions palette menu.

If you want to build an action but aren't quite sure how to approach it, try examining the actions that come with Photoshop. They may contain useful examples.

What You Can and Can't Record

You can record any step that involves concrete values, such as applying a dialog box, transforming (moving, resizing, and so on), or changing values in the options bar or in a palette.

You can't record brush strokes (including strokes by image-correction brushes like the healing brush, dodge and burn, and rubber stamp), path drawing or editing steps (such as drawing with the pen tool), or commands that appear on the View menu or Window menu. However, you can save freeform selections, such as those you create with the lasso tool.

If an action requires painting, drawing, or manual retouching, you can choose Insert Stop from the Actions palette menu and type instructions for the person using the action, telling them what to do at that point.

Although you can't record view changes, there is a way to add some view changes to an action, because you can add any menu item to an action using the Insert Menu Item command. The Insert Menu Item command is also a way to add a command to an action when for some reason a command wasn't added to an action when you were recording.

To add any command:

1.   In the Actions palette, select the action step before the place where you want to add the menu item.

2.   Choose Insert Menu Item from the Actions palette menu.

3.   Choose the command you want to add. You can choose commands from the menu bar or from a palette menu (the round button in the top-right corner of a palette), but not pop-up menus in palettes.

4.   Click OK.

 TIP   The Insert Menu Item command is also useful when you want to open a dialog box at its default values, instead of the values that were used when you recorded the action.

OPENING AND SAVING DOCUMENTS IN ACTIONS

Although in many cases you may run an action on an open document, you may want to design an action that opens a document. It can be tricky to open and save documents in actions, because filenames and folder paths are involved. The problem with recording the Open command is that you record opening one specific document—when you play it back, it will always open the same document. If you want an action to open a set of documents that aren't open, use the Batch dialog box (Chapter 18) with the source set to a folder or selected documents in Bridge.

Saving new documents is slightly less tricky. When recording an action that includes the Save As dialog box, touch only the options you actually want to change. Options you don't change take on the document's existing settings. For example, suppose you want an action to alter documents and then save the altered versions as JPEG documents in a new location without renaming them. To achieve that goal, you would record choosing File > Save As, changing the format and folder location, but leaving the filename untouched.

If you edit the filename while recording the action, the action records the new filename and gives it to all processed images—producing one document that's continually overwritten by each subsequent file, instead of a number of uniquely named documents.

When including the Save As command in an action, specify a folder location that's always going to be there. If the folder recorded in a Save As step isn't there or was renamed, an action will fail. For actions that I use all the time, I have a permanently designated output folder on my hard disk, and that's where the action's Save As step is pointed. Another advantage of a permanent output folder is that it can serve as an intermediate checkpoint where you can verify that the documents the action produced are correct. If they are, you can then move those documents to their final destination. If they aren't, you throw them out, adjust the action, and try again.

Testing Actions

Actions do exactly what you tell them to do. When an action is properly made, you can create 100 perfect documents very quickly. On the flip side, if your action contains an error, it's going to produce 100 documents worth of garbage. Before you use an action for actual production work, test it. Use expendable test documents in a test folder. Also, make sure your test files represent the range of documents you'll actually use. You might try different document sizes, or documents saved in different locations.

If you're having a problem with an action and you're trying to identify the problem itself, you can change the playback speed. To change how the action plays back:

1. Choose Playback Options from the Actions palette menu.

2. Select Step by Step to see more clearly what happens at each step; or select Pause and enter a time interval for Photoshop to pause after each step (**Figure 17.7**).

Figure 17.7

3. Click OK.

If you need a more specific indication of an action's playback progress as you debug it, you can insert alert dialog boxes near the steps in question. The dialog box pops up at its point in the sequence.

To add a dialog box to an action:

1. In the Actions palette, select the step before the place where you want to add the dialog box.

2. Choose Insert Stop from the Actions palette menu.

3. Enable the Allow Continue checkbox. If you enable Allow Continue, when the dialog box appears it displays Stop and Continue buttons. If you disable Allow Continue, the dialog box displays just a Stop button and you won't have a way to continue testing the action any further (**Figure 17.8**).

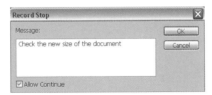

Figure 17.8

4. If you want to display a message in the dialog box, enter it.

5. Click OK.

 TIP It's a good idea for the first step in an action to save a snapshot in the History palette so that it's easy to return to the state of the document before you ran the action. This is especially useful when an action hasn't yet been fully tested. The actions that come with Photoshop create a history snapshot as a first step.

Editing Actions

Editing a step in an action is easy—simply double-click the step.

If an alert appears telling you that the feature is not available, that means there's a missing condition that the feature requires. For example, if you try to edit a step that uses the Free Transform command to apply rotation, but nothing is selected, the Free Transform command can't be used. Before you can edit that step, you need to select what you want to transform in that step.

You can also edit actions in other ways:

■ To rearrange the sequence of steps in the action, drag steps up or down in the list.

■ To record from any point in the sequence, select the step before the point where you want to start recording, and then click the Begin Recording button in the Actions palette.

■ To display a dialog box for a step, click the dialog toggle icon next to the step in the Actions palette (**Figure 17.9**). When the dialog toggle is enabled for a step, the action pauses at that step to display the dialog box so you can enter values. When you click OK, the action continues.

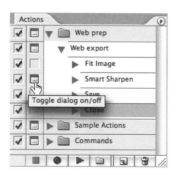

Figure 17.9: **When the dialog toggle icon is enabled, the dialog box for a step is displayed when you play back the action.**

■ To adjust the playback speed of an action, select the action (not a step) and choose Playback Options from the Actions palette menu.

■ To adjust how the action is displayed in the Actions palette and set a function key shortcut, double-click the empty area to the right of an action name, or choose Action Options from the Actions palette menu.

While testing my Web export action, I discovered that some files didn't process as I expected. As a result of testing, I decided to add the following steps after step 1 of my original plan (see the earlier section, "Planning an Action"):

■ Flatten the document. Layered documents take more time and memory to process, so flattening speeds things up a bit.

■ Convert the document color space to sRGB. I might be preparing documents that exist in the Adobe RGB or ProPhoto RGB color spaces, and if they aren't converted to sRGB before uploading to the Web, the colors look washed out.

■ Convert the document bit depth to 8 bits per channel. I've learned that some steps don't work on 16-bit documents, so it's good to get this out of way early, too.

Here's how my final action looks after I add the steps suggested by my test results (**Figure 17.10**):

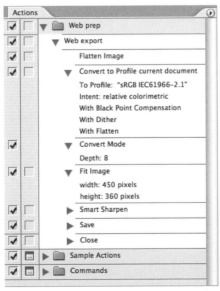

Figure 17.10: My final Web action includes the steps I originally recorded and the new steps I added after testing.

Here are a few tips you can use to help an action run faster and more smoothly:

■ Reduce the amount of data to be processed by including steps that merge or flatten layers, lower the document bit depth, and reduce the document dimensions before applying steps that involve a lot of processing, such as the Smart Sharpen filter. Of course, only add those steps if they're acceptable for your final result (don't flatten if you want the final document to retain layers).

■ If you include a step that resizes an object, and you want the action to resize the object in proportion to its size, enter the scaling value as a percentage instead of as an absolute number.

■ When you're done testing and editing an action, choose Playback Options from the Actions palette menu and select Accelerated.

Enhancing Your Actions

After you've mastered the basics, try these ideas to power up your actions:

■ **Run an action on many documents** in a single run (batch processing), or save an action as a droplet that you can leave on your desktop so you can process documents by dragging them to the droplet. For the details, see Chapter 18.

■ **Build complex actions out of several simpler ones**, by running one action from inside another (**Figure 17.11**). While recording an action, record a step where you run another action. In other words, you use one action as a step in another action. This can simplify maintenance of many actions that use the same step. If you update the action that's used as a step, any actions referring to the updated action benefit from the update the next time you run them.

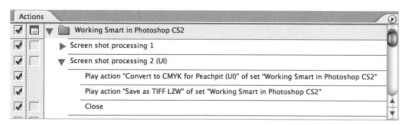

Figure 17.11: One of my actions simply plays back two other existing actions in a specific order.

■ **Trigger an action with a Photoshop event.** Choose File > Scripts > Script Events Manager to run an action when specific events occur, such as saving or printing. Although the Script Events Manager is primarily intended to run scripts, it provides an option to use an action instead. For more information on the Script Events Manager, see Chapter 19.

■ **Build tutorials with actions.** You can use the Stop feature to guide students through a sequence by inserting a dialog box message after any step. To do this, select a step and choose Insert Stop from the Actions palette menu. Enter a message, be sure to enable the Allow Continue checkbox, and click OK. You can combine tutorial actions with how-to tutorials that you add to the Help menu (see Chapter 5).

■ **Document your actions.** The Insert Stop command is useful for instructing users of your actions when you want to explain what a step does, or when users need to perform a manual task in the middle of an action, such as making a selection.

■ **Organize your action sets.** It's a good idea to keep your actions in a set separate from the action sets that come with Photoshop. Use the Save Actions command on the Actions palette menu to save action sets to disk in order to archive them and make them available for reinstallation if you upgrade, migrate, or re-install Photoshop. If I create actions for a specific project, I make a separate action set for that project which can be backed up along with the rest of the project files and fonts.

Links About Actions

On the Web, you can read more about actions and download free actions others have created. Here are a few links to resources for actions:

Adobe Studio Exchange

    `share.studio.adobe.com`

Fred Miranda

    `www.fredmiranda.com`

Action Addiction

    `www.actionaddiction.com`

Action Central

www.atncentral.com

ActionFx Photoshop Resources

www.actionfx.com

National Association of Photoshop Professionals (requires membership)

www.photoshopuser.com

CHAPTER EIGHTEEN

Batch Processing and Droplets

AN ACTION CAN REMOVE THE DRUDGERY OF APPLYING a sequence of steps to one image, but it's still drudgery if you have to run that action over and over again on 100 images. Fortunately, there's no need to put up with that in Photoshop, because you can use the Batch command to apply a Photoshop action to any number of files. You can also save a batch process as a *droplet*—a batch action saved as a shortcut. Just drop documents on the droplet to process them.

Although the Batch command is powerful, it's also a little on the complex side. Photoshop also includes the Image Processor, a more user-friendly batch processor that focuses on a few common conversion tasks.

Using the Image Processor

Before getting into the Batch dialog box itself, you should first take a look at the Image Processor. Originally developed by Russell Brown as an add-on and now included with Photoshop CS2, the Image Processor performs many of the more common tasks you might try to set up on your own with actions and the Batch dialog box. In other words, if the Image Processor does something you want to do, you don't have to build your own action to do it.

The Image Processor is designed to convert selected documents to JPEG, Photoshop (PSD), and TIFF file formats (all optional), and you can run an action on the processed documents.

To use the Image Processor:

1. Choose File > Scripts > Image Processor.

2. In step 1 of the Image Processor dialog box (**Figure 18.1**), select which images to process. If you enable the Open First Image to Apply Settings checkbox, you can specify options that apply to all of the other images you process.

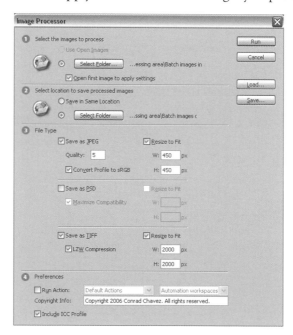

Figure 18.1

3. In step 2 of the Image Processor, specify where to save the processed documents.

4. In step 3 of the Image Processor, enable the checkboxes for the file format copies you want to make. Some of the available options are particularly helpful:

- For all formats, Resize to Fit scales each image within the height and width you specify, maintaining proportions and without cropping.

- For JPEG, Quality is the same scale used in Photoshop (1 is lowest quality, 12 is highest). Convert Profile to sRGB is very useful when processing images for the Web or when sending images to others.

- For PSD, Maximize Compatibility adds a composite version so that layered files can be read by other applications that support Photoshop format.

- For TIFF, LZW Compression applies lossless data compression.

5. In the Preferences dialog box, you can specify an action to run, enter copyright information, and embed the ICC profile with the processed image. If color reproduction is not critical, and the processed images are in the sRGB color space, you can save smaller files by disabling Include ICC Profile.

6. Click Run.

 TIP   If the Image Processor doesn't quite do what you want, try Russell Brown's expanded set of free tools, Dr. Brown's Services. I cover them in Chapter 6.

Using the Batch Dialog Box

To run an action as a batch process (**Figure 18.2**, next page):

1. Choose File > Automate > Batch.

2. In the Play section, choose an action set and an action. Of course, the action and its set have to be loaded in the Actions palette before you can choose it in the Batch dialog box.

3. From the Source pop-up menu, choose which documents to process:

- To process all eligible documents in a folder, choose Folder and then click Choose to specify the folder.

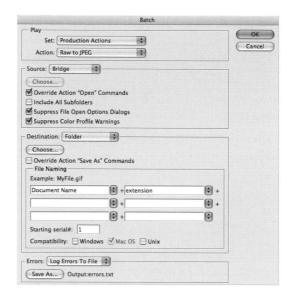

Figure 18.2

- To import and process PICT documents, choose Import and choose an option from the From pop-up menu. (PICT files were in use in older versions of Mac OS, so you probably won't use this option often.)

- To process documents currently open in Photoshop, choose Opened Files.

- To process documents selected in the frontmost browser window in Adobe Bridge, switch to Adobe Bridge and choose Tools > Photoshop > Batch. You can't choose Bridge from inside Photoshop; you must start from selected files in Bridge.

4. Enable any of the following checkboxes as needed:

- If the action doesn't include any Open commands, don't worry about the Override Action "Open" Commands checkbox. If the action does include an Open command, see the nearby sidebar "Override Action Commands . . . What the Heck?" to determine what to do.

- To run the action on the documents inside folders contained within the folder you specified, enable Include All Subfolders.

- In most cases, enable the Suppress File Open Options Dialogs checkbox. If you disable this option, every time the action opens a document in a format that displays options in the Open dialog box (such as a raw file), the action pauses and waits for your input, which defeats the purpose of fast batch processing.

■ In most cases, enable the Suppress Color Profile Warnings checkbox.
If you disable this option, and the Ask When Opening checkboxes in your
color settings (Edit > Color Settings) are enabled, every time the action opens
a document that conflicts with the Color Settings dialog box, the action
pauses, and a dialog box appears asking you what to do. Instead, depending
on the color-management requirements of your workflow, you can make the
color spaces of opened documents consistent by converting them to the desired
color space before running the action; or you can edit the Color Management Policy in the Color Settings dialog box so that the Ask When Opening
checkboxes are disabled.

5. In the Destination pop-up menu, choose how and where completed documents
are stored:

■ To leave each document open after the action is complete, choose None.
I choose None when I have a Save step in the action itself. This can be a good
way to double-check the results of an action when you run the action on
just a few documents. However, if you run many documents through the
action, the completed open documents pile up and occupy RAM, and if
Photoshop were to crash, you'd lose all of the results. The more documents
you want to process, the more you should choose one of the other commands
in the Destination pop-up menu.

■ To save each processed document and then close it, choose Save and Close.
This is typically not a recommended step if you process original documents,
because a mistake in the action or its settings can ruin your originals. It's OK to
choose Save and Close if you're processing copies of your original documents.

■ To save all processed documents to a specific folder, choose Folder. You
don't have to choose this if there's a Save step in the action itself. If you
choose Folder, click the Choose button to specify the folder and enter any
file-naming options you want.

■ If the action doesn't include any Save commands, don't worry about the
Override Action "Save As" Commands checkbox. If the action does include
an Open command, see the nearby sidebar "Override Action Commands . . .
What the Heck?" to determine what to do.

6. For Errors, it's usually better to choose Log Errors to File and then click
Save As and specify where the log text file goes. If you choose Stop for Errors,

you might walk away after starting a batch on many documents, and come back much later to find it never got past the third document because of an error on just that document. It may be a good idea to choose Stop for Errors if you are still testing an action and want to be aware of any problems right away.

7. Click OK to start the batch process.

OVERRIDE ACTION COMMANDS . . . WHAT THE HECK?

The two most confusing options in the Batch dialog box are the Override Action "Open" Commands and Override Action "Save As" Commands checkboxes. The confusion stems from having to convey a complex concept in a short label for a checkbox, and the label isn't very good. Both options do the same thing, but one applies to opening documents, and the other applies to saving documents. When you use either option, you use the filename and location specified by the Batch dialog box, not by any steps in the action. The only two attributes these options override are the filename and location. Any other options available in the Open or Save dialog boxes are still controlled by Open or Save steps in the action.

If the action includes an Open step, in most cases you should enable Override Action "Open" Commands so that the action doesn't always open the same document you used to record the action. If the action includes an Open step, and you want the Open step to always open the same document (as in an action that combines a document with another document that the action opens), disable the Override Action "Open" Commands checkbox. The most common reason to enable the Override Action "Open" Commands checkbox is when you include an Open step for a raw file because you want to apply the Adobe Camera Raw settings you recorded in the Open step (such as document dimensions, bit depth, and color space).

If the action includes a Save step, and you choose Save and Close or Folder, you should typically enable the Override Action "Save As" Commands checkbox, so that the file naming and location options in the Batch dialog box control where the final documents are saved. It doesn't override options in the Save As dialog box, such as the file format. If you leave Override Action "Save As" Commands disabled, you may get unexpected results, such as 100 documents processed but saved to the same filename and location, leaving you with just one document (the last one processed).

If you want an action to save its documents to the same folder every time, but a different folder than other actions use, it may be best to set the Destination pop-up menu to None and let a Save action in the step control where files are saved. If you do this, be sure to record the Save As dialog box step without editing the filename or you'll save all documents under the same filename. Using a Save step can be easier than changing the folder in the Batch dialog box for different actions.

Batch Processing Examples

The Batch dialog box is overwhelming enough that it helps to have an example or two. I've got two. They're similar, but that's on purpose so that I can point out why I decided to set up each action the way I did.

I often produce compact JPEG files from camera raw files. I could use the Image Processor, but there are specific features I like to apply, and I frequently tweak the settings depending on the content. For example, I might decide to apply the Shadow/Highlight command to the images of a high-contrast subject. Or I might adjust the noise-reduction settings depending on the camera I used. For those reasons, I decided to create actions and use them with the Batch command.

There's a complication in that opening camera raw files involves settings that aren't present for other file formats like TIFF. That's the main reason I have two actions, and I explain that a little later.

I run these actions from Bridge (Tools > Photoshop > Batch) after selecting documents in Bridge, as described in Chapter 6. In the future, I may decide to save each variation as a droplet if I don't want to examine and possibly edit the action's settings before running it.

Producing JPEG Files from Camera Raw Files

In Chapter 17, I use the example of producing JPEG files for the Web. The action in this example, Raw to JPEG (**Figure 18.3**), uses the same planning philosophy, but this action can produce JPEG files for uses other than the Web. Let's look at the action from the top down:

■ At the top is an Open command that specifies settings for the Adobe Camera Raw plug-in. If I didn't include this step, Camera Raw would open a raw file using the last settings used, which may have no relevance to the raw files I'm converting. I recorded this step to control those settings.

■ Next are three Fit Image commands, and only one is enabled. What's going on with those? There are three main sizes at which I usually create JPEG files: 2000 pixels on a side, 1440 pixels, and 320 pixels. I enable the size I need for a particular batch and make sure the other two are disabled (by enabling or disabling the checkboxes in the first column of the Actions palette). The details of each step aren't visible in the screen shot, but remember that clicking a disclosure triangle expands a step to reveal its details.

Figure 18.3: **My Raw to JPEG action includes an Open step to specify settings in a camera raw file.**

In the future, if I learn how to write scripts (Chapter 19) that can present dialog boxes, as the Image Processor does, I may turn the three Fit Image commands into three radio buttons in a dialog box.

■ There's a Shadow/Highlight step. For some batches, I want to apply Image > Adjustments > Shadow/Highlight. If I need it, I enable this step.

■ Some batches need noise reduction, so I include a Reduce Noise step (Filter > Noise > Reduce Noise) if I need it.

■ Next you see three Smart Sharpen steps. Again, there are three settings that I tend to use most often, so I keep them all in here and turn on the one I think will work best for a specific batch of images.

■ The Save step is actually for the Save As command. I recorded it with specific JPEG compression settings and set the destination to be a specific output folder I created on my hard disk. I have that folder saved in my Bridge favorites so that as processed images arrive in that folder I can watch them show up and examine them to make sure everything's going as planned.

■ The last step closes the file without saving it. It's already saved by the previous step, and I want it out of the way so that each successive file doesn't stay open, occupying valuable RAM.

When I run this action from the Batch dialog box, I enable Override Action "Open" Commands because I want the currently selected raw files to be the ones I specify in the Batch dialog box, not the specific raw file I used to record the Open command. Photoshop still applies the settings in the Open step for the Camera Raw dialog box.

For the Destination in the Batch dialog box, I choose None because I let the Save step in the action control where the file go. When recording the Save step, I was very careful not to touch the filename so that Photoshop would simply use the name of the source file. Of course, the file is saved with a .JPG extension instead of its original raw format extension.

Producing JPEG Files from Other Formats

At first glance, my To JPEG action (**Figure 18.4**) looks like the Raw to JPEG action in the previous example. There are a few differences, for the following reasons:

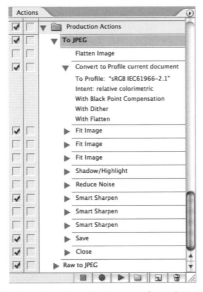

Figure 18.4: My To JPEG action includes steps that can conform documents that aren't flattened or in the sRGB color space.

■   There isn't an Open command, because non-raw files don't open through the Camera Raw dialog box as in the other action. The non-raw files are opened by the standard Open command, so I let the Batch dialog box handle that.

- There's a Flatten Image step in this action. That's because I might run layered Photoshop or TIFF files through the action and I want to flatten them to reduce the amount of time and RAM required to process them.

- I also include a Convert to Profile command that converts the document to the sRGB color space. I didn't need this step in the other action because the Camera Raw dialog box was set to output sRGB.

The rest of the action is the same as the other one. Because the two actions are similar, I could have left them as one action and simply remembered to turn on or off more checkboxes depending on the documents I was feeding into the action.

When I run this action from the Batch dialog box, I disable Override Action "Open" Commands because there isn't an Open command in the action. If I forget to do this, the action doesn't work correctly. For the Destination in the Batch dialog box, I choose None, just as I do for the other action.

The way I've set up these actions is not necessarily the best way to implement them, and they may not be the best solution for everyone. I hope they at least provide insight into the decisions and considerations you may want to anticipate when you build your own actions.

 TIP   If you want to apply a batch action to files in more than one folder, use Adobe Bridge to tag those files with a unique keyword or label and then choose Edit > Find in Bridge to gather those files by performing a search from a folder that contains all the folders of images you want to process. This works as long as you enable the Include All Subfolders checkbox in the Find dialog box in Bridge.

SAFETY FIRST

Even actions you test can cause unwanted results if you process a document that has an attribute you didn't originally test, or when you accidentally change a setting in the action and don't catch it before running the action. The risk is magnified when you apply batch processing, because instead of potentially ruining one document, you could ruin an entire shoot of many images. You can avoid damaging original documents by designing your actions workflow with document safety in mind.

One overarching guideline is to never let an action save over your only original document. Here are more specific ways to protect your original documents:

■ Process copies of the original documents. If you do this, you don't need to use the rest of the recommendations in this list.

■ If you decide to run an action on original documents but need to save the processed document, make sure the action includes a Save As step that copies the processed documents to another folder.

■ If you plan to use an action for batch processing, make sure the action closes the original document without saving it and make sure there are no Save commands anywhere in the action (Save As to a new name or location is OK).

■ If an action leaves an original document open, you might want the first step to be a new snapshot in the History palette so that you can easily back up if the action doesn't work correctly. Notice that the actions that come with Photoshop create an initial snapshot for this reason.

Using Droplets for Instant Batch Processing

If you've got an action that you throw images at all day long, and you're getting tired of mousing your way through the Batch dialog box every time you use that action, consider saving the action as a droplet. A droplet is like a shortcut to an action: Instead of directing Photoshop to files, you drop files on the droplet, and the droplet handles the rest. You can store the droplet anywhere you'd store a file or folder; if you make a droplet from an action you use all the time, you can leave the droplet on the desktop for very convenient dragging and dropping.

There is one thing to watch out for with droplets. Once you save them, they're done. If you want to modify the settings of a batch action, you'll have to do it from the Actions palette or the Batch dialog box. Also, a droplet doesn't update if you edit the action that it's based on—if you want to update the droplet, you'll need to create it again. Therefore, the best time to create a droplet is after you've thoroughly tested the action you're using to create the droplet.

To create a droplet from an action:

1. In Photoshop, choose File > Automate > Create Droplet (**Figure 18.5**).

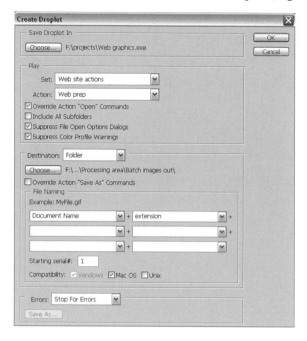

Figure 18.5

2. Under Save Droplet In, click Choose and specify where you want to save the droplet. You can always move it later.

3. Specify all settings as described in the section "Using the Batch Dialog Box."

The only difference between the Create Droplet dialog box and the Batch dialog box is that instead of specifying a source for the files, you specify where you want to save the droplet, which is where you'll drag files later.

4. Click OK.

To use a droplet, simply drag any number of documents onto the droplet.

CHAPTER NINETEEN

Automating with Scripts

IF YOU'VE GOTTEN PRETTY FAR WITH PHOTOSHOP ACTIONS, you've probably started running into some of their limitations. Although actions are easy to create, an action can't perform calculations or adjust to various conditions. For example, you can use both an action and a script to scale a layer to a specific size, but only a script can calculate how many of those layers can be duplicated across and down a particular document size, duplicate the layer until you have an entire row of them, and then duplicate the row all the way down the page—suddenly, you have a page full of business cards in one click.

Scripts are definitely more powerful than actions, but as you might expect, there is a tradeoff: Scripts are harder to create and edit because they consist of lines of code. You have a lot more options, but those options can make it more challenging to perfect a script.

You can make good use of scripts even if you don't know how to write code. Many scripts are available on the Web—many for free—so all you have to do is run those. Also, if you have an idea for a script that doesn't involve calculation or decisions, you can actually use Photoshop to record the script, make a couple of easy changes, and play it back when you need it.

If you have a programming background, you can take advantage of scripting rather easily. If you want to create advanced scripts, but don't have a programming background, you'll need to understand some of the concepts behind scripting that I briefly introduce in this chapter.

Like many Photoshop users, I come from a creative background, not a programming background. In this chapter, I introduce scripting and show how anyone can use it. If you want to write scripts from scratch, you'll need a lot more information than I can fit into this book. Fortunately, Adobe provides extensive scripting documentation with Photoshop. I tell you where to find that and also where to look on the Web for more information.

Scripting Languages You Can Use

Photoshop supports three scripting languages: JavaScript, AppleScript (Mac OS X), and VBScript (Windows). Here's how to decide which language to use:

- If you want to be able to run a script that works with both the Mac OS X and Windows versions of Photoshop, use JavaScript.

- If you want to be able to write a script that drives Photoshop and other programs, use AppleScript or VBScript. For example, you can write a script to move a document among multiple Adobe Creative Suite programs, processing it each step of the way.

- If you only need to control Photoshop and don't need cross-platform compatibility, you can use any of the three languages. In addition, on Mac OS X you can use any language that supports Apple Events, and on Windows you can use any language that supports OLE Automation.

Running Scripts

Anyone can run a script, because it's easy as choosing a menu command. You can try it right now, because Photoshop comes with some sample scripts.

To run a script from within Photoshop:

1. Open a test document (something expendable).

2. Choose File > Scripts.

3. Do one of the following:

   ■ Choose a script from the Scripts submenu, if any are listed.

   ■ Choose Browse to look for a script. The sample scripts that come with Photoshop are located inside the Adobe Photoshop CS2 application folder, in

   `Scripting Guide/Sample Scripts/JavaScript.`

4. Click Load.

In this example, I pointed you to the JavaScript folder because you can open those from within Photoshop. AppleScript and VBScript scripts operate at the level of your operating system, so you can run those by double-clicking them from the desktop.

You can also trigger a script when a specific event happens in Photoshop. For example, you can use a script to control what happens when someone chooses File > Save. You set this up in the Script Events Manager.

To associate a script with an event:

1. Choose File > Scripts > Script Events Manager.

2. Make sure Enable Events to Run Scripts/Actions is enabled.

3. Choose an event from the Photoshop Event pop-up menu. For the Save example I mentioned, choose Save Document.

   ■ To use an event that isn't listed, choose Add an Event from the Photoshop Event pop-up menu. In the Add an Event dialog box, enter the Event Name and Descriptive Label. You must choose from the list of events in Appendix A of the Adobe Photoshop CS2 JavaScript Scripting Reference (see the section "Scripting Documentation" later in this chapter); the Descriptive Label must be one of the Event ID Codes listed in Appendix A.

4. Choose a script from the Script pop-up menu. For the example, choose Save Extra JPEG.jsx.

5. Click Add. The event you set up is added to the list at the top of the Script Events Manager dialog box (**Figure 19.1**).

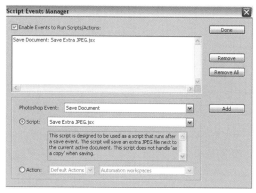

Figure 19.1: **Use the Script Events Manager to run any script when a specific event happens in Photoshop.**

6. Click Done.

To test the Save example, open a test file, choose File > Save, and save the PSD file in a convenient location. Look in the folder where you store the original test document—a copy of the file with a .jpg filename extension should now exist next to it. (The sample script applies the last-used JPEG settings, as if you had chosen the JPEG file format and simply clicked Save.)

I use the Script Events Manager again later in another, more specific example.

 TIP   To edit the list of Photoshop Events in the Script Events Manager, edit the file Script Events Manager.xml, located inside the Adobe Photoshop CS2 Settings folder.

How Scripting Works

If you intend to write your own script code from scratch, you need to know how to use a script to select an object and do something to it. In the programming world, the rules by which you do that are known as the *object model*. The scripting object model for Photoshop is hierarchical, like the folders on Web sites and your hard drive. When you want to open a specific Web page, you specify a URL that digs through the Web site (as in www.example.com), a top-level folder (www.example.com/products/), and more specific folders until you get to the file you want to view (www.example.com/products/appliances/ovens.html). In Photoshop, your script must identify the application (Photoshop), the document, and the type of object you intend to change, such as a layer, a selection, or a history state.

Once your script identifies the object, you can use a scripting command (AppleScript) or method (JavaScript and VBScript) to change the properties of an object. This is like selecting a layer and changing the values in a dialog box or palette.

A script can also define *variables*, placeholders that store a value that can change as the script runs. A variable can change because the script performs a calculation on it, or because Photoshop replaces the variable with values you enter or from an external file. For example, in the business card example at the beginning of this chapter, a Photoshop script could start with a blank business card document, duplicate the business card to fill a page, and populate each card with a different employee name read from a text file.

You can see more details about the Photoshop object model in the *Adobe Photoshop CS2 Scripting Guide* (see the section "Scripting Resources").

Scripting Resources

Adobe is nice enough to include extensive scripting documentation and tools with Photoshop, which means you already have them on your hard disk. In addition, many script-oriented Web sites provide free scripts and forums where you can ask questions and exchange ideas and code.

Scripting Documentation

In the Scripting Guide folder inside the Adobe Photoshop CS2 application folder, you'll find the following documentation for scripting:

- *Photoshop Scripting Guide*

- *AppleScript Reference Guide*

- *JavaScript Reference Guide*

- *VisualBasic Reference Guide*

The first PDF you'll probably want to read is the *Photoshop Scripting Guide*, because that document gives you an overview of scripting in Photoshop. After you read that, refer to one of the other three documents for the specific scripting language you want to use.

Loading Scripts

Photoshop loads scripts from the Scripts folder, located inside the Presets folder in the Adobe Photoshop CS2 application folder. You'll find a number of sample scripts already stored there, and it's where you should store scripts that you want to see in the File > Scripts submenu in Photoshop. The scripts in the Scripts folder also appear in Bridge, in the Tools menu.

In Photoshop, you can also load scripts from any disk or mounted volume by choosing File > Scripts > Browse.

Scripting Utilities

Photoshop installs a few utilities that help you create and use scripts, which are all located inside the Adobe Photoshop CS2 application folder. You can also use other utilities that are included with your operating system. Here's an overview of what you already have:

- **ExtendScript Toolkit.** Use this utility to write, edit, and debug JavaScripts. It's documented in the *JavaScript Reference Guide*. On Mac OS X< ExtendScript Toolkit is installed in your Utilities folder, which is inside your Applcations folder. On Windows XP, ExtendScript Toolkit is installed in:

  ```
  c:\Program Files\Adobe\Adobe Utilities\ExtendScript Toolkit\
  ```

- **Script Listener.** You'll find it in the folder Adobe Photoshop CS2/Scripting Guide/Utilities. You do need to install it; do that by dragging it into the folder Adobe Photoshop CS2/Plug-Ins/Adobe Photoshop Only/Automate. Then restart Photoshop. As long as it's installed, everything you do in Photoshop is recorded as JavaScript in the file ScriptingListenerJS.log which appears on the desktop (Mac OS X) or at c:\(Windows XP). I show you how to use it in the example later in the chapter.

- **Script Events Manager.** This is the utility I mentioned earlier that runs a script when something specific happens in Photoshop. You run it by choosing File > Scripts > Script Events Manager.

- **A text editor or log reader.** You can use a text editor to write or edit the scripts you create or want to modify. Both Mac OS X and Windows come with text editors. On Mac OS X, you can use TextEdit. On Windows XP, you can use Notepad or WordPad. You can also use a text editor to examine script log files such as ScriptingListenerJS.log, but it's usually better to use a log reader such as Console on Mac OS X, because a log reader can continually update the log.

Web Sites About Scripting

There are many Web sites where you can find scripting tutorials, information, discussions, and examples. Here are just a few to get you started; a search engine will turn up many more:

The Adobe Design Center, which contains scripts for Photoshop

    share.studio.adobe.com/axBrowseSubmit.asp?t=74

Adobe Design Center scripts for Bridge

    share.studio.adobe.com/axBrowseSubmit.asp?c=222

JavaScript Reference for Bridge

    www.adobe.com/products/creativesuite/pdfs/bridge_javascript_ref.pdf

The Adobe User-to-User Forum for Photoshop Scripting

    Go to www.adobeforums.com/, then click Adobe Photoshop and ImageReady, then click Photoshop Scripting.

Jeff Tranberry's Photoshop scripting page

    www.tranberry.com/photoshop/photoshop_scripting/index.html

The Fotofects scripting tutorial

    fotofects.com/articles/362/1/Photoshop-Scripting-Basics

Example: Creating and Installing a Simple Script

I'm going to show you how even a former art major like me can create a simple yet useful script to change how Photoshop works. I don't have any programming experience, but the built-in tools will help me get it done. I came up with the idea for the following script after seeing an example on Jeff Tranberry's blog (blogs.adobe.com/crawlspace/2006/05/installing_and_1.html).

My script solves a specific problem. I use a laptop and often plug in an external monitor or projector. Every time the monitor configuration changes, Photoshop decides to reset the palettes the next time I open it. I'm quite picky about my palette arrangement, so it's annoying when my palettes aren't the way I like them. I've already saved my favorite palette arrangements as workspaces, and I realized that if I recorded a script that chose my favorite workspace, I can use the Script Events Manager to run the script every time Photoshop opens. That way, no matter what Photoshop wants to do with the palettes, my favorite workspace will be applied without my having to manually select my workspace every time.

Here's how I did it:

1. I install the Scripting Listener plug-in (see "Scripting Utilities" earlier in this chapter).

2. I start Photoshop.

3. I choose Window > Workspace > PowerBook monitor. That's the name of a workspace I created, so if you try this, choose the name of a workspace you created.

4. On my Mac OS X desktop, I double-click the file ScriptingListenerJS.log, which opens the log in the Console program (**Figure 19.2**). On my Windows desktop, I would navigate to c:/ and double-click ScriptingListenerJS.log, which opens the log in the Notepad program.

   ■ I see a few lines of JavaScript code that recorded my workspace selection. I can see the name of my workspace in the code ("PowerBook monitor").

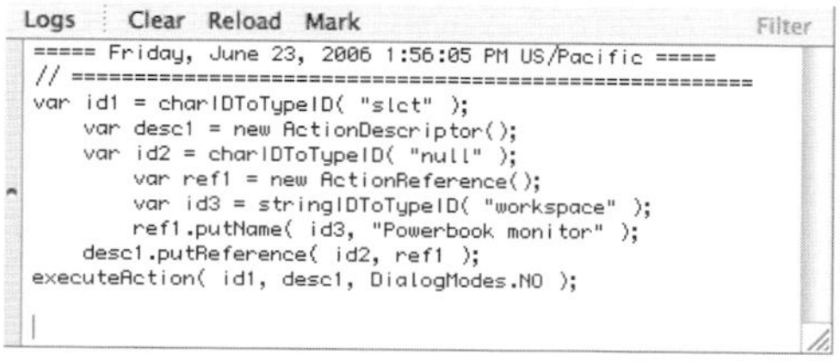

```
Logs    Clear  Reload  Mark                              Filter
===== Friday, June 23, 2006 1:56:05 PM US/Pacific =====
// =====================================================
var id1 = charIDToTypeID( "slct" );
    var desc1 = new ActionDescriptor();
    var id2 = charIDToTypeID( "null" );
        var ref1 = new ActionReference();
        var id3 = stringIDToTypeID( "workspace" );
        ref1.putName( id3, "Powerbook monitor" );
    desc1.putReference( id2, ref1 );
executeAction( id1, desc1, DialogModes.NO );

|
```

Figure 19.2

5. Because I can't edit text in the Console program I'm using, I copy and paste it into a text editor (TextEdit).

6. I add two lines to the top of the text: A description on the first line and a comment on the second line. I copied the format from one of the Photoshop sample scripts (**Figure 19.3**).

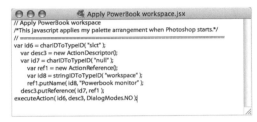

Figure 19.3

7. I save the script as a text-only document with the filename Apply PowerBook workspace.jsx. The .jsx extension identifies the document as a JavaScript.

■ If I was going to run the script from the Scripts submenu, I'd save it in the Scripts folder (see "Loading Scripts"). However, because I plan to run this script only by using a Photoshop event to trigger it, I save it in the Event Scripts Only folder inside the Scripts folder.

8. I choose File > Scripts > Script Events Manager.

9. I choose Start Application from the Photoshop Event pop-up menu and choose Apply PowerBook Workspace from the Script menu.

10. I click Add, and the new event appears in the list at the top of the dialog box (**Figure 19.4**). Then I click Done.

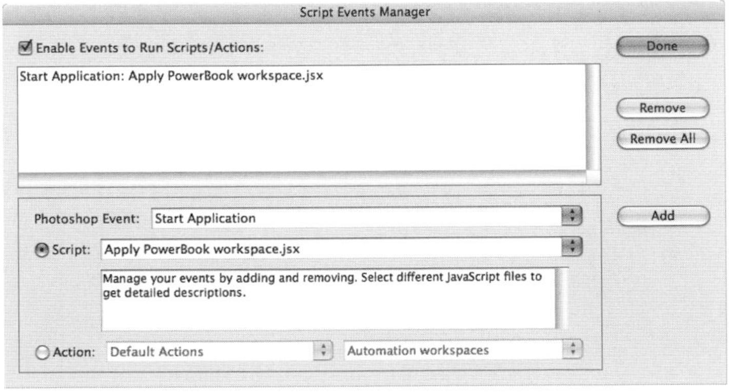

Figure 19.4

11. I test the script by moving some palettes around and restarting Photoshop. Sure enough, as soon as Photoshop loads, my palettes are arranged according to my PowerBook Monitor workspace. Success!

If you simply want to run a script from the File > Scripts submenu, you don't need to perform steps 8 through 11. As long as you've moved the script into the Scripts folder, just restart Photoshop, and the script appears on the File > Scripts submenu.

 TIP   You can use the Scripting Listener plug-in to observe what happens when you change settings in dialog boxes and palettes. You can then use the code from the log to build scripts that open a dialog box and fill it with settings of your choice.

CHAPTER TWENTY

Generating Data-Driven Graphics

Many PEOPLE USE PHOTOSHOP TO PROCESS one document at a time. When creating groups of files that share common elements, such as a stack of baseball cards, the usual approach is to design a document, make copies of it, and manually edit the text information and images for each player. With Photoshop CS2, there's a more automatic way to generate groups of documents that use the same layout but have different images and text. That way involves *variables*, placeholders in a file that maintain position but contain contents that can be swapped out automatically by Photoshop from a defined set of images or text. Think of it as similar to a mail merge between a mailing list and a word processor, but more visually interesting.

Data-driven graphics require a template, variables, and a data set. You design a template in Photoshop using layers as variables that can contain text or graphics and define the names of the variables. In an external file, you set up a data set of text and graphics that uses names that correspond to the variables. Photoshop takes the template document and makes copies of it, and in each copy Photoshop inserts a different instance of the data to replace each variable in the document. In the end, you get a complete set of documents filled in with unique combinations of text and graphic data.

Using variables doesn't save very much time on a short run of similar documents, such as a set of posters promoting the five plays in a theater company's season. However, in the previously mentioned example of baseball cards, variables can save great amounts of time and easily maintain consistency across documents, because hundreds of documents are involved. Using variables also saves time when the data is already available in a database or spreadsheet program, because Photoshop can import the commonly used tab-delimited or comma-delimited text files that you can export from a database or spreadsheet.

In some cases it may be better to generate data-driven layouts using a dedicated layout program such as Adobe InDesign. But if producing Photoshop files is a more direct route to a final image format such as JPEG for the Web, Photoshop may be a more straightforward alternative.

Creating the Template

A Photoshop template gives the underlying structure to the data-driven graphics. The template not only contains the visual design for the graphics, it also houses the variables you fill in with data. When you design a template, plan to set aside a layer for each variable you need.

I'll use the example of building coupons from a list of products and their prices, and the images that go with them. Each coupon must contain the coupon background (which won't change) and also a layer for each of the variables that will change for each coupon, which are the product name, its price, a picture of the product, and whether it was grown organically (**Figure 20.1**).

Defining Variables for Layers

Once you've got a template, you define which layers of the template will be replaced by data. A Photoshop layer can contain any of three kinds of variables:

- **Visibility.** Is the layer visible or not? You control that with this simple on/off variable.

Figure 20.1: My template (left) contains top and bottom bars that won't change, along with layers for the variables. In the Layers palette for this template (right), I grouped the template and variable layers separately, for clarity.

- **Pixel replacement.** Replace a layer with an image so that each instance can have a different picture.

- **Text replacement.** Replace a layer with text.

In my example, I have four variables:

- **Product.** This is the name of the product, and I define it as a text-replacement variable.

- **Price.** This is the sale price of the product, which I'll define as a text-replacement variable.

- **Image.** This is the image of the product, to be defined as a pixel-replacement variable.

- **Organic.** This indicates that the product was grown organically, and I define it as a visibility variable, because the only thing that changes is whether this type layer is displayed or not.

To define a variable:

1. Choose Image > Variables > Define.

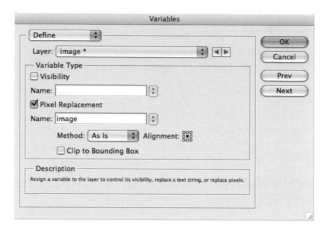

Figure 20.2

2. From the Layer pop-up menu, select a layer that you want to assign to a variable. My template contains a layer for each variable I want to use (**Figure 20.2**).

3. Under Variable Type, enable the checkbox for the variable you want to use. Enter a new variable name or select an existing variable name of the same type by clicking the pop-up menu to the right of the name.

4. If Pixel Replacement is available and you enable it, you can specify how images of different sizes should fit on the layer:

■ The Method pop-up menu specifies which resizing method to use; select one and read the help text at the bottom of the dialog box to see if it's the right choice. I'm using As Is because all my images are already sized properly.

■ The Alignment proxy anchors a resized image to the center or an edge; click a point to set it. The Alignment proxy doesn't apply in my case because I selected the As Is method.

■ Clip to Bounding Box, when enabled, doesn't display areas of an image that are scaled beyond the edge of the image's original bounding box. Disable it to always display all of the image.

5. When you're done defining one variable, you can do one of the following:

■ To assign a variable to another layer, click the Prev or Next button.

■ To continue on and work with data sets, choose Data Sets from the pop-up menu at the top of the screen.

■ To close the Variables dialog box, click OK.

Creating a Data Set

The other essential piece of a data-driven graphic is the data set, which is the actual content Photoshop uses to fill in the variables. You can define a data set inside Photoshop or in an external document. In my example, this is where I associate each product with its price, image, and organically grown status. To start with, I'll make data sets for pears and bananas.

To define a data set inside Photoshop:

1. Choose Image > Variables > Data Sets, or if you're already in the Variables dialog box, choose Data Sets from the pop-up menu at the top of the dialog box.

2. Click the Create New Data Set button and then enter a name for Data Set. In my example, I make one called Pears (**Figure 20.3**).

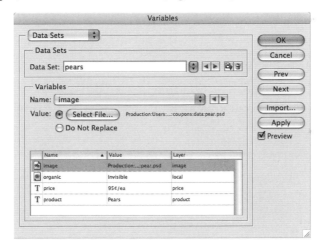

Figure 20.3

3. In the Variables section, choose a variable from the Name menu or click a variable in the list.

4. For Value, specify the value of the variable you selected.

In my example, for my variable named "image" I clicked Select File to locate the pear.psd file that is the image that goes with the pear product.

5. Repeat step 4 for every variable in the list. For the pear coupon I'm making, I enter the product name ("product" variable), its price ("price" variable), and set its "organic" variable to Visible.

6. Click Apply.

7. Repeat steps 2 through 6 for each data set. I did that for each product that needed a coupon. You can navigate among existing data sets by clicking the pop-up menu button or the arrows to the right of the Data Set name.

Changing data sets changes all the variables over the template. In my example, the Organic type layer appears only with the pear data set because its "organic" variable is set to Visible for that data set.

You can also set up a data set outside Photoshop using a database or spread-sheet program and then export the data set as an ordinary comma-delimited or tab-delimited text file. I'll show how my example would look coming from Microsoft Excel.

To create a data set outside of Photoshop:

1. Use a database or spreadsheet program to create a record of each data set, its variables, and their values (**Figure 20.4**). My example shows Microsoft Excel.

Figure 20.4

Path names to image files must be absolute path names that are legal for your platform. For example, a path in Windows XP should look similar to this:

```
C:/My Documents/<folder name>/<filename>
```

A Mac OS X path should look similar to this:

```
Macintosh HD:Users:<username>:<folder name>:<filename>
```

2. From the database or spreadsheet program, save or export the document as tab-delimited or comma-delimited text.

In Microsoft Excel, the option to save as comma-delimited text is available in the File > Save As dialog box. Tab-delimited and comma-delimited formats produced by Microsoft Excel and common database programs should work fine. If you're generating your own, the full requirements for the data set text file format are in the Photoshop help file in the topic "Importing Data Sets from External Files."

3. In Photoshop, choose File > Import > Variable Data Sets; or if you're already in the Data Sets dialog box, just click Import.

4. In the Import Data Set dialog box, specify options and click OK (**Figure 20.5**). You can usually leave the Encoding set to Automatic. Enable the Use First Column For Data Set Names checkbox if the original spreadsheet listed the data set names down the first column instead of across the first row.

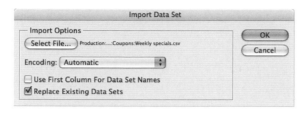

Figure 20.5

 TIP   In the Variables dialog box, leave the Preview checkbox enabled to see if the variables affect the document correctly.

Generating the Final Documents

After your variables are defined, and your data sets are set up, you can test the data sets by choosing Image > Apply Data Set and selecting a data set with the Preview checkbox enabled. When you click Apply, you change the current layer content.

If the test is successful, you can then generate the final documents—one document for each data set.

To generate data-driven documents:

1. Choose Export > Data Sets as Files (**Figure 20.6**).

Figure 20.6

2. Specify the folder, which data set to export (or all of them), and how you want the files to be named.

3. Click OK. Photoshop generates the documents in the folder you specified (**Figure 20.7**).

Notice how the product image, name, price, and Organic label change in each of the final files, corresponding to their data sets.

Figure 20.7

> **TIP** Positioning images can be tricky if you don't want them to be centered. Try setting up the image variable layer by starting with a blank layer, drawing an object at the exact center of the document (I used a gray dot), and then using the move tool to drag your center marker to the location where you want the image variables to appear. Image variables follow the position offset of the layer that contains them.

CHAPTER TWENTY-ONE

Using Photoshop with the Adobe Creative Suite

ALTHOUGH PHOTOSHOP HAS A LONG AND STRONG HISTORY as a standalone software product, it is also available as part of the Adobe Creative Suite collection of Adobe graphics programs. The goal of the Creative Suite is not merely to sell several Adobe products in one box, but also to integrate their functions. For example, using non-Creative Suite programs you typically need to convert copies of graphics to a common file format before importing them into another program. Using the Adobe Creative Suite, you can take advantage of Photoshop features such as layers and styles and then import the Photoshop document into an Adobe InDesign or Adobe Illustrator print layout without further conversion. By supporting the Photoshop file format directly, you can avoid making additional documents, which simplifies file management.

Adobe Creative Suite integration goes further than file format compatibility. In many cases, importing a Photoshop document into other Creative Suite programs is as easy as dragging and dropping.

Instead of having to learn the complete tool sets of several different programs, you can take advantage of the consistent user interface across Creative Suite programs. If you know how to use the direct selection tool in Adobe Illustrator, you already know how to use that same tool when editing paths in Photoshop. In addition, Adobe Bridge ties together all of the Creative Suite products, making it easier to manage projects and preview and identify the documents you want to use in your projects.

Adobe Creative Suite comes in two versions: Standard and Premium. The Standard suite includes Adobe Photoshop, Adobe Illustrator, Adobe InDesign, Adobe Bridge, Adobe Stock Photos, and Adobe Version Cue version-tracking and collaboration software. The Premium suite adds Adobe GoLive and Adobe Acrobat Professional.

Adobe InDesign

Because Photoshop has a long tradition of processing documents for print, it's only natural that Adobe would work extra hard to streamline the connections between Photoshop and InDesign. If you're used to saving Photoshop documents as TIFF or EPS documents before importing them into a layout program, that isn't necessary with Photoshop documents. Adobe InDesign reads Photoshop documents directly, preserving Photoshop features such as layers and transparency.

You can import a Photoshop document into InDesign by dragging and dropping the Photoshop document from the desktop or Adobe Bridge right into an InDesign document window, or in InDesign you can choose File > Place. InDesign preserves any transparency that exists in the Photoshop document (see Chapter 13). Once a Photoshop document is in an InDesign layout, you can modify the Photoshop file to a limited extent within InDesign or make more extensive edits back in Photoshop.

Jumping Back to Photoshop

To open a Photoshop document from InDesign, select a Photoshop document on an InDesign layout and choose Edit > Edit Original. This is handy when you're in InDesign and you want to edit a Photoshop document without having to figure out where it is on disk. When you save the Photoshop document and switch back to InDesign, the Photoshop document updates right on the InDesign layout.

TIP Instead of choosing Edit > Edit Original, a faster way to edit a Photoshop document placed in InDesign is to Option/Alt+double-click the Photoshop document.

Controlling Photoshop Layer Visibility

You can use InDesign to control which layers are visible in a placed Photoshop document. This is useful when you've built a Photoshop document that contains different design variations using various layers or combinations of layers saved as layer comps. Instead of having to save, manage, and track several copies of a Photoshop document, you can set up your common elements in Photoshop using layers, place more than one instance of the document in InDesign, and simply hide and show different layers in each placed instance. InDesign also recognizes Photoshop layer comps.

To control Photoshop layers from InDesign:

1. Select a Photoshop document on an InDesign layout and choose Object > Object Layer Options.

■ Click any eye icon to show or hide the Photoshop document layers in the Adobe InDesign CS2 document, or choose a layer comp from the Layer Comp menu (**Figure 21.1**).

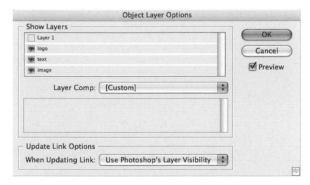

Figure 21.1

■ To always preserve the layer visibility settings you applied to the Photo-shop document in InDesign, choose Keep Layer Visibility Overrides from the When Updating Link pop-up menu. If you choose Use Photoshop's Layer Visibility, every time InDesign updates the link to the Photoshop document InDesign will check the settings saved by Photoshop and use those, removing any layer visibility overrides you applied in InDesign.

InDesign indicates placed documents with layer overrides in case you want to troubleshoot why an element isn't visible. When layer overrides are applied to a Photoshop document in InDesign, a red eye icon appears next to the Photoshop document name in the Links palette in InDesign. When you pre-flight the InDesign document (File > Preflight), the Links and Images panel in the Preflight dialog box indicates how many placed documents use layer over-rides; to see if a document has layer overrides select it in the list and see what it says for Layer Overrides.

 TIP   You can control layer visibility as you import a layered Photoshop file into InDesign, by enabling the Show Import Options checkbox in the Place dialog box (in InDesign) and clicking the Layers tab in the Image Import Options dialog box. But it's often easier to place the file first and see how it looks on the layout before changing layer visibility.

If you use the Object Layers Options dialog box to apply different InDesign layer over-rides to several instances of the same Photoshop document, make sure the When Updating Link pop-up menu is set to Keep Layer Visibility Overrides in InDesign. If you don't do this, the next time InDesign updates graphics links, all of the Photoshop documents will be reset to the layer visibility settings originally saved by Photoshop, making all of the placed instances of the Photoshop document look the same again.

Creating a Contact Sheet in InDesign

Although you can create contact sheets in Photoshop (File > Automate > Contact Sheet II), you can also use InDesign to make a contact sheet of any documents that are in formats InDesign can import. The file formats that InDesign can place and Photoshop can save include Photoshop native format, JPEG, and TIFF; the file formats InDesign can import are listed in InDesign Help under the Graphics topic.

Why would you want to use InDesign instead of Photoshop? When you create an InDesign contact sheet, you have the option of specifying an InDesign template. If your organization's visual identity is built on InDesign templates, you can use InDesign to create a template for contact sheets so that your contact sheets are consistent with your other materials such as business cards and letterhead. Also, if you plan to archive the contact sheets, InDesign documents will take up less disk space than Photoshop contact sheets because they link back to the images you use, instead of copying all of the images into the InDesign document.

To create an InDesign contact sheet:

1. In an Adobe Bridge browser window, select the images you want to include in the contact sheet.

2. Choose Tools > InDesign > Create InDesign Contact Sheet.

3. Specify options in the Contact Sheet dialog box (**Figure 21.2**). The options that could use more explanation are the following:

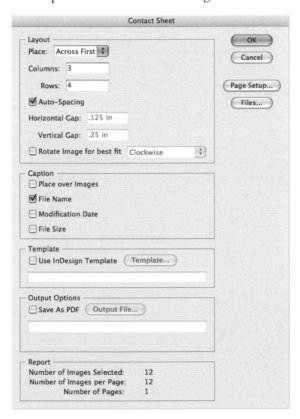

Figure 21.2

- ■ **Page Setup.** InDesign needs to know the dimensions and printer margins of the page you want to use to build the contact sheets, so it's important to click Page Setup and make sure the selected printer, paper size, and margins are correct.

- ■ **Template.** If you have an InDesign template you'd like to use, this is the place to tell InDesign where it is.

- ■ **Output Options.** If you already know you want the contact sheet in PDF for easy distribution, enable Save as PDF and click Output File to specify a filename and location. This way you don't have to generate a PDF from the resulting InDesign document—InDesign simply continues on to the PDF export stage after the contact sheets are built.

4. Click OK.

Using an InDesign Layout in Photoshop

There may be times when you want to use an InDesign layout in Photoshop, such as processing a magazine cover as a graphic for the Web. All you have to do is export the InDesign layout in a file format that Photoshop can import, such as EPS, JPEG, or PDF. Using PDF is a good bet, because it preserves type and vector objects for higher-quality scaling.

In InDesign, you create an EPS, JPEG, or PDF document by choosing File > Export and choosing the format from the Format pop-up menu. The PDF presets are the same as those in Photoshop (see Chapter 4).

You can then drag the exported document from Bridge or the desktop to the Photoshop program icon (Mac OS X) or program window (Windows XP). If you're using the exported InDesign layout as part of a Photoshop document, in Photoshop choose File > Place so that you can use the InDesign layout as a smart object (see Chapter 10).

 TIP   Whenever I say you can drag a document from the desktop to Photoshop, that automatically means you can also drag the same document from Adobe Bridge to Photoshop.

Adobe Illustrator

You can drag Photoshop documents directly into an Illustrator document. As in InDesign, drag-and-drop placing is the same as placing by choosing File > Place.

You can also drag Illustrator documents to the Photoshop program icon (Mac OS X), program window (Windows XP), or to a Photoshop document window; or in Photoshop you can choose File > Place to import an Illustrator document. Photoshop displays the Import PDF dialog box, because Illustrator CS2 uses PDF as its native file format. For more information about the options in the Import PDF dialog box, see the next section, "Adobe Acrobat and PDF."

You can also copy and paste one or more paths from Illustrator to Photoshop. When you do, a dialog box appears asking you how you'd like to paste the path. You can choose from the following options (**Figure 21.3**):

Figure 21.3: In the Paste dialog box, you decide how you want Adobe Illustrator paths to import into a Photoshop document.

■ **Smart Object.** If you want to preserve both the ability to update the Illustrator path and how the path looks in Illustrator, select this option, which pastes the Illustrator object as a smart object in the Photoshop document. Because it's a smart object, you can double-click its thumbnail in the Layers palette in Photoshop to open up the smart object back in Illustrator so you can update it.

■ **Pixels.** Click this option to rasterize the Illustrator path you're pasting, which turns it into pixels. You won't be able to update the path using Illustrator because it won't exist as a path any longer.

■ **Path.** Click this option to paste the Illustrator path as a Photoshop path, which means it appears as the Work Path in the Paths palette in Photoshop. You might choose this option if you want to use the Illustrator path as the basis for a selection or channel.

■ **Shape layer.** Click this option to paste the Illustrator path as a vector shape layer. You might go this route if you wanted to draw a shape layer that you could accomplish more quickly using the vector drawing tools in Illustrator, compared to the more limited vector drawing tools in Photoshop.

Adobe Acrobat and PDF

You can open or import a PDF document into Photoshop the same way you can with the other compatible file formats I mention in this chapter—by dragging the document to Photoshop or by choosing File > Open or File > Place (in Photoshop). You can open or import only one page at a time, because Photoshop doesn't have multiple-page capability.

When you open a PDF document, the Import PDF dialog box appears (**Figure 21.4**). In this dialog box, you convert a PDF document into pixels in Photoshop. Many of the options are similar to those you use to set up a new Photoshop document, but concentrate your attention on three options:

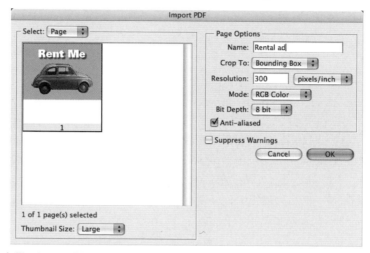

Figure 21.4: **The Import PDF dialog box appears when you open a PDF document in Photoshop.**

■   Select Page/Image lets you decide whether you want to import entire pages from the PDF document, or individual images. Whichever one you choose, click which page or image you want to import.

■   Crop To fine-tunes the image area that's converted. For example, because PDF documents often come from page-layout programs, you might receive a PDF that's a small ad sitting on a much larger US Letter paper size, which means there's a lot of empty space all around the ad. When you import the PDF document, you may want to choose Bounding Box instead of Media Box from the Crop To pop-up menu, because the Media Box includes the entire paper size indicated in the PDF document. The way programs use the Crop To sizes can vary, so it's usually best to try out all of the options in the Crop To pop-up menu to make sure you're getting what you want, keeping an eye on the preview thumbnails.

■   Resolution is the pixels per inch at which the document is rasterized, based on its print dimensions in the PDF document. If you want a US Letter-sized PDF document to reproduce at US Letter size at 300 pixels per inch, enter 300. If you plan to resize the document later, make sure you enter a value large enough to accommodate later resizing. For example, if you plan to use Photoshop to later double the height and width of the above example and still print it at 300 pixels per inch, enter 600 pixels per inch so that the final resolution is 300 pixels per inch after a 200% enlargement.

When you place a PDF document into an existing Photoshop document, the Place PDF dialog box appears instead. The Place PDF dialog box is the same as the Import PDF dialog but with far fewer options, because the PDF imports as a smart object and so rasterization is deferred until final output.

Going in the other direction, from Photoshop to PDF, Photoshop provides ways for converting one Photoshop document or several. When you choose File > Save As, you can choose Photoshop PDF from the Format pop-up menu in the Save As dialog box. Also, you can convert multiple Photoshop documents into a multiple-page PDF document or presentation (slide show); choose File > Automate > PDF Presentation. Whenever you create a PDF, you need to select a PDF export preset so that the PDF is optimized for its final output or distribution; I describe each PDF preset in Chapter 4.

Adobe GoLive

You can drag a Photoshop document directly to a Web page document in GoLive. The Save for Web dialog box appears, where you can optimize the document for the Web. The fastest way to optimize in the Save for Web dialog box is to choose a preset from the Preset pop-up menu before you start changing individual optimization settings. You might find that one of the presets already works well for your image. If none of the presets is quite right, you can choose the most appropriate one and then change individual optimization settings to get exactly what you want. For more details on the Save for Web dialog box, see Chapter 13, where I describe preserving Photoshop transparency for GoLive.

When you import a Photoshop document into GoLive, it becomes a smart object in GoLive. To update the Photoshop document that's in GoLive, simply double-click it to open the original document in Photoshop. When you're done editing, save the document in Photoshop and when you switch back to GoLive, the Web version is automatically updated—now *that's* smart.

When generating data-driven Web pages using GoLive, you can use a Photoshop document as a template if you've defined variables in the document (see Chapter 20).

You can't import a GoLive HTML document or Web site into Photoshop directly, because Photoshop isn't a Web browser. To show a Web page in a Photoshop document, your best bet is to load the GoLive page in a Web browser, take a screen shot of the Web browser window, and then open the screen shot in Photoshop.

 TIP   In the Save for Web dialog box, always click the Image Size tab and make sure the pixel dimensions fit on your Web page. Many Photoshop documents—particularly those coming straight from a digital camera—have pixel dimensions that are too large for a Web page. If you adjust the image size, be sure to click the Apply button, otherwise your changes won't affect the exported Web graphic.

Adobe Bridge

Bridge is such a natural extension of Photoshop that I cover many of its Photoshop integration opportunities in Bridge's own chapter (Chapter 6). In general, think of Bridge as the place to go when you want to do the same thing to more than one Photoshop file. Here are a few more integration tips that haven't been mentioned yet:

- To make sure all Creative Suite programs use the same color settings, synchronize them. Choose Edit > Creative Suite Color Settings, select the color settings that most closely match your primary workflow, and click Apply.

- To send files from Bridge to other Creative Suite programs, select files in Bridge, choose File > Place, and select a program from the Place submenu. If a program is dimmed, that usually means you must have a document open in the destination program to receive the file.

- You'll find most Photoshop integration opportunities in the Tools menu, in the Photoshop Services and Photoshop submenus.

CHAPTER TWENTY-TWO

Jumping Directly to Other Programs

PHOTOSHOP IS OFTEN IN THE MIDDLE OF A WORKFLOW chain involving multiple programs. An image you edit in Photoshop may have come from digital-camera software or Adobe Camera Raw, and when you finish editing an image in Photoshop, you may be passing it on to a more specialized image editor such as Adobe ImageReady, or to a Web-site editor like Adobe GoLive or Dreamweaver.

Although your habit may be to close and open the document repeatedly as you switch from program to program, you can send a document from Photoshop to another program in one step from within Photoshop.

Jumping Between Photoshop and ImageReady

If you often correct images in Photoshop before sending them to ImageReady to more thoroughly prepare the images for the Web, you can save a lot of time by using the direct links between Photoshop and ImageReady.

Photoshop gives you two quick ways to move a document between Photoshop and ImageReady. The fastest way is to click the Edit in ImageReady button at the bottom of the Tools palette in Photoshop (**Figure 22.1**). Going the other way, you'll find the same button in the same location on the Tools palette in ImageReady, which you can click to send the image back to Photoshop.

Figure 22.1: **Click the Edit in ImageReady button at the bottom of the Tools palette to open the frontmost document in ImageReady.**

If you prefer to choose a command, you'll find both by choosing File > Edit in ImageReady when you're in Photoshop, or File > Edit in Photoshop when you're in ImageReady. Of course, the command has a keyboard shortcut—Shift+Command+M/Shift+Ctrl+M.

When a Photoshop document is open in ImageReady, you can't edit it in Photoshop until you bring it back. The filename of the document appears on the Window menu under an ImageReady label, and if you choose it you do bring the document back to Photoshop.

Jumping to Other Graphics Programs

If you're interested in using the jump feature with more programs, you certainly aren't limited to ImageReady. Photoshop and ImageReady provide the Jump To menu at the bottom of the File menu, and although it may be empty at first, you can easily add your favorite programs to the menu.

ImageReady's Jump To submenu comes with a couple of twists. First, it separates the Jump To submenu into two sections: graphics editors and Web-page editors. The Jump To editor in ImageReady also includes the Other Graphics Editor and Other HTML Editor commands, so that you can jump to programs that you haven't added to the Jump To submenu.

You add programs to the Jump To menu using the Helpers folder, which is inside the Adobe Photoshop CS2 application folder. Inside the Helpers folder are two more folders: Jump To Graphics Editor and Jump To HTML Editor. All you have to do is make an alias (Mac OS X) or shortcut (Windows) of a program and move it into either of those two subfolders inside the Helpers folder (**Figure 22.2**). Photoshop and ImageReady share that folder, but only ImageReady uses the Jump To HTML Editor folder.

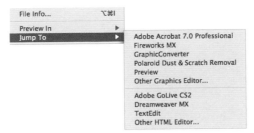

Figure 22.2: **Adding shortcuts to the subfolders in the Helpers folder adds programs to the Jump To submenu, shown here in ImageReady.**

After you've added the aliases or shortcuts, restart Photoshop and ImageReady. When a document is open, you can now choose File > Jump To and choose a program from the Jump To submenu. If you use ImageReady to jump to an HTML editor, the Save Optimized dialog box appears so that you can specify a folder where ImageReady can save an HTML page that contains all of the slices and other Web features you've added in ImageReady or Photoshop.

As you might guess from the folder names, you can add only graphics-editor programs and Web-page design programs to the Jump To submenu. More specifically, you can add any program that can use its Open command on the file type you have open in Photoshop. For example, if you've opened a layered Photoshop document, you can use Jump To to open it in Adobe Illustrator, which can preserve the individual Photoshop layers (although from that point on you'd save it as an Illustrator document, instead of sending it back to Photoshop).

Index

Photoshop
    and Acrobat, 273–275
    activation process, 26–27
    allocating RAM to, 9–13
    application folder, xii
    assigning scratch disk for, 17–19
    and Bridge, 276. *See also* Bridge
    building computer for, 28
    deactivating, 27
    and GoLive, 275–276
    as graphic design tool, 169
    how RAM is used by, 5–9
    and Illustrator, 272–273
    and ImageReady, 278–279
    and InDesign, 268–272
    installer, xii
    jumping to other programs from, 277–279
    keyboard shortcuts. *See* keyboard shortcuts
    license agreement, 26
    manual, 95
    menus. *See* menus
    monitor considerations, 23–24, 34–40
    optimizing computer for, 1–28
    and other Creative Suite Programs, 267–276.
        See also specific programs
    vs. other image editors, 1
    palettes. *See* palettes
    performance bottlenecks, 2, 28
    presets. *See* presets
    working smart in, ix
    workspaces. *See* workspaces
Photoshop Help command, 95
Photoshop PDF format, 86, 87, 275
Photoshop Professionals, National Association
        of, 236
Photoshop Scripting Guide, 253, 254
Photoshop Services submenu (Bridge), 120, 276
Photoshop submenu (Bridge), 120, 276
Picture Package command, 219
Pixel Replacement variable, 261, 262
pixel-based layers, 153
pixels, 7, 207, 210, 217, 273
Place PDF dialog box, 275
Place-O-Matic, Dr. Brown's, 123
Play Selection button, 225
Playback Options command, 231, 232, 234
plug-ins
    Bigger Tiles, 13–14
    Disable VM Buffering, 15
    disabling, 14
    Dr. Brown's Services, 122–123, 239
    and RAM, 5–6
plus (+) key, 51
PNG format, 193
pointing devices, 25. *See also* mice

polygonal lasso tool, 148
pop-up menus, unlabeled, xii
Portable Document Format, 85. *See also* PDF
Preferences command, xiii
Preferences file, xiii
Preset Manager dialog box, 84
presets, 67–94
    backing up, 84
    for brushes, 70–72
    for Camera Raw, 166–167
    for contours, 77–79
    creating/using, 68–81
    vs. defaults, 68
    deleting, 84
    editing, 82, 89
    for exporting PDF files, 85–92
    for gradients, 73–74
    importing, 84, 93
    kinds of, 70
    for layer styles, 74–75, 172
    loading, 93
    managing, 83–85
    naming/renaming, 84, 93
    for patterns, 76–77
    purpose of, 68
    RAM considerations, 72
    resetting default, 85
    saving to disk, 84, 93–94
    for shapes, 79–82
    for swatches, 72–73
    for tools. *See* tool presets
    viewing, 82–85
press output
    Adobe PDF presets for, 86, 87
    file formats for, 205, 206, 209
    and transparent backgrounds, 189
Press Quality preset, 87
print, creating transparent background for,
        189–192
print colors, soft-proofing, 219–222
Print command, 215
Print Size command, 216–217
Print with Preview command, 216–217, 218, 219
processors, 2–4, 28
Proof Setup command, 220, 222
ProPhoto RGB color space, 207, 208
proxy images, 216, 219
PSD files, 86, 238
Purge Cache command (Bridge), 131
Purge submenu, 14

R
RAID, 19
RAM, 5–16
    allocating to Photoshop, 9–13